THE BODACIOUS OZARKS

True Tales of the Backhills

by Charles Morrow Wilson

PELICAN PUBLISHING COMPANY
Gretna 2002

Printed in the United States of America
Published by Pelican Publishing Company, Inc.
1000 Burmaster Street, Gretna, Louisiana 70053

Contents

	Preface	1
I	Glimpsing the Ozarks Backhills	15
II	Any Day Is Tramping Day	29
III	Whuppin' Holler	43
IV	Soundly Unlawful	51
V	Gobble Drovers	58
VI	Favorin' Foxes	69
VII	The Right and the Wrong of It	75
VIII	The Ozarks Storyteller	90
IX	It Gits Mighty Durn Cold	99
X	It Can Git Spirited, Likewise	106
XI	The Wonder of It	112
XII	To Tell of Many Things	120
XIII	Way Folks Say It	141
XIV	Way Folks Serve It	150
XV	The Thoughted Change-Over	166
XVI	Roads of Destiny	180
XVII	Ballets and Play Parties	190
XVIII	A Ballet Singer Bears a Son	207
XIX	Everlasting Ozarks	226
XX	You Take That There Road	237

THE
BODACIOUS
OZARKS

Preface

THERE IS GOOD reason to believe that the Ozarks are the oldest land surfaces on the Western hemisphere and that to a considerable extent they have waited apart for millions or tens of millions of years. Geological evidence suggests that the Ozarks began as a towering mountain range, the inaccessibly tall Himalayas of an era perhaps hundreds of millions of years ago, and that rivers and perhaps other erosive forces wore down those vast mountains and remade them into a plateau which may have covered as much as a third of the present U.S.A. In time the great central plateau was covered by seas, presumably impounded by the explosive uprising of younger mountain ranges to the east and west. In any case, the sea beds were spilled over with vast deposits of silts and sands and filled in farther by shells and bony residues of marine lives.

Then, apparently, the bed of the great sea was again raised or blasted up into another range of tall and faulted mountains. Again these cloud scrapers were worn down by erosion to far-stretching and swampy flatlands. These inaccessible mires were once more raised explosively and shaped into considerably smaller but very tall mountains. These, in turn and in millions of years of time, were worn down to the general dimensions and contours of the present-day Ozarks plateau or uplift.

The geological remoteness which had persisted through eons of earthly time appeared to remain a heritage of what eventually became the human populations of the Ozarks. Respected archeol-

1

ogists are disposed to agree that the first Ozarks people were of the Toltec Indian civilization. For one reason or another the Toltecs settled only the southern and western fringes of the plateau.

In more recent pre-Columbian times, Siouan Indians, including the Osage and Quapaw tribes, made limited settlements into the plateau. But here again the penetrations were limited and apparently the larger tribes withdrew, leaving the Ozarks as seasonal hunting grounds and as refuges for maverick or itinerant Indians who endured only as small clans or bands. Archeological evidence indicates that the wanderers were disposed to take shelter under riverside cliffs or in shallow caves rather than in well-established villages. Their hunting trails, in part still well-marked by arrowheads and spearheads made of flint, frequently connected the larger springs and other water sites. But the remoteness of the region appears to have remained potent.

The earliest white settlers, for the most part itinerant trappers and fur traders, principally of French or French-Indian origins, apparently touched only lightly into the Ozarks, taking little and giving nothing except a rather widespread scattering of French names, such as *Petit Jean* (mountain), *bois des arcs* (tree), and French adaptations of Indian place names, such as *Ozarks*.

As the nineteenth century came into orbit, the American fur trade, powerfully stimulated by the materializing Napoleonic Wars and the actions of Russia, Prussia and Sweden to winter-garb their expanding armies with American furs, tended to move north and west to more productive pelt stations.

Spain, which held treaty sovereignty over the Ozarks between 1762 and 1802, did little to change the situation. Beginning in 1776, the Spanish Crown instituted the issuance of baronial or "caretakers'" grants in a few select areas to a few, presumably select henchmen. Very few of the grants took cognizance of the

2

Ozarks and from appearances none served substantially to overcome Ozarks remoteness.

France's dominion of the Ozarks (as part of the Louisiana Territory) endured only thirty-three months. Perhaps that was just as well. France's Napoleon I did not see fit to confirm any of Spain's baronial grants in the Ozarks or elsewhere in the Territory. Instead, the dictator from Corsica appeared to oppose settlement of any of the upper Territory, having bluntly forbidden private ownership of lands north of parallel 35.5.

This situation changed with the Louisiana Purchase. Thomas Jefferson and his counsellors moved to make at least the easternmost lands of the great Territory immediately available to settlement. By 1808 formal "government title" for land ownership was made attainable throughout the Ozarks. But takers were few and Ozarks remoteness endured. By 1810 a very sparse trickle of durable settlers began moving into the northern Ozarks, for the most part from the hills of Kentucky and Tennessee and in less part from Pennsylvania and North Carolina. Springfield, Missouri, the oldest of the present major Ozarks towns, was first incorporated during 1812.

The War of 1812 added considerable impetus to settlement of the northern or Missouri Ozarks. The impetus grew noticeably with hard-hitting depressions which followed that hot little war. During the 1820's abstracts of land titles in various areas of the Ozarks began showing a sprinkling of German and Polish names, and more than a few Irish. The northern Ozarks received a scattering of settlers from the Ohio Valley and the nearer Great Plains. By the 1830's the Arkansas Ozarks were receiving settlers from the south and southeast, in greatest part from the hills of Alabama. But the name "Arkansas" was only beginning to appear on maps. Missouri Territory had been established by an act of the Congress, June 4, 1812, and it included virtually all of the Ozarks plateau.

3

PREFACE

On the last day of 1813 the Territorial Legislature of Missouri had established Arkansa County (named for the Arkansa Indians). It included most of the present area of Arkansas.

A little more than three years later (March, 1817), President James Monroe signed a Congressional act changing Arkansa County, Missouri, to the United States Territory of Arkansas— the final "s" was apparently contributed by the erstwhile law clerk, James Monroe. In any case the revision of spelling and map designation had no effect on the isolation of the lands described. The Ozarks continued to wait apart. Their rivers carried little of the white man's traffic. The first passenger-carrying steamboat did not navigate the comparatively mighty Arkansas River until 1820. Nearly ten years passed before the first mail route was opened between Springfield, Missouri, and Fort Smith, Arkansas. Transcontinental stagecoach lines did not dip decisively into the Ozarks until 1858.

Meanwhile, the ancient plateau remained remote. The covered-wagon routes skirted it to the north and west. River shipping skirted it to the south and west. On many other frontiers white settlers were able to follow Indian trails and to be guided by Indian precedence in the selection of farm lands and water sites. This was not the case in the Ozarks, which even in the middle nineteenth century were commonly regarded as being "farther off route" than the Great Plains or the intermountain West.

In 1845 Abraham Reynolds, onetime Jesuit, schoolmaster and perceptive historian of frontier St. Louis, noted that the Ozarks were the "most lost" country in all the "near West"; adding that they were absorbing only a slight back-splashing of the already impressive population movement to the Great Plains. Reynolds also pointed out the ironic fate of the principal Indian tribes of the region who were being driven through the Ozarks by duress, even while white-skinned Americans were entering the area laboriously and in great part leaving—also laboriously. (Throughout the

4

1820's and early 1830's such eminent Indian tribes as the Caddoes, Choctaws, Osages and Quapaws, and the confederated clans of the illustrious Cherokee Nation, previously headquartered in Georgia and the Carolinas, were being "pressed" through the Ozarks under Federal goading to resettle on assigned lands in what is now the State of Oklahoma.)

The Indians had no chance to settle in the Ozarks or elsewhere en route. They had been relentlessly uprooted from their homelands by both Federal and State governments and numerous political conspiracies thereof, and under like auspices the tribespeople were being herded toward and dumped on an approximate no man's land to the west. Thus many Indians traveled through the Ozarks lamenting, suffering and dying. For the most part they blazed their own trails and buried their own dead. The Cherokee "Trail of Tears" was the best marked of the routes.

Ozarks remoteness clung. In 1836, when Arkansas gained admission as a state, thereby marking both the Arkansas and Missouri Ozarks as "slavery territory," the Federal estimate of Arkansas' census was 55,000; the entire census of Missouri, 170,000. According to Andrew Jackson's Presidential Summation of 1835, the total population of all the Ozarks was guessed at 20,000. There was still but one post office in the entire state of Arkansas and (apparently) only one in the Missouri Ozarks. And there was still not one through road!

Even so, the not especially good year 1836 marked the beginning of a quarter-century of unprecedented census growth for the region. During the twenty-five years between Arkansas' statehood and the Civil War, the over-all census of the Ozarks area appears to have increased somewhere near tenfold. The Federal census estimate compiled in 1860 indicates that the population of what were then the twenty Ozark counties totalled approximately 310,000 persons. Interestingly, at least seven Ozarks counties had more people in 1850 than in 1950. For one example, Madison

5

County, Arkansas, had an estimated census of 20,000 in 1850; 23,400 in 1900, and as this book is written, 11,230.

There is a great deal of evidence that the deliberate quest of remoteness motivated a sizable share of the early settlement of the Ozarks. There were scatterings of renegades and instances of pursued refugees. But a much greater proportion of early settlers, like the youthful Dan'l Boone, simply did not elect to have neighbors within the sound of musketshot or the sight of chimney smoke. There were still more who brought with them from other mountain lands the compelling quest of subsistence and isolation.

It followed that many early settlers came in afoot or rode along dim trails, or took directly to grassy valleys or tillable hilltops without benefit or convenience of roads. The ancient Southwest Trail out of St. Louis skirted only the western fringe of the Ozarks and, as already noted, all the principal covered-wagon routes avoided the plateau. At least twenty Ozarks rivers were navigable in some part, yet their traffic remained severely limited or nonexistent. The raft, canoe and small rowboat stayed the principal river transport, such as it was.

The 1850's were the first decade to witness any appreciable road building in any part of the Ozarks, and these rather sporadic efforts tended to concentrate in the northern and western fringes. During 1858 the first transcontinental stagecoach service dipped into the northern Ozarks. During the same year, Springfield, Missouri, became a "relay depot" for the Butterfield Stages to San Francisco. When the Civil War began three feeder stage lines had been extended southward into some of the more accessible Ozarks, and a first telegraph line had been put through between St. Louis and Springfield, Missouri, and presently extended to the Indian "Enforcement Base" at Fort Smith. But coordinated road systems came excessively late.

Throughout the writer's boyhood, and well beyond the era

of the First World War, Ozarks travel by auto ranged from the improbable to the impossible. In terms of language, folk beliefs, agriculture and rural living, the marks and patterns of isolation remained clear and strong.

A dozen years after Armistice Day, the writer, as a distinctly temporary and expendable employee of the Arkansas Highway Department, had a slight part in locating first through roads in a sizable area of the southwestern Ozarks. I noted with penitence that neither the livestock nor the human population had learned to respect the deadliness of the automotive age. For the first time trucks and autos were getting in and out of dozens of far-back communities. The country people were only beginning to learn to get out of the way of the omnipotent internal combustion engine, but the chickens, guinea fowl, household cats and hounds, horses and mules, and the freely ranging cattle and hogs were comparatively slow, too frequently fatally slow to learn the all-important lesson. I once accompanied the highway commissioner on an inspection tour and slithered into a ditch to avoid premature slaughter of a sow and seven accompanying pigs. The highway commissioner was furious at my clumsiness and insisted on taking the wheel. Within the hour he collided head on with a ranging steer, wrecked the auto, destroyed the bovine and fractured his gesturing arm.

The prolonged sparsity or absence of Ozarks roads was the number-one factor in perpetuating isolation. But there were paralleling factors and scarcities. These included public education. Public schools like public roads, entered the Ozarks by way of Missouri, but likewise few and late. By 1869 there were sixteen public schools in twenty-two counties of the Missouri Ozarks, but only three in all the Arkansas Ozarks. In 1890, when Harvard was noting its two hundred and fifty-fourth birthday and Vermont's public school system was marking the centennial of the nation's oldest state school system including four years of state-supported college attendance, the entire State of Arkansas had only twenty-five public schools with a total enrollment of 410. The public-school census was then somewhere near one-fourth of one percent of the total population. As noted, the 22,300 square miles of Arkansas Ozarks had only three public school systems or districts. Meanwhile the Merrill Report, published by the U.S. Senate in 1869, estimated that fully 80 percent of the Ozarks population was illiterate.

"Intellectual" isolation vied strongly with physical isolation. The 1870's were to materialize as a founding era of district schools, preponderantly one-room all-graders, throughout most of the Ozarks. But the public-school obstetrics were made difficult by deeply-rooted opposition to what politicians of that era still dubbed extravagant man education. The Negro was already a principal target of this opposition. During 1845 the still new State of Arkansas enacted laws to make the private "education" of slaves a felony. Here is a record instance: During 1859 my father's mother was arrested, brought to court, prosecuted, fined and severely reprimanded for the then felony of "teaching a slave child to read and write."

In the course of directing an unsuccessful defense of his wife, my grandfather, Alf Wilson, at the time U.S. prosecuting attorney for western Arkansas, pointed out that Arkansas then had at least 60,000 Negro children who were "lawfully condemned to lifelong illiteracy." He lost the case. The circuit judge tagged my grandmother with a fifty-dollar fine and "instructed" her that the schooling of minor slaves was a willful menace to the integrity of the Anglo-Saxon race.

The slave girl, Mary, carried her learning well. She was fifteen when she was lawfully freed by the Emancipation Proclamation. On two earlier occasions my grandparents had sought to "free" all their slaves. On the first try made in 1852 all the Negroes voted against it. They saw "freedom" as abandonment and eventual starvation. In a thought-provoking journal record, my grandfather noted several dilemmas which he declared to be common to slave ownership in the Ozarks and comparable backwoods areas throughout the South and border South. He noted that neither he nor his wife believed in the "moral correctness" of slavery. They had never deliberately purchased or otherwise acquired ownership of any human being. He insisted this point of view was quite commonplace throughout his own and many neighboring communities where, in the main, the slaves were inherited properties.

My grandfather insisted that slavery had long since become a weighty, even a ruinous obligation to the owners and was a prime detriment to the valid growth and development of the Ozarks as a whole. The hilly lands contained few farming sites where slaves could be profitably employed at producing crops which were marketable for profit. Cotton, on which the economy of slavery in the South so largely depended, had already turned out to be a very poor harvest for the Ozarks where neither soil nor climate is suited to growing the most-used fiber crop. The same was generally true of tobacco and in the main of cattle raising.

By basic geography and economy the Ozarks never were suited to the obligations of slave ownership. Yet, ironically, the ratio of slave-owning farmers, which in 1860 averaged between 15 and 18 percent of active landowners throughout the entire South, apparently applied to the Ozarks in almost the same ratio. In instance after instance settlers who could not feed themselves adequately were "carrying" slaves—perennially on the brink of starvation. "I'm nigger poor," was a repetitious lament of Ozarks farmers, most of whom were small holders. Alf Wilson continued to point out that all too many Ozark settlers, including himself,

9

were continually buying land which they could not afford in a usually futile attempt to support slaves whom they could not afford, did not need, and could not "conscience."

After my grandmother's death and my grandfather's departure to join the Confederate Army, the newly freed slaves remained with and on his two farms. When the war ended, most of the Negroes drifted away. Mary, who had taught the "home class" which included my father, three of his brothers and several slave children, became a domestic in what is now Kansas City and presently one of the first, possibly the very first Negro woman superintendent of a public-school system anywhere in the United States.

Following the Civil War, and for the most part despairingly, the Negroes drifted out of the Ozarks, at first mostly to the south to become share croppers of cotton. The few who stayed had the distinctly wretched choice of retreat to the poorest or previously abandoned hillside farms or of moving into towns to loll in the "pools" of unskilled labor, hoping for occasional employment as ditch diggers, wood choppers or domestics.

The loss of the Negro was unquestionably the gravest sociological loss suffered by the Ozarks region. More than any other one component of frontier population the Negro had added depths and richness to the folk culture of the region and to its potential scientific and economic development. George Washington Carver, born and raised a slave in the lower Missouri Ozarks, typified the magnificent Negro talent which, due to avoidable mass prejudice and degeneracy, has been substantially lost to the region.

The Negro a century ago was ready-proved as the most valuable balance factor of the Ozarks. In pre-Civil-War times the Negro slave was the premier hewer of wood, drawer of water and builder of roads in a land where the felling of timber, the utilization of surface water and road-building were basic definitions of community and countryside self-realization and, in many instances, survival.

PREFACE

The inevitable exodus of the Negro served to restore isolation and to return the frontier roads to an era of prolonged lapse. The half-century following the Civil War was the nation's most definitive era of land travel and settlements along or by means of through roads. For the most part the Ozarks lacked the latter and in great part they were by-passed by the most historic of Westward migrations.

In the later 1860's Sanford C. Faulkner's saga of the *Arkansas Traveler* depicted the persisting dilemma of lower Ozarks roads in the following dialogue: When the Traveler said, "My friend, can't you tell me about the road I'm to travel tomorrow?" the Squatter said, "Stranger you won't git out'n these diggin's fer six weeks. But when it gits so you kin start, you see that big sloo over thar? Well, you'll have to git crost that, then you take the road up the bank and in about a mile you'll come to a two-acre-and-a-half corn patch. The corn is mitely in the weeds, but you needn't mind that, jist ride on. About a mile and a half, or two miles from that you'll come to the damndest swamp you ever struck in all your travels, it's boggy enough to mire a saddle blanket. Thar's a fust-rate road about six feet under hit."

Traveler: "How am I to get at the road?"

Squatter: "You can't git at hit nary time till the weather stiffens down some. Well, about a mile beyont, you come to a place where thar's two roads. . . . You can take the right-hand ef you want to, you'll foller it a mile or so and then you'll find it runs out. . . . Comes then, you'll be obleeged to come back and try the left-hand fork. When you git about two miles on that, you may know you are wrong, fur there ain't no road thar. You'll be figgerin' by then you kin find the way back to whar you started from . . ."

Half a century after the Arkansas Traveler's hypothetical times (1865–75), the status of Arkansas roads and that of Ozarks roads in general had not been impressivly changed. The covered-wagon routes had bypassed the Ozarks. The horse-and-wagon age came in a generation later. The auto age came puttering in at least a decade after it had invaded the United States as a whole.

I caught my first glimpse of an automobile during 1910. The gasoline buggy was owned by a countryside medical practitioner who was usually too drunk to walk, though he drove the auto quite ably so far as he had a road to drive on—which wasn't very far; never more than five miles from the place of cranking. Twenty years later prospective auto buyers of the nearby town were still insisting they'd be hanged if they bought any auty-mobile until they'd seen and felt it navigate the road to Winslow, a hill-country village about twenty miles south of my native countryside.

The prime problem of the Ozarks then, even as today, was how to adjust to adjoining frontiers and how to live with and in the nation as a whole. Today, as a century or centuries ago, the Ozarks are preponderantly a backwoods region; the real sense of "backwoods" being timbered or partly cleared lands beyond immediate boundaries of towns or cities.

Every county in the Arkansas Ozarks and all except two or at most three counties in the Missouri Ozarks are still backwoods in terms of principal areas. It is well that they are. Continuation of backwoods supports the great resources of native timbers and the key industries of fishing, hunting and tourist catering. It sustains the convincing cultural resources of the Ozarks and does most to save what remains of the tillable soils.

Only the Ozarks backwoods keep the region in the bona fide foregrounds of literate and widespread public interest. This, too, has been true for a very long time. It was conspicuously true back in the early 1830's when my forebears first settled in the Arkansas Ozarks. It was consistently true throughout my father's eighty-seven-year lifetime, all spent in the Arkansas

12

PREFACE

Ozarks. It has never ceased being true during the more than half-century of my own firsthand and native's knowledge of the Ozarks.

I have been viewing anew and pondering again my native land, viewing and pondering as a changed man, noting a rather baffling intermingling of changed and comparatively unchanged countrysides.

In earlier years I first viewed and pondered Ozarks places and peoples as a newspaper reporter and intermittently as a writer for magazines and reviews. Most of my published work was factual. Most of my editors accepted or rejected it as such. My primary interest was in the individual and mainly rural people of the Ozarks. Here again my editors employed free choice of acceptance or rejection. A few, including the lucidly pompous Ellery Sedgwick, late editor-publisher of *The Atlantic,* and my long-time boss on the St. Louis *Post-Dispatch,* the mellowed but brilliant realist Paul Greer, had chided me for the habitual favoring of rural Ozarkers. "You're much too damn sweet with your fellow hillbillies," Greer had shouted. "You'd sweet talk the devil himself if you chanced to find the Old Persuader going around in patched overalls held up by a single gallus buttoned with a bent nail. . . ."

Then, shortly after Mencken's *American Mercury* published two of my earlier efforts in Ozark fiction (it was clearly labeled "fiction"), the redoubtable Sage of Baltimore wrote me waspishly ". . . I've now had opportunity to glimpse and smell a few of the quaint Ozark folk whom you adore so avidly. I can't prove they are any lower than whale manure on the ocean bed, but I doubt if they are very much higher and I can only rate you as an incurable romanticist . . ."

By strange coincidence, I rated Henry Louis Mencken as an incurable romanticist, meaning the antithesis of a factual reporter. This prejudice became stronger when the Great Man later told me (in person) how he had once traveled through the Ozarks on a railroad which "parallels the western boundary of Arkansas" and watched the natives "lousing through the tree-tops." I never saw anything like that in the Ozarks or, indeed, in any other of the thirty countries in which I have traveled or worked or soldiered. I never saw that railroad which parallels the western boundary of Arkansas—in some part, at least, because there is not and never was such a railroad.

Many years later it was as a would-be homecomer that I strove to report and appraise the Ozarks, not for a newspaper or a magazine, or even—heavens to Betsy—a book, but rather for my own guidance. Accordingly I encouraged myself to peer closely and feel personally.

But this undertaking and resolve would not obliterate some of the more essential way markers. Beginning with the absolute fact that the Ozarks as a whole remained a frontier. Not a frontier of fertile lands virtually free for the taking, but rather of a preponderance of comparatively poor land, in great part badly used, yet in greater part distinctly restorable to worthwhile uses including grasslands, water sites, woodlands, wildlife preserves, vacation ranges, and so on.

The Ozarks are no longer frontiers in the sense of being farthest outposts of a nation's territory. Yet they are frontiers of viewpoint and spirit and of opportunities for restoration to usefulness. I found dozens of instances of everyday people in the process of restoring farms, forest lands, hunting lands and valuable rangelands, and by so doing restoring themselves. I met city physicians in the process of establishing rural practices primarily for the fun of it; city pastors who were serving country churches primarily for love of it. I noted that far more conspicuously than before, the Ozarks have people coming in as others go out, which is still another mark of a self-perpetuating frontier.

CHAPTER I

Glimpsing the Ozark Backhills

GRANDPA WILSON settled in the Arkansas Ozarks in 1836. It was something of an accident. The same held for his brother Greene, the artistic member of the family.

Alfred (my grandpa) was sixteen and Greene was seventeen when they headed west and south out of the far coves back of Fayetteville, Tennessee. Alf took off in broad daylight, goading a pair of wild young oxen yoked to a two-wheel cart. Uncle Greene headed west about a week later aboard a sound, fleet Morgan horse, a situation which necessitated his leaving after dark. Both passed through Chickasaw Bluffs (now Memphis) and ferried the Mississippi aboard Gaither's Tow Barges, perhaps on the same day, but the brothers did not meet. Grandpa Wilson took the wrong turn at Cypress Stages a couple of days beyond the ferry site. He didn't find out he was on the wrong road until he was in the far and largely roadless hills about halfway to Fort Smith, Arkansas.

15

THE BODACIOUS OZARKS

Winter was settling by then. On a snowy afternoon, Alf Wilson's cart bounded down the side of a boulder outcrop and broke a wheel. When he saw the damage was irreparable, the youngest of this flock of nine Wilsons burned the broken wheel and presently the rest of the cart in order to keep from freezing to death during the bitter night. Next morning he led his oxen into the saloon-littered stagecoach terminal which he presently joined in naming Fayetteville, Arkansas.

There Grandpa swapped one of his steers for two weeks' lodging at one of the stage taverns and bartered the other steer for a set of law books. He didn't exactly cherish the law books, but the owner had died and bequeathed the law books as a first and, as things turned out, the final payment on his tavern bill. Lacking feed for his final ox, Alf Wilson begrudgingly swapped the hungry steer for the law "library." Lacking other occupation, he settled to reading the books, then to lawyering, then to farming, then to politics, and eventually to the gratis and unrequested title of Old Legal.

Meanwhile, Alf's artistic brother was winning the durable designation of Old Illegal. My great-uncle Greene managed to take the right road out of Cypress Stages, but apparently he took the wrong way to Little Rock. I never identified all that happened; I do know that Great-Uncle left Little Rock headed for the far-back Ozarks with a sheriff's pistol slug in his right leg and the Pulaski County sheriff in better than lukewarm pursuit. The Morgan horse, as a breed, was one of the fastest and toughest ever begotten of earth, air, water, and male and female horses. And Greene Wilson's horse was true to the breed. In any case, he outran the sheriff's horse and Uncle Greene reached the limestone-cave country of what are now the Carroll County, Arkansas, Ozarks with his horse and fiddle intact but with his right leg amputated—in deference to the gangrene which had directly settled around the sheriff's bullet.

16

By 1854, when President Pierce appointed my grandpa Federal prosecutor for the western district of Arkansas, Great-Uncle Greene had settled down to counterfeiting. Solid money, rather than sloppy greenbacks or bank script, appealed to his subtle artistic heritage. In the beginning Great-Uncle Greene struck off a few kegfuls of lead dollars. They were strikingly original and quite pretty, but apparently nobody except possibly a blind bartender ever seriously considered accepting them in lieu of money.

Some said the lead dollars came out bulgy in the middle and ragged at the edges because the bronze molds Uncle Greene used couldn't be clamped tight enough. But presently Greene began counterfeiting and gold-dipping ten- and twenty-dollar gold pieces —eagles and double eagles. Even the experts found them lifelike and fairly negotiable. When the U.S. Treasury Department finally got out warnings, my grandfather, as the local Federal prosecutor, was understandably embarrassed. By special messenger he sent word to Greene that he would hate mightily to be obliged to prosecute his own brother. I have a copy of Uncle Greene's reply: "Dear Bro. Alfey: Don't feel too bad. They'll have to ketch me first. Your Loving Bro. Greene."

During May of 1861, when my grandpa set out for Little Rock to be sworn in as the customary colonel in the Confederate Army, brother Greene began supplying counterfeit U.S. gold for the aid, comfort and advancement of the Confederacy. Apparently the spurious coinage gave the Boys in Gray considerable aid and a lot of comfort. It showed up in bawdy houses as far north as St. Louis and in some part may have helped supply other military requirements. In any case, Uncle Greene counterfeited like crazy throughout the Civil War.

After the Struggle between the States was momentarily concluded, my grandfather, understandably, was no longer a U.S. attorney, and his gratis title of Old Legal was temporarily of no particular significance. But his brother Greene was going strong with his counterfeiting, his fiddling, singing and folkish antics. Travelers told of hearing wondrous fiddle music pouring out of cave entrances or far backhill meetin' houses even before they could hear the stomping of dancing feet inside. Federal men reported that Uncle Greene's artistically funny money kept cropping up all the way from St. Louis to the Portlands, i.e., Maine and Oregon.

Beginning in the early 1890's the family began getting dribbles of dependable information about its estrayed artist member. These came directly from Uncle Fred Morrow, my mother's younger brother, who had worked his way through a medical school in Memphis and, diploma in hand, set out for the backhills to pick himself a location. He rode a livery-stable horse into the wilds of Carrol County, Arkansas, as far as a crossroads village called Green Forest where the rented horse abruptly sank down dead. Fred Morrow, M.D., diagnosed this as a heart attack, buried the horse, and set up practice in and around Green Forest, in truly backhill Ozarks.

His first case was a gunshot wound, his second and third were knife wounds. Then came an influx of babies, followed by a virtual epidemic of gunshot wounds. Among the latter were two members of a U.S. marshal's party who had ridden out into the lime-cave hills to haul in Old Illegal, alias Greene Wilson. Four law men rode out. Only two rode back. The other two returned to the village face downward in a rented farm wagon. Both the wounded had been shot in the buttocks. That looked very much like the antics of Old Illegal. My doctor uncle tweezered out the bullets; both were home-molded minie balls obviously fired from a muzzle-loader with low powder charges. When the marshal asked what the young doctor made of it, my medical doctor uncle answered: "I've seen that mold of minie balls before.

18

'Pears to be where Greene Wilson customarily shoots the federal men."

The marshal interrupted to explain that insofar as he had personally winged Old Illegal, the aforenamed criminal would unquestionably be calling for medical attention in the very near future, at which time it was the doctor's bounden duty to turn the desperado in. Uncle Fred didn't see it that way. He figured that whoever truly needed his services would get them and U.S. marshals could go mix their own juleps. The marshal and his men were hardly out of sight when a puny little boy, garbed in a long yellow shirt without breeches, came riding in bareback and lickety-split to summon the doctor and trail him back to Old Greene Wilson's hideout.

Uncle Fred advised the pantsless Mercury to simmer down and prior to setting out treated the youth to a fifteen-cent lunch at the local snackery. Then he saddled his horse, took up his surgery kit and with the boy leading the way rode up into the cave country.

Young Doc Morrow knew whom he would be treating. He didn't know that he would be obliged to tether his horse, light a pine-knot torch which the way-shower had readied, and slosh and stumble more than half a mile into a cave. Uncle Greene was a cave man, all right, and a badly shot cave man. My medical uncle succeeded in kindling a fire with discarded bedding straw, heating a pan of water and lighting a knee-high kerosene lantern with a cracked chimney. He washed the chest wound, dug out the bullet, heated his "brandin' irons," cauterized the surface areas, then dressed and bandaged the old man's chest and shoulder. During the long ordeal my great uncle didn't cry out once. Instead, he asked questions, all quite rational. How long before he could play his fiddle again? What did the doctor recommend? What was the prescription and how much was the charge?

My doctor uncle favored with forthright answers. Having first made the slender old man as comfortable as possible on the floor bunk, he pronounced: There was a fair chance the old man's shoulder and arm would presently recover sufficiently for fiddle playing. Nobody could be sure, but the least the doc could do was to come back and recheck the wound the following day and a couple of times after that. The doc would also send back the little boy with a supply of food and some cooking utensils; having first endeavored to tell the brat how and what to cook. Uncle Fred then checked the obviously homemade peg leg which just as obviously had never come any ways near fitting. "After your shoulder heals, I'll get you measured for a decent wooden leg. You'll have to pay for this. As for me, I don't require any funny money. I got funny patients."

Uncle Greene seemed hurt by the reference to funny money. He vowed he had quit counterfeiting nearly ten years before; he was a reformed and a double-baptised and duly saved Foot-Washing Baptist, and a bill-paying, law-abiding American citizen. Young Doc Morrow said that was all very gratifying and he further recommended that as soon as possible the old man get the hell out of the dark, stinking cave, and bunk up in a log cabin the same as any other law-abiding, properly-saved Ozarker. Uncle Greene promised to do just that.

The reformed one recovered from his wound. When Uncle Fred drove out in a surrey with an artificial-limb salesman to help make the measures, Uncle Greene had moved into an abandoned loggers' shack a couple of miles out of Fingle's Rim. The location was considerably less accessible than the cave, but at least somewhere near averagely liveable.

Uncle Greene welcomed his professional callers with an improvised fiddle concert of Irish jigs. As they hauled the old man down the gulchy mountainside, Uncle Greene made quite a ceremony of tossing what he said were the last of his coin molds into a deep pool of the Little Buffalo River.

For many years the kin across in Washington and Benton counties "follered" the doings of Uncle Greene by way of Doc Morrow's occasional reports and the less reliable hillside grapevine. The general understanding was that among his numerous goings and comings Old Illegal had turned out to be quite a salvationer. Armed with his fiddle and hymn book he was getting to be a soul-saving circuit rider with music, but without compensation.

There were the inevitable I-hear-tell stories about Greene Wilson. The one I liked best dealt with a brush arbor revival meetin' near Savoy, Arkansas, where the itinerant preacher was leading a community prayer for rain. It happened on a blistery September night. As was and still is too frequently the case, the Ozarks had been punished by a demon of a drought so ruthlessly prolonged that poor people were already going hungry and facing the prospects of a starvation winter.

The preacher was praying for a divine recurrence of the parable of feeding the hungering multitude. After a time, he began calling on the faithful to testify individually. When the fiddler's turn came, Uncle Greene opened: "O, Lord, go ahead and care for each one accordin' to his needs. Grant every household a barrel of cured pork, a barrel of molasses, a barrel of flour, a barrel of salt, a barrel of pepper—aw, hell! that's too damn' much pepper!"

The Life of Salvation went hard with Uncle Greene. Crippled, past seventy, and scarecrow poor, he fished, hunted and hobbled and scratched out a living as a backhill searcher man. He trailed down wild honey; dug and sold ginseng root; picked, hulled and peddled chinquapins, chestnuts and black walnuts; and otherwise scrambled for the makings of a nickel here and a dime there.

21

For better or worse, and at best it was pretty bad, Old Illegal remained invincibly law-abiding. And even as he grew feebler and ever more ragged, he refused to have business with anything even faintly resembling handouts. Every time my grandfather sent or overtured to send money or goods, his brother Greene spurned the would-be gifts. He also refused to take money for his music. "I already got charity," he explained, "and I sure as hell don't take handouts!"

Finally, during the ruthlessly hot summer of 1916, Uncle Greene scrawled and mailed a note to my grandfather: "Bro. Alf: I have got to die. It would oblige me mightily if you would come and see me. Your brother Greene."

My grandpa had died seven years before, so the letter was passed on to my father who accepted the invitation. To my profound gratification, he took me along. We hitched one of the broncos to the one-horse spring wagon and set out to locate Uncle Greene. My father had taken for granted that the old-timer was on or near his deathbed. As we soon discovered, that was nowhere near the truth. On the second day out, we stopped to buy some provisions in a loggers' village called Loafer's Glory. The storekeeper reported that Uncle Greene had driven up to his store less than a week before—behind a lawfully borrowed mule team—with his fiddle and a red kerchief filled with fine ginseng root (to barter with) in the front seat and a hen crate full of cats in the wagon bed.

"Why the cats?"

The storekeeper indulged in a sad, understanding smile. "Old feller 'pears to be tetched in the haid. When I ast him 'Why the cats?' he says he is collectin' cats for to haul to Eureky. So, when I asks what in tarnal he aimed to do with cagefuls of cats in Eureky, the old man says, 'Sell to the moneyed bastards fer a dollar apiece.'"

The narrator again indulged in a sad and understanding smile. He told us that Uncle Greene had spent about half the afternoon playing his fiddle for the entertainment of the usual gathering of store loafers. Also that the old man had practically started a riot by stating an outrageous question and following it with an even more outrageous answer. Question: Two adder snakes are egg-zactly thirty inches long. One day the two snakes get into a fight and each one commences swallering the other one at the rate of one inch a minute. At the end of thirty minutes, what would be left? Answer: There wouldn't be nothing left.

Next day, at Avoca, we came upon a still warmer trail. Our Uncle Greene had been through only one day before. He was still collecting cats—all kinds, toms, tabbies, strays, house, barn, porch, and wild, but recruiting on a very high ethical level. Yessir, it was for shore our Uncle Greene was no common cat thief. He was getting hold of the cats square and honest. He would hobble to a cabin door, knock, and ask in his courtly manner if the folks happened to have any cats they chose to get rid of. As a rule, they did. Reportedly one family contributed sixteen surplus cats to the roundup. Several had surpluses of half a dozen or more.

The storekeeper at Avoca reported that by then our aged uncle had three chicken crates, all smackdab full of cats. "Ever' kind of fool cat you ever see," the man of commerce affirmed. "Tiger stripers, yellers, whites, blacks, grays, blues. . . . Big cats and li'l cats and quite a lot of fat cats."

Having refreshed himself from a grayish clay jug, the storekeeper allowed the cats were all getting fatter on account of Uncle Greene had been feeding them real good. "I give the old man a mighty good dicker on some canned sal-mon that had got rusty on me. . . . Onderstand, now, it was good sal-mon fish . . . only the tins had got a mite rusty."

My father promptly identified that the dicker had been a good one for the storekeeper. Our uncle had swapped a pound of dry ginseng roots worth at least six dollars for four dozen cans of pink salmon. At least nobody could doubt that the confined cats were being properly fed.

"Your old tetched uncle man done a funny thing while here," the storekeeper related. "In his fiddle case he carried one of them round handglasses that make things look lots bigger'n they really is. So, after we'd finished swappin' the old man asked me could he take a look at what gold coins I keep in the cash box. So I let him do it. . . . One after the next, he stood there peerin' at them gold pieces through that there magnifyin' glass like a child peerin' at a brand new playpurty. After he'd finished lookin', I see him count the coin back into the cash drawer, fair and square. Then the old man commenced to play his fiddle and sing. And man, I'm tellin' you that even iffen your old uncle does look to be a hundert years old, the old sawbuck can still sing like a martingale."

My father began seeking out the motive for Uncle Greene's cat collecting. The storekeeper staggered to the doorway and favored the rising breeze with a tremendous charge of tobacco spit. "My notion is this . . . poor old Uncle Greene has met up with mighty hard times since he quit counterfeitin'. He's a-gettin' old and as I figger it, turnin' honest might of tetched him in the haid—proved too much fer his jedgment. Anyway, its seems some mis-chievous durn clodhopper convinced him he could make himself some good money by ketchin' up a wagonload of cats and peddlin' 'em in Eureky where the new-come rich folks is fresh out of cats and panicky to buy 'em at a dollar apiece . . . I tried to tell your uncle diffrunt, but didn't do no good."

As we shall presently notice in better detail, Eureky, listed on contemporary maps as Eureka Springs, is an ever astonishing mountainside town in what were then backhill Ozarks of Carroll County. At the turn of the century, the discovery of allegedly medicinal waters in the uniquely vertical settlement had drawn a stampede of real or would-be sick people, ranging from the hopelessly stricken or violently insane to the usual majority of comparatively healthy hypochondriacs and their accompanying kin. Thus, almost overnight, the peculiarly inaccessible moonshiners' outpost had been changed into the biggest as well as the flimsiest town in the Arkansas Ozarks, with a transient and immigrant population of at least 25,000. Most of the influx presently seeped and simmered away, but at the time of our pilgrimage to Uncle Greene's, Eureky was the wealth-and-wonder capital of the Ozarks.

My father drove hard in hopes of overtaking our tetched uncle before his certain-to-be-unfortunate arrival in Eureka Springs. But overtaking was made completely impossible by the goat trail of a road which even now is probably the steepest, curviest, and most "scenic" main road in all the Ozarks. Once more we arrived only in time to hear about what had "fresh happened." We learned that Uncle Greene and his cargo of cats had pulled into Eureky around the middle of the previous afternoon. Apparently the loud and boisterous behavior of the cats was aggravated by the rough and bouncy ride and by the fact that Uncle Greene had filled one crate exclusively with adult tomcats.

In any case, the cat-peddling venture was badly snarled long before the vendor got as far as the bandstand which had been built under a limestone ledge near the middle of the town. A horde of boys took in after the cat wagon at the high bend near Streepey's Wayside. In practically no time the natural caterwauls and miscellaneous uproar was being exceeded by man-made kinds. Uncle Greene was visibly upset. When he undertook to call out his wares—"Cats . . . I got all kinds of cats . . . Who needs

a good cat? . . . Good ratters, good mousers . . . for a dollar?"
—his rather appealing voice was completely drowned out by the
mingled yowling of the cats and the curiosity seekers.

The old man flapped the lines and headed for the fringe of
grass which comprised the public green, such as it was. There
he hitched his mules, hobbled back to the wagon load of squall-
ing cats and took out his ever shiny fiddle from its beat-up
wooden case. He struck up a tune. But this time his music failed
to still either the savage humans or the unhappy cats. Indeed,
it seemed to make a bad situation worse.

Then Uncle Greene reached his decision. The closer and more
attentive onlookers heard him speak gently and resignedly. "So
you smart alecs don't like honest peddlin'! So you'd ruther act
stinky and not buy nothin'. So I won't disaccommodate you for
to buy no cats. . . . I'll give 'em to you, for free . . ."

The old man replaced his fiddle in the battered case which he
laid fondly on the front seat of his wagon. Then he hobbled to
the rear of the wagon, let down the backboard, and began opening the poultry crates. Cats began pouring out, in feline deluges.
They bounded over the fringe of park, leaped and skipped across
the dusty road, eagerly resumed their fighting and courting along
the board sidewalks and in the storefronts.

A friendly witness told us the story in explicit detail. "Hit
was just egg-zactly the right thing that he done." The witness's
brown cheeks were becoming streaked with tears brought on by
laughter. "Ef the old coot was my great-uncle, I'd be the proudest
man in Eureky."

"What's to become of the cats?" I inquired.

"You needn't worry your stoopid little haid about that, Sonny,"
the informant assured me. "They is plenty of openin's hereabouts
for cats, on account of Eureky is a right big town." The skinny
onlooker concluded thoughtfully, " 'Nother p'int is that cats
can take a sight better care of cats than people can take of people."

26

Next day, when we finally trailed him to his shack, our Uncle Greene spoke similar sentiments. But his total outlook seemed benevolent. Before he had finished welcoming us into his home, he explained that he had late changed his mind about dyin' off. . . . He said that in the course of his otherwise lossful trip he had discovered a wondrous health-restoring drink. The name of the drink was strawberry sody pop. He hadn't hardly no more than swigged down two bottlefuls and by next morning his bladder aches were just about all gone. He had swigged down maybe a dozen bottles since and he was fresh decided to live another thirty years. (He did live about three more.)

I remember that we made so many misturns that we didn't arrive at Uncle Greene's shack until very late in the day. There had been a shower earlier in the afternoon. The grass was almost magically freshened. The oak leaves showed a metallic luster, and a golden green mist blew up from the valley.

In that setting even the one-windowed, weather-gray shack built of pole-size logs chinked with brown-red clay seemed beautiful. So did my great uncle. Old Illegal looked almost exactly as I had imagined he would. He was a tall man, with a thin face, high forehead, and silky white hair. His eyes were large, almost grass green, and superbly expressive of practically every mood or emotion, except fear or hatred. There was nothing in his eyes or his thin and sensitive lips or his generally poetic face to indicate that he had ever feared or hated. His voice was amazingly clear and young, as was his laughter.

I was disappointed in his fiddle playing because it seemed to waver and rasp with encroaching age. But his singing delighted me. It had a lyric gaiety which I could feel and enjoy powerfully without being able to explain.

From the moment he asked us into his one bare-floored room, Uncle Greene was in high spirits. He talked of old times until wet darkness settled. Then he permitted me to build a small fire in the blackrock fireplace and to set up a big iron pot which contained the squirrel-and-rabbit stew which, supplemented with Nancy Hall sweet potatoes roasted in hot ashes, provided our supper.

After supper Uncle Greene and my father talked on and on. After a while the family's artist member began speaking of the Ozarks. "Used to be a real happy land for us outlaws," he recalled. "But for us reformed sons-of-bitches no country ain't no great sight better than no other country. . . . But I still say . . . pious bastard I've turned out to be, that whichever the country, hit's the backhills that stay interestin' and closest to everlastin' . . ."

I agreed with Great-Uncle Greene at the time. I still agree. The Ozarks are some fifty thousand square miles of mid-continent frontier which is above averagely durable. But its backhills remain the storied bulwarks, its undying stronghold of whimsy and engaging truth.

Listening to the allegedly reformed counterfeiter recite glorious stories of his preponderantly inglorious past warmed my already budding desire to seek out and write down the stories, the enduring breath of these remote roughlands. The desire grew like a poke shoot in early spring. By the following year, and newly turned seventeen, I began tramping the backhills on my own impetus and feet.

It began as an intermittent kind of tramping, necessarily interspersed with farm work with my father, with splurges of schooling and presently with more laborious splurges of newspaper reporting. But backhill tramping became my particular joy. All the more so because of its wondrous talents for dropping one into the long-gone past and hoisting him into the near or distant future. The Ozark backhills are still like that. They are where yesterdays touch discerningly or leap bodily into tomorrow.

CHAPTER II

Any Day Is Tramping Day

THE TIME WAS late April, 1920. The place was northwest Arkansas. It was spring again. I still believe that in April the Ozarks are the youngest of all lands of the earth. And I was one with the April and getting lost in it.

While seeking to locate the old Wire Road, so named because it was the route of the first telegraph line into regions southwest, I met an old woman who was heading for her sassafras-hedged garden. She was tall and spare and tented in billowy gray calico. Her slender, pitying face was almost lost in a pale blue sunbonnet which had a scoop brim, known locally as a foreshader, almost as big as a peach basket. I spoke good morning.

She dispensed with salutations. "Hit's spring ag'in" she shrilled. "I got radishes most big enough to choke a cow on. Got mule-ear lettuce most of a size to wrop a goose egg in. Got reddenin' star-berries . . . most enough to make a short starberry cake . . . yup," she continued, "and in case you be lookin' for the Wire Road,

29

you only got to foller that sloppy ole rail fence. Hit'll take you out'n this pertater knob and hit'll lead you to wheresome ever you needs to go. . . . Likewise to some places you shouldn't ought to of got into . . ."

Cows, dangling old brass bells, munched at what once had been roadside pastures. The new green grass was generously scattered with midget bluet flowers. A line of wind-swayed daffodils marked the site of a cabin long since rotted away. At a zigzagging edge of scrub-oak forest I saw a squat figure which I first took to be a less than teens-age boy with unusually broad shoulders. The little one turned toward me. Then he lifted off his ragged-brimmed straw hat, and I saw that his hair was beer-foam white.

I joined him in what apparently had been a cattle trail of earlier years. When I spoke howdy the undersize told me that his name was Sam Blankhall. "I ain't no boy," he added with deep conviction. "Pervidin' I live till then, I'll be sixty-seben, comes my next birthday."

He noted, too, that he kept a five-acre patch of ground in Tater-knob Holler, about four turns and a rock-throw down the trail and about the same closeness to the old Wire Road. He next explained matter-of-factly that he came of a long line of little people —good folks, only somehow or other they seldom ever got their growth. In a fairly abrupt onrush of confidence he told me he used to keep a country store near Shell Knob. He'd done right good with it until one night the store somehow got burned flat down to the ground. Without so much as a nickel's worth of in-surance and without so much as a lucky quarter in his jeans, there he was, full obliged for and owing for a whole stock of store goods, a good part of which he had never unpacked. "For a biz-ness man," Sammy summarized, "that makes it rocky."

After we had walked the specified four turns and a rock-throw, Sammy asked me into his single-room log cabin. A corner was piled high with ready-hulled black walnuts, well-dried and waiting to be "jabbed out." My host explained that he was paying off his indebtedness to the wholesale grocery firm which had "trusted" him with the fire-destroyed stock by picking out walnut kernels and selling them to the town drug stores. He figured he could maybe be squared with the wholesaler in maybe five to six years.

Sammy invited me to set a spell and wet my gullet with a dipperful of persimmon beer. The latter proved to be a murky pink syrup which fortified a honeylike sweetness with a rocking, hammerlike blast of alcohol. "A reel friendly drinkin' licker," Sammy said. "Next to starberries and walnuts, ripe persimmins is the best flavor they is . . . meanin' persimmin beer is the best made drink they is. . . . Pervided," he amended, "hit's made proper to leave a man the strength to swaller and keep on settin' or walkin' . . . persimmin beer keeps a man young . . ." My host qualified the analysis: "Pervided a man waits till December freezes to skin up the trees and pick off the persimmins. . . . Big thing is," Sammy refilled our pewter cups, "the beer keeps a man young enough to skin up the tallest trees where the persimmins grow honey-sweet and apple-big . . ."

Sammy was filling the cups again. "There be times when I gits the notion that this here persimmin beer keeps me so durn young I get borned afresh comes each A-pril."

After a brief convalescence, I walked out into the green golden noontime where the light qualities were undergoing changes not entirely attributable to the persimmon beer. Clouds were piling in from the west. A line of white-bodied sycamores marked the course of a little river which meandered to the southeast. From the next hilltop I looked down on a great sweep of valley where yellow fennels bloomed in ungrazed pastures. There was rain in the hills. A green-gray mist was sweeping up the valley and slate-gray clouds were banking to the west.

31

THE BODACIOUS OZARKS

As I approached a sway-backed wooden bridge I was overtaken by the hard-laboring remains of a topless Model-T Ford auto. "Hop in, Tall Shorty!" The driver was a tiny man with an impressively deep voice and an almost bald and egg-shaped head which bobbed beside and slightly above a yellow-lettered wooden placard. The latter advised: U.S. MAIL—KEEP OUT. THAT MEANS YOU.

Except for a moldy canvas bag on the front seat, there was no visible indication of U.S. mail. The back seat was crowded with a dozen or so white hens, lying prostrate, their legs bound with strips of flannel, their beaks open, their bright little eyes quickly opening and slowly closing. The other occupant of the unsheltered back seat was a black-and-tan hound with distrustful eyes, an enormous mouth and a lusty aroma of vanquished skunks.

"You can set on the empty mailbag!" the driver bellowed. I obeyed, reflecting that in the Ozarks the tiniest men seem to have the biggest and most thunderous of voices. "By all that is pea-green monkey spit," the driver roared, "here comes the ga-damn rain!" He waved a sunburned hand to indicate the auto's complete lack of a roof, swore loudly as the first big drops began pelting us. The carrier scowled at me with unremitting ferocity. "Ga-damn mail's got to git through!" he roared.

At that moment the loud little engine popped like a medium-size firecracker and just as abruptly expired. As the narrow-tired vehicle sluffed to a halt, the carrier hoisted his skinny little legs over the doortop, dropped to the rocky earth, and still cursing, began cranking. On the fourth or fifth spin the auto began to quiver and backfire. Then the little engine began to pop again. The driver climbed back into the seat and stamped the foot pedal with great violence. As the auto lurched forward, the driver began scuffling frantically with the big wooden steering wheel. With almost superhuman effort he managed to turn off on a side road.

For a few frenzied minutes the little auto went bounding up an extremely steep and boulder-strewn aisle through a forest of giant white oaks. Here the rain changed to blowing mist, then abruptly vanished and became replaced with greenish sunlight.

"Where you headin'?" the carrier queried. Without waiting for an answer he continued to shout. "I'd aimed to sell them chickens down Avocy ways. But I'm takin' this mailbag back to Monkey Run. You goin' that way?"

"Been there already."

The mail carrier eyed me resentfully. "Hell of a place! Hell of a name. *Monkey Run!* Bet they ain't now, nor never was, a ga-damned monkey in a thousand miles to any side!" His tone of resentment lingered. "Who you doin' bin-ness with in Monkey Run?"

"Nobody," I admitted, "I was only passin' through, headed west."

The mail carrier's resentment seemed to change to dark suspicion. "You shore as hell ain't headed west now." He stopped the auto abruptly. "Who you lookin' for, nohow?"

Explanation had grown extremely difficult. "Old man Abel Clark. Used to be secretary to President Grant . . ."

The mail carrier took time to dissect a corner from a large black square of chewing tobacco. He thrust the dark triangle into his tiny mouth, chewed ferociously—with only one tooth visible or indicated, then spat into the wind. "Ole Abe Clark! I know him and his old woman. Live like mountain goats. . . . Run off from people forty years ago. Likely ain't looked at a dozen two-legged things since then!" He resumed chewing, and I prepared to duck the imminent side spray. "That's another thing I *don't* like about this country. . . . Hit's sprinkled with hiders outers—bank robbers, big-town whores, counterfeiters, train wreckers, hoss thieves. . . . Guess you done found that out."

He blinked sadly. "Speakin' personal," he said, "I don't rightly belong back in these here wild-hawg playgrounds. I come from a big town—Joplin, Missour-a. Used to keep live-ry stable there. Got myself sickened. Doctor commenced pleadin' I should get off down here to rest and re-cuperate. Said I'd get a lot out'n it." Again he spat violently. "All I got out'n it was to get stuck—with a extry wife. Had me one woman in Missour-a. She was one too many! So I come and latched onto another 'un down here in Arkansaw." His china-blue eyes seemed to plead for understanding. "One woman's more'n aplenty. But two women! Creepin' Jesus!"

"Lemme tell you somethin' else, Tall Shorty! This here Ozarker country is due for change." With meticulous care he now drew an undersize banana from his jacket pocket and began peeling it. "First thing you know, they'll be cee-ment roads into these bresh jungles. By that I don't mean wild-hawg and panther trails like we got now. I mean real roads straight through from Missour-a to Li'l Rock and such fur-off places as that. Them roads will be pasted down so damn hard that ever' time you dray your feet on 'em your boot nails will scratch up sparks big enough to start a far."

Unexpectedly the mail carrier stretched himself in the general shape of a capital Y. "Whenever them wide roads gits built, they'll be bound to get traveled by autos and trucks and people from ever' which side. First thing you know, these here crossroad and penny-whistle settle-ments will take and fade off—like the last stink of a dyin' pole cat. . . . I ain't here to tell you for shore how this Ozarker country will change over. But one way or the next, hit's bound and beholden to change over."

He permitted the auto to roll forward thereby enabling the engine to reawaken itself. The roadway led past a scattering of hillside cabins, then to a paintless little roadside store, with a

long window waveringly lettered with the intelligence: POST OFFICE
GEN. STORE: EAT . . .

Once more the mail carrier kicked the brake pedal. "Far as I
go for now," he explained. Then he added emphatically, "Ain't
took you no more'n ten miles off'n your road . . ."

That night I lodged in another log cabin. This one was the home
of a countryside herb doctor who called himself Prophet Milsap.
Among other intriguing revelations, the Prophet disclosed that
stars are God's lanterns rightly hung in the heavens to show fal-
tering man the time and season and the ways to correctness; that
the sun is God's own and very special heating stove and that the
moon is God's very special signal lamp hung in the sky to show
people the way toward Wise and Rightful Wisdom and Understanding.

My host's blue eyes sparkled and his blanketing white beard
parted in a sort of Santa Claus laugh. "My pappy learned me early
about how to read them holy sky lights. Since then I been en-
joyin' my way through life—same as Pappy done his . . ."

In the Prophet's windowless loft, on a pallet stuffed with oat
straw, I went to sleep reflecting that even if backhill living, like
straw-stuffed pallets or Prophet Milsap's conversation, is poor in
terms of comfort, it is rich in revelation.

Next morning I headed west and north again, walking into the
wind. The east was blotched with red-fringed remnants of storm
clouds. Early air was distinctly chilly, but walking was good and
well before mid-morning I was within sight of Elk Horn Tavern
and the Civil War battlefield not far beyond.

Sixty years had come and gone since they fought the battle of
Pea Ridge. Sixty winters had watered the poor land-sedge grass
with cold rains and buried the fields in intermittent snow and ice.
Sixty springtimes with south winds and warming rains had brought

35

the breath of life to the trees and grass and made the valleys green again. Through that circus parade of years a hand-hacked pillar supporting a square-headed angel had stood as a monument to the borderland volunteers who there had fought and slaughtered and died. Shattered sunlight fell on the silk-blue hills. A rumbling farm wagon echoed forgotten cannonades. A slate-gray catbird shrilled her song to the coming spring.

I strolled to the tavern porch where an old man was ready ensconced in the only available rocking chair. He told me that his name was Timothy Cox and that he had very personally heard and lived through the great battle.

"Confederate Army moved acrost in the dead of night . . . from out'n a cave it'd been ahidin' in . . . acrost Bentonville way. Federal Army come pullin' acrost the ridges comes daybreak.

"All hell commenced to break loose. Farm folks tore out for the cellars and caves. Back in them days, my folks owned this here tavern. My pappy opened the cellar to us kids and near neighbors. . . . My maw, she took over as doorkeeper. Close on fifty people countin' grown folks and young'uns and soldiers as didn't feel for fightin' stole into that cellar . . .

"Round the noontime I slipped past Maw and slunk out to see what was happenin'. Maw cotched me and drug me back and give me the awfullest lickin' I ever got. Couldn't nobody hear me yell on account the noise of the war.

"We stayed put till we got bloodied out. Comes afternoon, the Yankees commenced makin' hospital out the tavern. Blood came drippin' through the floor. Purty soon it got worser inside the cellar than in the outside battlement."

At that point the recounting changed to comic whimsy and near merriment. I reflected on this transition while tramping down the Wire Road into the warming midday. As I tramped around

36

Redbud Bend I looked down on Garfield Village and its ragged scattering of shacks which garnished the solitary store.

Even before I sighted the sagging ridgepole of Kennicott's Arkansas Store (the foresign bore the character R, followed by a picture of a can, then a picture of a handsaw), I heard laughter. On the next turn I noted that the narrow front porch of the store building was ornamented with a swinging bunch of ripe bananas; below this stood a wooden tub about half full of newly "cut" wild greens in which a bluish-gray mama cat was fast asleep and a stack of slatted and empty poultry crates. The store porch was vitally occupied by seven country men all garbed in varying shades and conditions of denim overalls and faded work shirts. Four sat on the shady edge of the porch. Two sagged against the graying four-by-fours which held up the porch roof insofar as it was held up at all. The seventh lounged in shady seclusion on a remnant of grass. As I was soon to learn, the off-sider was Billy Skeets, Homer Leathers' hired boy.

The adolescent Billy opened in dialogue with his employer. "Homer, how'd hit do fer me to ride your hoss home?" The employer quivered perceptibly. "Wouldn't do so good, Willie. Got to ride 'im myself." Homer's smile broadened. "Mought be I'd leave you walk alongside me . . ."

The hired boy leered up at his employer. "No siree, bob! Reckon I'll be pattin' on down the road by myse'f. Was I to walk aside you I'd have to open and shet every gate and fencegap between here and that."

With that the afternoon's flow of merriment was opened. Still shaky with laughter, Homer Leathers peered down at his lolling hired help. "By the way, how come you ain't workin' today?"

With extreme deliberation the youth pushed the shapeless remains of a much ventilated felt hat low over his ears, and again leered up at his employer. "I *was* workin'. Only I got hurt. I was plowin' corn in that fur squirrel patch field and drekly I come to the end of the fust row . . . I fell off and wronched my knee."

A graying hunchback took the cue to recount how he had once come horrifying close to falling off the field of grace and wrenching his fine moral principles. "Whole thing commenced with readin' books . . ." the old-timer revealed. "Hit was back before I got snow-blinded by the winter of eighty-eight. Fust book done me a sight of good. Hit was a new Bible Test-a-ment that I traded a thirty-pound turkey gobbler for. Recollect, I was courtin' back in them days and when Truetta asked me what I was readin', I told her I was lookin' up names for our chilluns. That there was the Gawd's truth. Account of after we got wedded five young 'uns come to us—fust a row of three boys, then a girl, then another boy. So I named 'em Matthew, Mark, Luke, Ann and Jawhn."

Truth and fable frolicked side by side. Another lounger was somehow reminded of the unknowing sheriff from acrost ridge-tops in Newton County. Sheriff Heffilfinger was forming a posse to recapture a culprit who had broken jail while the overweight arm of justice and defender of the peace was sampling some moonshined drinking whisky—naturally in line of duty. A perceptive local citizen reported that the fugitive had spent most of the afternoon filching Fig Newton cookies and plantin' peanuts from Lyin' Johnny Wells' store, then was seen strolling south toward Hemmed-In Holler. The observant countryman added that he personally had seen the sheriff pass by the escaped prisoner hardly an hour before.

The sheriff nodded violently. "I seen him too—passed him on Town Branch—passed and spoke howdy to him. But I didn't know the lowdown bastard was outta jail!"

I pondered again the intriguing absence of continuity of discussion or correlation of episodes. Another lounger began reciting ancient whimsey about the Alpena rustic who was taking his very first train ride. When the news butcher came through, shouting "Chawklet, sody pop, bernanners!" the backhills youth invested in one of the latter. On his next round the vender stopped to inquire as to the merit of his merchandise.

"Mister, I can't say so bodaciously much for it. Fust place, it was mostly all cob; and when I'd throwed that away, what little was left was bitter and right 'onery to eat . . ."

Store-porch talk had drifted around to the chinch bug, a dastardly sucking beetle which recurrently had plagued the tasseling corn. On the same store porch a short while before a traveling salesman, new out of Saint Loois, had there inquired what a chinch bug is and what it looks like.

"You say it's no bigger than a seed tick? Well, I wouldn't have my crops ruint by little suckers like them!" The sitters nudged one another. One inquired what the traveler would do about them.

"Do about 'em? I'd get me a good two-handed brush and frail 'em plum' off my place . . ."

I reflected that the backhill merriment was and, from all appearances, is destined to remain dependent on ignorance and the hopes and quandaries which rise from ignorance. The newcomer who undertakes to shoo the gluttonous songbirds out of his cherry orchard; or to frighten the corn-hungry raccoons from his patch of roasting ears; or the outlander who seeks to bridle his horse and let the horse mouth the bit later; or the countryside justice of the peace who interprets *habeas corpus* as the right to keep a corpse in his settin' room—as if any dang fool could be that much of a dang idiot. Or the hymn-scraping fiddler who steps pompously to the preacher's side to strike up *Redeeming Grace, How Sweet Thy Name,* only to discover that some little hellion had larded his fiddle bow so it wouldn't make as much noise as a smothered lightnin' bug (firefly).

THE BODACIOUS OZARKS

For its enduring life the far-back Ozarks humor stays rooted in a sustaining earth and nurtured by abundant time and tranquil waiting. The merriment gains pertinence from the ways of its people, their deliberate speech and magnificent languor of postures and inflections.

Merry quips mellow with age and soften with countryside traditions. Thus it suffices grandfather, father and son alike to recall and recount that Uncle Ameriky Hansen got religion at the Schooner Bald revival meeting only to lose it again when his buggy bounced off a ledge boulder and broke an axle. Or that Aunt Marthy Piffitt put eggs beneath twenty-six settin' hens which responded to the cause by hatching out three pullets and three-hundred and ninety-six roosters; or that the near-sighted Parson Womack once trapped, skinned and ate a weasel mistaking it for a gray squirrel.

Throughout the backhill pilgrimages I kept hearing the time-worn chromos; such as the one about the youth from Gulch Hollow who, on first coming to Springdale, Arkansas, was lured by the bizarre and tempting yellowness of the exotic fruit which had been put in the show window of Gollehar's Grocery. The hillside visitor had never seen lemons before and he aimed to sample them. Accordingly, he bought a dime's worth and settled himself to their conquest.

The first bite revealed an appalling mistake, but before an assembly of town loafers the Gulch Hollow youth did not once hesitate. He ate the first lemon whole; not only the first, but the second, and—after a nonchalant, if considerably puckered pause —the third. Then through writhing lips the rustic teen-ager addressed the astonished onlookers: "Yes suh, fer a mighty long spell I've been honin' to git my fill of these here trupical fruits . . . I shore pleasure in the taste of 'em and bein' in town I aim to revel in 'em . . ."

40

Or the time the neighbor people were having a moonlight supper up at the Brushy Ford schoolhouse and Uncle Zeb Hatfield, who hadn't been to any socializin' for a month of Sundays, got nervous and chanced to pour buttermilk, instead of common milk, into his coffee. Nonchalantly, Uncle Zeb blew at the appalling mess and assured all present that he invariably took buttermilk in his coffee.

Usually there was, and still is, gentleness in the tone of narration, and a peculiar verbal poetry in the language of recall or the recountings of the old-timer who could never get any true satisfaction out of reading the dictionary on account of it changes the subject too blamed often. Or the clodhopper who overwhelmed the schoolteacher's suggestion that the burning of Mart Miller's barn must have been the work of an incendiary with, "Incendiary, hell! Some mean bastard sot it afire!" Or of the Southern sympathizer who stood by to view the Battle of Pea Ridge at a safe distance. When a scurrying cannon ball came slittering across the cleared field, Uncle Luke gave the Yankee callin' card a contemptuous kick, and thereby lost his right foot.

Or the tribulations of the near-sighted gospel singer who set out to cross Peckerwood River by walking the fallen elm tree that served as a bridge. It was a moon-bright winter's night and naturally the hymn singer missed the real log and approached instead a long black shadow which extended across the water. The man of the mighty voice decided he would just hunker down and 'coon across what he took to be the log bridge. So, he knelt, and putting his elbows forward, most painstakingly tumbled head first into the icy river.

The humor incident to misunderstanding is as invincible as it is old. Back in 1920, much more than at present, widespread illiteracy was one of its principal pegs. As my late country neighbor, Bill Coldiron, recited: "Over past Loafer's Glory settlement, where my folks come from, is the reel bresh. Used to be Leander Frost was the only man in all the bend and holler as knew how to read or write or pencil figger. Come a summertime, the rest of us chipped in and buyed the noospaper from Springfield, Missour-a, so as Pappy Leander could read it to us.

"One day we was settin' around listenin' to Pappy who was readin' where the paper said ever'body ought to plant corn early on account a powerful bad drought was set to come our way. Back in them parts 'dry spell' was what we said when there didn't come no rain. . . . Anyway, Mart Miller rared his chair back and chawed his terbaccer and petted his chin whiskers till finally he says, 'Now, what's a drought?'

"Pappy puzzled for quite a spell and finally said, 'Speakin' back-actual and open, I ain't shore. But iffen I ain't mighty fur wrong, a drought is one of them newfangled varmints that's a cross betwixt a wild hawg and a 'coon. . . . Whatever hit be for fair, hit shore is hell on the corn crop . . .' "

CHAPTER III

Whuppin' Holler

THAT NIGHT I took lodging in the windowless attic of a crossroads store. There was no charge and very little sleeping. The space was bare except for a row of dusty wooden churns, a rack of mildewed buggy whips and a feather-stuffed floor pallet covered with a lone and ragged quilt. The pallet was noticeably damp and before midnight I was awake and shivering. At least two chilly hours before dawn I slipped on my shoes and walked out into the waning moonlight.

The sun was all of an hour high before I reached the next crossroad. There I found one slaunched-roofed store which in turn had one window branded with three words all lettered in wavery scrawl: POST OFFICE—EAT. I undertook to purchase a glass of milk and a sandwich. The proprietor slipped down from his high stool and looked me over with great thoroughness. "You ain't in no trouble?" he inquired.

I told him I hoped not. The storekeeper allowed he hoped not

43

likewise. "You ain't been time-beatin' with ary them Tannehill gals?" My interrogator added darkly. "Onderstand, I ain't pryin' into your business. But ef you don't already know, you're headed into some real tough settlements. . . . Gals come fat and smiley, but menfolks come lean and wicked strong." The storekeeper leered at me. "Mebbe you already know . . ."

I assured him I didn't and asked again of the chances for buying a glass of milk and a sandwich. The storekeeper weighed my query with evident disapproval. "Got no milk. Ole cow died off in Jenewery. Heiffer ain't come fresh yit."

"How about water?"

"Yup, how about water?" Begrudgingly, the storekeeper wandered out of sight and after an almost frighteningly long wait returned with a dipperful of water in one hand and an extremely rough-hewn sandwich in the other. The water tasted strongly of sulphur; the sandwich turned out to be two chunks of hard bread propped apart by a roughly hacked chunk of slightly mildewed cheese. I munched at the bread ineffectually, then tasted the rancid cheese, and fed the greater part of both to a beggar hound with eloquent eyes.

When I laid my dime on the table and turned to the open doorway the storekeeper continued to peer at me sadly. "Be careful, feller."

"Any particular reason?"

My counsellor examined the dime sadly. "Case you're headed to southeast, which I figger you be, this here road will take you into Whuppin' Holler . . ."

"So?"

"So if I was you, I'd stay shy of them gals that live down that-a-ways." The old man nodded with vehemence. "They's three broods of 'em all told. Mostly they is purty and fat and trouble

44

bestirrin'. That's how come the neighborhood got named Whuppin' Holler."

The flint-littered roadway seemed to beckon amiably. I followed it for more than an hour without meeting another user. Then as the road dipped into a curving descent, I saw two shapes strolling a side lane of bluegrass. An extremely tall young man in tight-fitting bluejeans and a ragged brown shirt was escorting an exceptionally plump young woman in an almost skin-tight purple dress. Both were dragging their feet. The girl's right arm circled the tall man's waist and her free hand was fondling an immense rip in the back of his shirt.

The young giant stopped abruptly and placed his big left hand on top of the girl's head which was piled high with red-brown hair. She smiled up at her escort and bent forward accommodatingly. The towering young man began spanking her resoundingly and from all appearances to her complete satisfaction. As I passed them he grasped the hem of her skirt and raised it to display leather-brown and extremely plump thighs.

At that the young woman protested meekly, "We ain't yet home, Marcus . . . and they's a young man a passin' by . . ."

"Been too damm many young man's a passin' too damn close by e'er since I marriet ye last Christmas. 'Fore New Years I'd seed ye triflin'." The young husband delivered an echoing smack and turned to glare at me.

I watched his left hand slip into his breeches pocket and emerge with an oversize knife. He flipped open the Bowie-length blade and took a long stride toward me. I stooped to pick up a throwable rock. The extremely tall young man commanded me to stop. "Tall Shorty," he continued, "I can throw this here knife a lot quicker than you can pick up ary a rock. . . likewise I can degut ye in half the time it takes to spit."

45

I watched the overweight bride hurrying to stand between us. She moved with remarkable grace and I noted that her features were quite pretty. Her oversize husband continued to glare at me. "You wouldn't be one of them fiddle-playin' roosters from over aroun' Sulphur Springs?" he demanded. "You wouldn't be one of them dudey birds that last night taken out my wife and her fat lil sister and bothered 'em while me and her pappy was gone 'coon huntin' down on Henbest branch? You wouldn't be . . ."

I interrupted to deny. "I'm not a fiddle player. I don't live at Sulphur Springs or anywhere near it. I never saw you or your wife or her sister before. . . . In fact I never saw your sister-in-law at all. . . . And I never was in this holler before now."

"Never was, huh?"

The plump bride was grasping his knife-bearing hand. For a moment he looked down on her with an almost angelic smile, then grasped her nose between two knuckles of his left hand. With a very quick flick of his knife he slashed open the front of her dress, thereby exposing her breasts which were big as medium cantaloupes.

The young woman began to whimper, then ducked free of his hold. "He ain't the one, Marcus. Honest to getout, I never see him before now." She sought vainly to cover her breasts with shreads of what had been her dress front. The young husband smiled down at her.

"So you wasn't triflin' last night?"

She circled his waist with her bare arms. "I already told you I was, Marcus. I already said you could whup me all the much you feel like I should git."

His smile broadened. "You don't sa-say!"

She stroked his right hand. "I done you wrong, Marcus. I'm due a whuppin'. But I want you should give me it at home. If you say so, I'll borry Pappy's braid whup."

The tall young man shook his head as if in disappointment. "Your Pap is usin' it on your big fat little sister."

"Rosy's done been corrected, Marcus. I heerd her hollerin' a hour ago whilst you was still searchin' me down. Pappy must of ketched her sneaking in the back door . . ." The erring bride stopped short, then added imploringly, "Marcus, do purty please take me home . . ."

The towering young husband continued to smile. He returned his knife to his pocket. Then with abrupt fierceness he tore off the remnants of her dress and for a moment permitted her to stand naked. Then he pushed down on her shoulders and delivered two sweeping, underhanded spanks.

He turned away from her, took out his knife again, and cut an oversize switch from a roadside cluster of saplings. I heard the switch whack loudly on bare flesh. As I walked along, the tempo of the whacks increased. But the young wife did not cry out.

A mile or so down the road the way forked puzzlingly. I followed the low road which paralleled a youthful and dashing river. Presently the road led directly into the river. I pulled off my shoes, rolled up my breeches legs and waded.

The current was swift and minnows darted at all sides like living arrows. Out of the chilly water I warmed myself on a sunny bank, then replaced my shoes and tramped on. The old road continued to follow the river. From beyond a bend of sumacs I heard merry laughter and a swishing of wet cloth. Then I saw two dark blotches climbing the miniature stone bluff which protruded into a deep pool. The blotches began taking definition as extremely bulgy dresses filled with large female forms.

Next I noted that the young women were protrusively plump and that both sported long and dripping braids of dark red hair. Both had pug noses, plentiful face freckles, full lips and eyes that appeared to be almost as green as the blades of young corn in the

47

field immediately beyond. Both grinned at me and retreated toward the field where they waited for a time, peering about and dripping profusely. Then the taller of the riverside Amazons strolled toward me and inquired if I had seen or heard anything of a black plowhorse. I hadn't.

By way of offering a neighborly exchange of queries, I asked how they found the swimming. Both smiled broadly. Then the larger one answered. "Still right chilly . . . but they's got to be a first time."

The smaller one, who barely missed being six feet tall, took the next line. "We been first plowin' and first-time hoein' our pappy's corn patch. Sun commenced a-warmin' our backs and so we figgered hit was time to try ourselves a swim. . . . While we was sillyin' around, the old hoss slipped his halter bit and strayed plum off. . . . Now we got to git back that hoss reel quick."

"Maybe he's strayed home," I suggested.

"Shore hope he ain't."

The big one interposed concernedly. "My sister ain't told you maybe. But our pappy don't favor havin' no women folks a-swimmin' perticular whenever they is been told to plow crops. . . . Our pappy figgers womenfolks and hosses is made for to work . . ."

"And to get whupped effin they don't," the smaller sister inserted forebodingly. "Should that hoss git to home afore we do, our pa will be waitin' us with his big mule whup . . ."

The larger sister nodded with enormous solemnity. "Even should he ketch us a-swimmin' our pappy would be shore to leave us settin' on blisters." She rubbed her immense hips apprehensively.

"Begin to see why they call this Whuppin' Holler," I hazarded.

Both of the wet Amazons nodded vehemently. "Hit shore is," the larger one peered down on me. "Our pappy is raised up seben gals of his own and two more adopted. He's wore out enough whups and switches on us to fill up a wagon box."

"Not countin' them bundles and piles of split oak shingles," the less enormous sister confided. She patted her protruding bottom. "But we got 'leven girl cousins . . ."

"Not countin' four adopted," interceded the immense sister.

"They all growed up with blistered tails. . . . Tannehills all calculate as how God put the devil into women and leaves hit to menfolks to whup the devil out of 'em . . ."

The oversize damsels turned at a common urge. I watched them trotting down a fencerow pathway and continued to look on until I saw them overtake the errant plow horse.

The road turned from the riverside and led into a great aisle through a hillside of squatty cedars. It was mid-afternoon before I reached the next crossroad where a solitary store waited paintless-gray and lacking customers. The storekeeper was a plump little man with bristly white hair, large poetic eyes and a violent twitching of the eyebrows. Having purchased a tin of salmon and a handful of heroic-sized soda crackers from an open barrel, I settled myself to self-service on the back counter. When I inquired about business, the proprietor confided there practically wasn't any. When I inquired of the crops, he allowed they were mostly meanness crops.

Then the storekeeper, his white patches of eyebrows twitching wildly began asking questions. "You new to these parts?"

"Just trampin' through."

"See anything oddish?"

"You might say . . ."

"I might say what?"

"Might say I'm pleased I'm not one of the young girls of these parts."

His eyebrows were twitching again. "Wouldn't do you no great good was you a *old* gal in these parts. This here is Whuppin' Holler. An hit's full up of big ole fat gals—mostly sisters or else cousins. . . . Mostly meaner'n bull nettles in early August." After a cautious pause he settled himself on the counter besides me. "Fust time I come through I was single and afoot, same as you be. I figgered hit was hurtin' hard—anyway on the womenfolks. Kept figgerin' so all the while I was courtin' Violy. . . . She's one of them Tannehill sisters. And she's makin' me a mighty fine helpmeet . . . now that she's my wife woman."

"That's good," I hazarded.

His eyebrows twitched again. "Hit's good, all right. And way I see it so was the way she was raised. . . . Like Violy says herself, she started off 'ornery mean, same as most young gals. Time she was fifteen when I marrit her, her big ole fat pappy had got the meanness purty well warped out'n her. Figger that saved me a mighty sight a troubles." He smiled agreeably. "Wouldn't you say so, too?"

I pondered the question with the knowing gravity of a seventeen-year-old. "Way it looks to me, women are people, same as men. I don't hardly see . . ."

The storekeeper interrupted, "Sweet Jesus, you don't hardly see a-tall, do you?"

CHAPTER IV

Soundly Unlawful

THE ROAD THROUGH Whuppin' Holler meandered to the east and south across a county line and groped its rocky way into an even more fluid capital of Ozarks individualism.

My great-uncle Greene, with mellow understanding of the advantages of directing the attentions of youth to notable and worthy followings, had suggested that I make the acquaintance of certain of his illustrious moonshiner friends. In particular he had recommended the Saulees whom he described as very cultural and the very best damned moonshiners in the entire Ozarks uplift.

I eventually located the revered subjects by making way through a waist-tall sweep of grassland which ends down where War Eagle River sweeps hard against a mile-long crescent of limestone bluffs. There, as recommended by an affably besotted roadside blacksmith, I searched until I had located a midget grove of pawpaw bushes among which I stood and whooped.

A halloo sounded far off down the valley. Presently, Grandpa

Dick Saulee, the senior partner, strolled out from among the adjacent grove of pawpaw bushes. He was a handsome citizen, medium tall, well muscled, wind-blown and distinctively gray. I had been advised in St. Paul village that Dick Saulee came of a moonshining family which had stilled good drinking licker for the Boys in Gray, and not to be small about it, the Boys in Blue as well. Dick himself had mixed, soured, stilled and sold close to twenty thousand gallons of good whisky and nary so much as a swaller of bad. According to his virtues, Uncle Dick had prospered moderately. He had bought and equipped two good farms; one for himself, the other for his son Alfred, his partner.

In discreet time Alfred strolled up from the far green-golden valley to join us. He, too, was handsome, well bodied and gracious. He told me that he was just back from a convention. I inquired if it had been a distillers' convention. Alfred replied, "Nope, Sunday School convention . . ."

The younger Saulee took a bottleful of light amber nectar from his hip pocket, explained it was a sampler from his latest run. He took a first swallow, and handed the bottle to me. I took a nip and passed the sampler to Uncle Dick. The elder Saulee tasted, cleared his throat judiciously, then spat out the intake. "Never drink the damn stuff!" He added, "My boy is a-learnin'. About all he needs is more time, copper coil and a copper-lined belly."

Uncle Dick allowed we might as well go up to his house and set a spell. His wife, Narcissy, a motherly woman dressed in prim, blue-dotted calico, greeted us in the doorway. I noted her flashing black hair, her handsome blue-gray eyes and her evident multitude of petticoats which caused her to move as if mounted on casters. She led the way into the settin' room which was newly painted, high-ceilinged, outstandingly clean, and furnished with very old beds and highboys and straight chairs, all built of walnut or wild cherry by an earlier generation of cabinetmakers. It was a gracious home.

The conversation got back to moonshining. Uncle Dick settled himself into a strip-bottom rocking chair. "Here's my way of lookin' at it," he began. "Human kind is a drinkin' kind. Me and Alfred plants our corn, raises it, shucks it and takes it to mill and gets it mealed. If my woman goes and makes a pone of bread, that there don't violate no law. Then why shouldn't we put part of our crop to licker? We put out the work and skill, we take the risk and losses. They's plenty of work and skill to give. Honest licker is bound and beholden to come out a crop. And back in these parts hit's our only chance for a fair crop. Anyhow back in these creek prongs that's the way it figgers with Alfred and me and most of the neighbor people."

With an artist's comprehensiveness Dick Saulee recited and presently demonstrated step by step the little-changing procedures for changing field corn to drinkable whisky. First he shelled the dry corn into wooden tubs, "douched" it with warm water, let it stand until the grain began to sprout. Then he had the slightly sprouted corn milled into a coarse meal. He changed the "sweet meal" to "wet mash" by adding boiling water. After a few days of "settling" the wet mash formed a hard cake. Uncle Dick broke up the cake and "dressed it over" with corn sugar dissolved in warm water. Within a few days the sweet mash changes to sour mash which means, technically speaking, that the sugar changes to alcohol and carbonic acid. The resulting liquid, called "whisky beer" is moderately sour, usually bitter, and only slightly alcoholic.

The "workin's" of the beer and in lesser part the mineral contents of the local water combine to produce superior whisky. To "settle hit for workin' " the Saulees poured the beer into the tank of the still, set the tank on a rock-built furnace and built a slow fire under it.

The first distillation of "low wine" dripped out of the delivery end of the long copper coil which was spiralled through a galvanized iron jacket. The resulting "low wines" were weak in alcohol, though fairly strong in terms of "fusel oil" and miscellaneous impurities. A second distillation changed the low wines to "doublings" and the beginnings of drinkable licker. The doublings have a pronounced "bead," small iridescent bubbles which rise to the surface when the container is tilted. But when the bubbles rise and stay put, the liquor is ready for the final cure. To effect this the Saulees poured it through a succession of charcoal filters, from which the liquid corn emerged colorless and otherwise watery but with a faint smoky aroma. Aging was the final step; preferably quiet storage in kegs or barrels of red oak staves. There are local and personal variations, but the foregoing remains fairly typical of the present-day procedures of the old-line backhill professionals.

Throughout the 1920's Dick Saulee estimated that the "hard money" cost of moonshining a gallon of drinkable corn whisky was about two dollars. That included approximately half a bushel of corn, six pounds of corn sugar, a quarter-pound of yeast and malt mix, about an eighth of a cord of firewood, and about two hours of attentive labor. His stillside selling price averaged about eight dollars a gallon.

Worse whisky was being made more cheaply. But even at its lower levels Ozarks moonshining was neither treasure finding nor gusher opening. All in all, it was a soundly unlawful and frequently an exceptionally successful agricultural industry in a place and time when law-abiding agriculture was failing on every side.

After leaving the Saulees I tramped farther upcountry to meet and learn from the Porterfield brothers who were comparatively recent joiners on. I liked the brothers enormously. Noah had been the perennially promising member of the family. He was a gentleman, hard-working, studious, even scholarly. Brother Sody had been the happy-go-lucky member with chronic leanings toward daydreaming and sitting down. The same autumn that Noah went away to study at the Russellville (Arkansas) School of Agriculture and Mechanical Arts, Sody got a job as clerk in Fietz's Store at Gordon's Gap. Four years later when Noah came home with a secondhand army locker full of books, a sheepskin diploma and debts totaling somewhere near seven hundred dollars, Stinky Fietz fired Sody for being too lax with the credit.

Noah took over the family homestead, planning to upbuild it by means of Modern Agriculture and Inventive Mechanical Arts. Sody undertook to sell lightning rods for the Protection of Homes and Loved Ones. In the course of seven months he disposed of one set to the countryside Bible scholar who meant well but was not able to pay; the Bible scholar was this writer's maternal grandfather.

Brother Noah, meanwhile, planted forty acres of bud-grafted apple trees and lost about four-fifths of them in the course of a merciless and typical Ozarks drought which set in the following year. Returned to his hilly homeland, Brother Sody took to peddling the Watkins Line of Helpful Household Handies. As he should have remembered, the backhill farm wives were usually lacking money and always limited in cash on hand. They were accustomed to washing their clothes in creek water, to making their own soap out of waste pork fat and lye leakings from wood ashes, and to seasoning their cookery with salt if at all. Like many before and after him, Sody Porterfield quickly proved that backhill peddling does not pay.

Brother Noah had gone far toward proving the same as regards backhill agriculture. But Noah Porterfield was a man of hope—

and meritorious reading habits. The latter brought him in touch with two publications of the University of Arkansas; bulletins entitled respectively "Profits from Peaches" and "Profits from Strawberries." Noah recognized both bulletins as being approximately one-fourth literate and one-half hopeful: by unchallengeable Mathematical Truth that estimate made the two together somewhere near half literate and wholly hopeful. Accordingly, Noah replanted the drought-ruined apple orchard with peach trees and established strawberries between the tree rows. Sody, in turn, tried selling Granite State Monuments, again without success.

But Noah stayed with Scientific Agriculture for another decade. During their sixth year the peach trees, which had survived almost miraculously a succession of two utterly ruthless droughts, yielded a crop large enough almost to pay for the required sprayings. For three successive years the strawberries produced an average net loss of only a trifle more than half a dollar a crate. The peach crop was frost-killed three years in succession, but during the orchard's tenth year the trees bore an enormous harvest. So did practically every other peach orchard in at least forty other states. Markets collapsed, commission brokers absconded, and approximately six thousand bushels of Noah's peaches produced a net loss of nearly fifteen hundred dollars. Immediately thereafter the trees ceased bearing and began dying.

With money borrowed at ten percent at the county-seat bank, Noah changed over to Modern Dairy Practices which, besides being an almost overwhelming work load, yielded during the first year a net loss of slightly more than forty dollars for each of the eleven Registered Jerseys. A year later, Noah succeeded in selling all of the cows for a mere six-hundred-dollars loss and used the money recovered for making a down payment on a John Deere tractor with Minimum Accessories. So equipped, he took a brief fling at mechanized hay farming. The tractor almost paid for itself in two years at which time it collapsed along with the rest of the enterprise in hay farming.

Meanwhile, Brother Sody had opened a country store, and as he presently confided, "Somehow sort of came in to meet himself going out to take the bankruptcy law." On a long, hot July night in 1920 the two brothers fell to comparing experiences and philosophies. Both were showing gray about the temples; both had worked out their best years; both were weary and debt ridden. So, as they rounded fifty, the Porterfield boys became partners in moonshining. Thereafter they began to prosper modestly by making and selling usually drinkable moonshine whisky to fairly responsible customers. Neither was a stupid man. But both passed the half-century mark before perceiving that for the blackhill economy, illegality is sometimes indispensable.

CHAPTER V

Gobble Drovers

QUITE CLEARLY, moonshining, the beady child of illegality, was in the Ozarks to stay, even as more lawful and no less colorful enterprises were doomed to fade. On the doomed list was turkey driving, more commonly designated as gobble droverin'.

I learned of gobble droverin' the following autumn (1921), after I had helped my father close out the crops. In this instance the story came to me. Barely a mile from home and on a dry and beautiful October day I was overtaken by a most exceptional river which came billowing across a forest road I had set out to follow.

First there was an audible rustling of new-fallen leaves. Then the peculiar river came flowing down upon me at the pace of a lazy schoolboy. Its principal color was a heavy slate gray flecked with bobbing highlights of red and occasional flashes of brown. I next noted that the stream flowed uphill as readily as downhill and that it tended to form dark eddies in the groves or undergrowths of sumac, haw trees, scrub oaks and chinquapins or dwarf chestnuts.

58

GOBBLE DROVERS

Back on the road, actually the dim remnant of a one-time logging trail, I found myself in the unannounced company of four other slow-moving youths and three plodding old men. Each of the boys carried a wooden bucket partly filled with shelled corn; each of the old men carried a ready-lighted lantern, even though late sunlight was still filtering through the yellowing treetops.

The peculiar river turned out to be an overland drive of turkeys newly recruited from open ranges. Most of the birds were big; their live weights averaged above twenty pounds. The majority appeared to be toms with droopy and bright red wattles, some with scraggly brushes of black hair protruding from their breasts. As I shortly learned, this was one of the last, perhaps the very last of the open-range turkey drives. Its destination was the nearest livestock siding on the Frisco railroad.

The drive had originated far out in the hills to the east, some seventy miles as the crow flies and between two and three times as far as the turkeys had browsed, drowsed, foraged and roosted. The drive was in its eleventh and final day. Starting with about four hundred birds, the flock had grown en route to some seven hundred, this by due process of swapping, haggling and otherwise buying, or by the discreet merging of feathered holdings.

The four boys and three old men had done the droverin'; three farm wives and a crippled man were taking turns at driving two supply wagons which were following the route with cargoes of grain, flour, bacon and coffee. One of the youthful drivers explained that the flow of the peculiar river was nowhere near as spontaneous as it might have appeared. The youngster's father and a couple of his uncles had "thunk out" the route well in advance. They had scouted and blazed the way to take the best possible advantage of surface water and forage, including seeded grasses, small acorns, native berries and dwarf chestnuts.

They had also located favorable camping sites and figured out routes whereby the supply wagons could keep within rendezvous distance. The astute way markers had by-passed towns and villages, where the tramping birds might be disposed to roost on housetops, and areas likely to be tenanted by foxes, bobcats, coyotes or other predators which feel for the tastiness of turkey. The strategy of driving was an intriguing merging of the respective intelligences of man and bird.

The turkey, of course, is a grouse, the true king of that great species. It is one of the most intelligent birds that ever flapped wings or built nests, and on occasions one of the most stupid. Turkey-trapping techniques are appropriately dunderheaded. When I was very young I helped raise turkeys for the market. I also helped my father trap wild turkeys which are endearing country cousins of the domesticated.

The wild turkey was the most coveted game bird of the first white settlers of the Ozarks, and most probably of the Indian hunters. The reasons are quite evident. The wild or native turkey is a most delicious fowl and one of the most compatible to convenient cookery. It can be baked, roasted, slow-smoked, or even boiled, and still be delicious. But old-time Ozarkers usually fried the bird—to a crisp brownness, this without heed of age or sex, or size, which averaged somewhere near half that of the domestic turkey. And the fried wild turkey, as I remember it, was as tender, and gamey and otherwise delectable. Exactly half a century before this page was written, I remember partaking of a feast of fried wild turkey in the cabin home of still another uncle who farmed and trapped in the brushy hinterlands of Pea Ridge, Arkansas. The gobbler dressed off better than twelve pounds, which is king-size for the wild bird. Having plucked and dressed off the prize, my uncle hacked it to pieces with a hand ax, then fried the pieces on three fireplace skillets. They came out golden brown, exquisitely tender and an epicure's delight.

Old-timers figured on trapping wild turkeys. In his younger days my father was a turkey trapper of considerable renown. He spent his hunting time searching far ravines and woodland edges for bird signs—paths or trails, or visible tracks or scatterings of feathers. Having located the run, my father would follow it to a level space and there build a poled pen about the size of a jail cell. If a rail fence were anywhere near, he would save himself the labor of chopping poles by borrowing enough toprails to build the sides of the pen to a height of around four feet. He would roof the trap with brush, then dribble a trail of shelled corn along the turkey paths either known or hypothetical, and cause the lines of spilled grain to converge at a foot-deep furrow which he dug beneath a corner of the trapping pen.

The free roaming turkeys would presently discover one of the corn trails and eat their way along it until finally they would push under the base rail and so become trapped. Inside the pen the inconsistent birds would begin looking for a way out. Almost invariably they would look up instead of down. Having flapped and pounded against the brush ceiling with imbecilic futility, the giant pheasants would spend fruitless hours striving to pry their ways through the cracks between the rails or poles. Finally, with misunderstanding heads abob, they would begin an unending tramp around the barricading walls.

Since open-range turkeys usually join in coveys following summer nesting, the catches sometimes numbered half a dozen or more birds. Under cover of darkness my father would return and grabble in the catch. His progress as a taker of wild turkeys was somewhat blotched when Uncle Tiz Rutherford (no actual kin) called the sheriff and reported, or at least implied, that my sire had been seen snitching Tiz Rutherford's gobblers from out of those sneaky rail-pen traps. The fact was, of course, that Uncle Tiz never fenced his own poultry and on occasions possibly one or two or just possibly more of his quasi-wild turkeys may have made their meddlesome ways into an a priori honest wild turkey trap. Life is like that. Also during those times—the 1880's and '90's—all the Ozarks were open range. As recently as 1930 practically all of the Arkansas Ozarks were still open range. This fact, plus the turkey's eminent talents for fending for itself in the open, and no sneaky traps present, made possible the great turkey drives.

Squire Noah Drake, who was boss of the big droverin' which now poured around us, explained the general background while resting against the trunk of a hickory tree and munching chinquapin nuts. "Turkeys," the Squire explained, "is the finest poultry there is. These birds here has got all the strongness of wild birds besides weighin' out two or three times as big. . . . Our gobble droverin' game is playin' out on account of jest one reasonin' cause. . . . We no longer got nowhere near enough acorn mast which these birds is mostly feeded and fattened on. We no longer got the chestnuts, nor chinkpins, nor the rest of the feedin' that rangin' turkey ree-quires."

The explainer spat out an accumulated mouthful of nut shells. "T'ain't the fault of the birds, nor the raisers, nor the drovers. Hit's the fault of these greedy-gut railroaders and all the rest of the furriners that causes all our good feed trees to be took out our woods." The old man sank to a nearby cushion of forest moss. "That there is why I'm a-sayin' this here is about shore to be the last big turkey drive any of you lil bastards will ever see go by."

I pondered the sight and strategy of a great crop, raised in the open and proceeding to market on its own feet and power. Squire Drake appeared to be reading my thoughts. "Hit comes by gittin' to be what you might say is turkey minded, feelin' and viewin' like a turkey bird. . . . And that there takes some doin' . . ."

The turkey-minded patriarch became more specific as regards

the less than casual feat of becoming turkey minded. Here again he agreed that most of the credit for the accomplishment was due the turkeys and the free-ranging life they led.

In late winter, beginning some time in February, the backhill growers participated in a few neighborly turns of helping along. In preparation for the laying season, which usually began late in March, they treated their open-country flocks with a "softener," made by boiling dry hay in wash kettles until the roughage was duly softened or "mellered." As soon as the laying began, the children or womenfolks began making a daily search for the turkey nests, which were almost invariably on the ground, though frequently hidden in tall grass or dense bushes. Each day throughout the laying season of five or six weeks the sharp-eyed searchers picked up and carried home the freshly-laid eggs which they washed in lukewarm water, dried in soft rags and stored between layers of feather mats or straw, and put beside the fireplace or back of the stove so that the "gobble fruit" would not chill. Then when the roaming turkey hens would begin to brood, as a rule during April, each brooding hen was provided with a setting of some twenty eggs taken from storage and placed in the hen's own nest.

The hens did the hatching, the gobblers or toms the guarding, and the women and children the spying. After the preliminary three to four weeks, the eggs would begin to hatch and the tenders would cover the hen and her nest with a slatted cage. After two or three days they would remove the cage and permit the hen and her new brood to "fend for theirselves."

Mortality among the poults ran high. Frequently no more than half of the initial hatches reached marketable sizes. Disease losses were slight to nonexistent, but predator losses were usually high, enough so to require armed onslaughts against resident foxes and weasels and prowling coyotes, wolves, bobcats or lynxes.

More provident growers would sometimes scratch-plow patches

or small fields in accessible hollows or flatlands and hand-saw them to a feed grain, usually spring oats or buckwheat. The growing and ranging turkeys would rarely take serious heed of the plantings until the grain began to ripen. Then they would invade the midget fields, eat all the grain and for good measure most of the stalk and stover.

Otherwise the birds lived in and from the open, following the sequences of natural feeds which increased as the summer progressed and arrived at a climax abundance as late summer merged into autumn. By then the roving birds had joined themselves in clans or coveys, in the manner of the smaller pheasants.

The ranging birds sometimes benefited by some turns of herding or "pastorin'." To facilitate this and to make ready for the long drives to market, the young'uns or womenfolks sometimes rigged one bird, usually a mothering hen, in each covey with a neck bell or "toller," usually a harness bell about the size of a Concord grape "latched" to the bird's neck with a leather thong.

The sagacity of the bell birds was duly storied and revered. Squire Drake spoke with particular fondness of his own "eddicated" hen, Nellie, whom he invariably took on the drives to market and dutifully hauled home again after she had "hoped out" the drovers. By way of illustration the Squire told of a time when one of them trashly riffraffers from Oklyhomy just happened to come by and toll off Nellie and her brood of nine half-grown poults. That night the Squire just happened to stroll past the shack where the toller-offer happened to be living and there called out, "Come Nellie! Come Nellie!"

In next to no time he heard the tinkle of her little neck bell, and he saw a feathery shape come plopping down from a haw tree that stood next the riffraffer's woodpile. Be damn if it wasn't Nellie! She stood and clucked a time or two, and one after the next all nine of her young'uns came hopping down from amongst the under branches and commenced to foller their old scraggly-feathered mammy back home.

Inevitably the big drives were the grower's principal obligation and challenge. The first step in shaping a successful drive was to select a route where acorns, or mast, and other natural feeds were abundant. These, plus water, enabled a market-bound flock not only to forage its way along but to gain weight en route. The basic economy and strategy was closely similar to that of the Chisholm Trail and other great grazing and watering routes on which rugged frontier cattle were "fed along" to railheads or outpost market pens.

Longhorn driving never came easy. Neither did open-range turkey driving. One "drover" for every fifty birds was the desirable driving strength; one per hundred birds was the stingy minimum. The customary wage was four bits (fifty cents) a day plus camp fare, such as it was, and the loan of a blanket for outdoor or under-the-wagon sleeping; six bits (seventy-five cents a day) when and if the drover chose to hustle his own fare. There was no "horsin' along." The drivers walked, worked, won or lost afoot.

Since late November brings Thanksgiving and the decisive marketing time, the long drives were usually begun in late October after the birds had been indulged freely on all available fattening ranges. The roundups and weigh-ins which necessarily preceded the long drives were usually laborious and time-consuming. They were usually cooperative enterprises to which several backhill neighbors contributed, since big flocks are far more manageable in the open than small flocks. Growers who had "friendlied up" their ranging flocks were at an obvious advantage. Sometimes the freely ranging birds were so very free that they could not be run down or even dawgged down and required trapping in

65

trappin' pens, even as wild turkeys. There were tall yarns about wild turkeys which were trapped along with the domestic or "tame" and driven along to market.

I tend to regard the latter stories as apocryphal. All the drive turkeys I saw were much bigger and heavier than the native wild birds; indeed the recruiters sought to load the drives with the greatest available number of heavy birds or "ground-bounders." This, of course, enhanced the hoped-for profits and reduced the losses from estrayals by flight. In early times dealers bought entire flocks by the head rather than by the pound, and paid a more or less traditional price of fifty cents a head.

Around the turn of the century when "pound buyin' " came in vogue, the backhill growers found themselves obliged to weigh in as well as count in the "recruitments." At first they sought to guess the weights. Because town or railside buyers were oftentimes disposed to guess differently, the more provident recruiters were obliged to borrow or otherwise acquire platform scales.

Launching the long drive was an open invitation to adventure. By natural history, the North American turkey is a clannish bird with an implicit tendency to follow its kind. But its flock behavior is willful and unique, oftentimes excitingly so. Consider the nightfall habits—as the cross-country drovers were obliged to do.

When dusk settled, or sometimes earlier, the ranging turkeys usually elected to get off the ground. Accordingly there was a very good chance that an influential gobbler or tom would cluck or chortle to his hens, or vice versa, flap his wings significantly and rise slowly in the air to settle on a tree limb. Flock members would follow leaders until the first chosen branch, and in time the entire tree, became blackened and bowed down with roosting turkeys.

Where no trees were available, the birds would usually even

if begrudgingly bed down on the ground, preferably in tall grass or low shrubbery. But when night overtook a droverin' flock anywhere near a settlement, woe was likely to befall the settlement. An inevitable boss bird would flap to a building top, select a perch on a ridgepole or other high point, and there settle for the night. In practically no time the entire roof would be dark and saggy with roosting turkeys.

If the building were less than superbly sturdy, a cave-in was possible or inevitable. When hundreds of itinerant turkeys, with average weights of better than twenty pounds apiece, chose to settle head-to-tail and wing-to-wing on a none-too-steady roof, the entire building could and in recorded instances did fold in like a hand accordion. To cite a single and sad example, back in the 1890's the Viney Grove schoolhouse was abjectly caved in by a passing and, alas, a roosting drive of turkeys. The teacher, working late, sprinted through the back door just in time. On viewing the situation next morning, the backbrush educator changed over to horse trading. It wasn't that he resented the natural history of turkey birds or the indigenous economy of droverin' them to market. He just didn't relish the prospects of rebuilding the schoolhouse after having first to clear away the turkey manure. Besides, horse trading paid a lot better.

So as a rule the old-line turkey drovers avoided all towns and villages and by-passed the greatest possible number of homesteads. They also sought to avoid the more traveled roads, on the proved ground that when night settles, or even when dark clouds cover the sky in daytime, a sizable droving flock could blockade a throughway tighter than the devil's tail is stuck on. They knew, too, that when a flock trailed into a deep or heavily shaded ravine, it was all too likely to bed down or fly up for a long sleep, quite regardless of the hour, or the swinging lanterns, or the allurements of the strewn grain.

67

They also knew that turkey birds, which were skittish as all get-out on home ranges, when inducted into a big drive were disposed to develop a convention-goer's conviviality. A moving flock would sometimes settle most familiarly on passing buggies or farm wagons, dealing horses, drivers, and vehicles a show of friendly confidence and uninvited baptisms of turkey manure.

All in all the drives to market, or railside, were slow—ten to twelve miles a day was a good "make," laborious and foot-punishing. But they were almost never dull. The annual turkey drives continued intermittently for more than a third of a century. Understandably, they were a limited phenomenon, limited by natural feeds, suitable home ranges, available foraging routes, and most decisively by the personal and community enterprise which permitted the drives to assemble, set forth and push through.

While leaderin' what he believed was the last of the big turkey drives, Old Noah Drake had been pondering all the foregoing items, and a lot more. On rounding out his last big gobble droverin', he found himself tired and feelin' old and rickety, and a ways crotchety.

But he summarized with undeniable sincerity, "Quite a mighty lot besides free-range turkey birds will be a-goin' out with this here drive. . . . It ain't the money we made, on account we didn't hardly ever make none to speak of. Plenty of times we lost our shirt tails. . . . Ain't the loss of the hard work. Any damm fool can find plenty a hard work and kill his fool se'f a-doin' hit. . . . Way I see it, and what I sorry at, is the losin' of a fine and friendly sport . . ."

CHAPTER VI

Favorin' Foxes

DURING THE SAME bright autumn I made the acquaintance of another distinctive backhill sport. Though even older than free and open turkey driving, it has refused in a mild and gentle way to accept extinction. This sport is Ozarks-style fox hunting. It is one of the more self-perpetuating of the indigenous country sports, the more so because its followers are gentlemen foresworn never to ride down, run down or otherwise catch, kill or grievously persecute any fox.

Hounds and foxes are the active participants; for people it is merely a spectator sport. While the hounds scent and chase, hound owners, fanciers, and other human participants merely sit and otherwise lounge about late-burning campfires on open hillsides, joining in yarn spinning, small talk and the sociable swigging of corn whisky, usually water-clear moonshine—the while listening to the trailing and chasing hound packs, identifying the "mouths" of the respective dawgs, thereby ascertaining even if rarely agreeing on the fastest packs and the most capable trailers.

In earlier times numerous backhill and side-road communities throughout much of the Ozarks cherished and boasted of fox huntin' as a community sport. By the turn of the present century the pee-culiar fox hunting tended to become a county-wide sport; this on the fairly rational principle that in contemporary times an entire county is required to produce enough good trailing hounds and sufficient families or clans of runnin' foxes to make the chases truly exciting. The most famous and prolific perpetrator of the oldtime sport is currently the Benton County, Arkansas, Fox Hunting Association, which was founded back in 1871.

Grandsons and great-grandsons of the founders and first spectators perpetuate the annual "encampment" which as a rule lasts an entire week in late October, when the hickory leaves dangle lemon yellow and frost-blued persimmons cling to the trees. Hunting sites are chosen painstakingly in sparsely settled roughlands where the foxes come lusty and gutsy.

Most of the foxes are now orthodox "midland reds," though clans of gray foxes also endure and whites or albinos are still to be found. Regardless of color, size or heredity, there is very real reason to believe the foxes enjoy the sport at least as much as the hounds, some of which are said to be direct descendants (however hard to imagine) of the Julys, Walkers and other "bloods" which headed up and bayed out the first Association hunt—three long-lived generations ago.

In earlier times Ozark fox hunters arrived at the hunt sites in farm wagons or logging buckboards loaded with chunks of salt pork, bags of beans and corn grits, earthen-jugfuls of moonshine licker, home-grown grain for horses and mules, and other essential supplies, their hound packs following free alongside.

Nowadays pickup trucks are the stand-by conveyances, with

the dawgs freighted along as cargo. The puttering invasion of the auto age has largely substituted rough-road commutation for the unsheltered week-long outdoor camps of old. For the most part glass fruit jars have replaced the earthen jugs as containers for the fluid inspiration so largely unchanged. Black, chicory-mixed coffee is still brewed over open fires in smudged and hard-used granite pots.

Back in my younger days I once asked Henry Broslin, veteran president of the Benton County Fox Hunting Association, a deliberately silly question: "How do you keep the hounds from catching the foxes?" The mood was that which years later prompted me to halt my auto in the thick of New York's Times Square and bellow at a scaly-faced mounted policeman: "Hey, George, what's the name of this town?"

Henry spat out an enormous cud of chewing tobacco. "Foxes see after that. These here foxes take out through the rough grounds where they was borned and raised. Always was they live and run amongst caves and briar patches and steep hollers, bluffs and limesinks where they can outsmart a dawg jest about a thousand times out of a thousand. A fox generally lives most or all his life in one big holler. Chances are he knows that holler better than he knows his front paws. A fox like this here cotton-white the dawgs is chasin' right now—you couldn't ketch him with ten thousand dawgs. . . . Believe me, that there cotton-white is havin' fun . . ."

I could believe him. Throughout a half-century of witnessing foxy ways of one kind or another, I have learned that native foxes do not run confusedly. One sees them jumping high in the air to look behind them, ingeniously reversing their trails to further baffle the hounds, which as a rule yap and bellow along a cooling trail even while the fox back-sweeps toward or takes short cuts directly through the human-populated hunting camps.

71

I took in the seventy-fifth annual encampment of the Benton County Fox Hunting Association appropriately in the company of Judge Lon Williams, keeper of the Benton County poorhouse, who had been a member in good sitting for at least fifty years. We climbed toward the nearest hillside campfire where a fiddle player was sawing away resolutely. As we approached, he stopped and waved his overlength bow. Around the rising fire we could see at least a dozen tranquil but heavily whiskered faces.

"Henree!" whooped the fiddler. From a dense cluster of blackjack bush there came an answering "Yeah?" "Let's git it started. The dawgs is scentin'." The assent was general. Lank countrymen were strolling out from misty fringes of night as nearer members began piling dead brush on the already lusty fire. Red flames shot skyward. Henry was taking over, a tall, hawk-featured citizen garbed in swashingly ample rough denim overalls. He took a couple of hitches in the forebuckle of his oversize galluses and pushed his pot-black hat to the back of his head.

"Gents, we got a vis'tor amongst us tonight. His name is called Homer Feets, and he comes from Missour-a. They tell me that Homer is got three of the finest fox-trailin' dawgs as ever wiggled noses in the Ozarks. I was wonderin' how it would be to give Ted the old cotton-white to hunt after, on account far as I know ain't no home dawg got a look at that there cotton-white in ten years. And maybe we'd ought to put one of our own boys with him. Walt Leathers—how'd hit be to put your pack out to help give Mister Feets' dawgs a race?"

Walt Leathers, a slight, gracefully built youth, raised himself slowly and protested that when and if matched against such eminent dawgs as Mister Feets', his puppies would look mighty pukey. Yet even while protesting Walt began unleashing his four hounds from the tail gate of his pickup truck.

Henry Broslin coughed and shrugged his lean shoulders. "That there could likely take care of the cotton-white. But I know of at least three red foxes as live up Honey Crick. Looks to me like Jake Billin's dawgs, and them kept by Tom and Sam Dowder and Tolly Weatherby and any other dawgs that is hongerin' to run, might could organize theirselves to handle them reds . . ."

Onlookers were sinking into the browning grass. We could hear the song of the little river which halfway circled the camp ground. The flint pebbles shone silvery in first moonlight. Presently a sharp-pitched barking broke the lull. "They've got ole cotton-white's trail!"

Hound owners last designated were leading out their packs. The waiting crowd began breaking up into secondary watching and listening parties. Newcomers joined us about the mellowing fire, among them a moonshiner, a guitar player, a circuit judge, and a water hauler. After prolonged pondering, the Hiwasse schoolteacher stumbled forward to suggest that we arise and settle on a bare-topped hill up underneath Orion.

Audibly, the dawgs were running hard, well settled on divergent fox trails. Otherwise there was silence. Presently a sergeant-voiced hound struck a warm trail and with a bellowing yup-yup-yup made for a far recess of valley. A skinny hill man ran a two-fingered hand through bristling gray hair as he summarized, "They's one pink skewbald dawg out there with a bark like filin' the drags off'n a crosscut saw. That one is my dawg. He comes out of the very first Arkansas pack of the gen-u-wine fox-huntin' dawgs, the gen-u-wine July Redbones . . ."

Small talk and tall yarns were flowing freely along with the licker. Jedge Lon's two-gallon granite-finished coffee pot was boiling violently on a bed of cherry-red coals. We listened to the men's talk and the trailing hounds until the moon had swung half across the sky and the chill of early morning called for replenishing the watch fires. Race after race followed over far hills and into farther valleys.

Presently what seemed to be the final bayings died away to thin and wavery echoes. Light wind played through the baring trees. Then a slight shadow approached, dim and inches narrow in the failing moonlight.

"That's about all," Henry summarized. "The dawgs is all trailed way and the hell past Viney Ridge. Ain't likely to git back before noon tomorry . . ."

CHAPTER VII

The Right and the Wrong of It

OZARK FOX HUNTING is the most gentle sport this reporter has ever watched and the most immaculate in terms of sporting ethics. As a roving and oftentimes astonished spectator I found the procedure intriguing. The ways and moods of the fox-huntin' encampments shed a succession of revealing lights on the eternal puzzle of backhill behavior which in turn is necessarily a prime ingredient of Ozarks stories.

But this prime ingredient can be, and oftentimes is, most baffling. Backwoods behavior is almost consistently paradoxical. It ranges readily and sometimes quite casually from crimes of sordid violence to the most sublimated virtues of gentility and noble charity. As one frequently bewildered reporter I used to seek more expert counsel regarding the strange ways of the backhills. For better or worse, I turned to country lawyers and lawmakers of the region, including still another relative; to another uncle. This one was my Uncle Bob, Robert Jeremiah Wilson,

75

who spent fifty-two years in elective offices, and seventy-five as a countryman's counsellor.

Uncle Bob, who presently made his exit at a healthy ninety-five and the oldest native of his county, was not a great man, nor a noble man. He used to describe himself as an in-the-middle-man, in the middle, that is, between his hordes of rustic clients and the forces and persons which appeared hell-bent on doing them in. This in-the-middle-man's function never made him rich nor especially well at ease. My legal uncle dressed shabbily, avoided temptations including strong drink and all noxious frivolities not excepting Bill Hart movies, Will Rogers wit, even legislature banquets; the latter beginning around 1909, when his natural teeth got to the place where they could no longer handle the celery.

Uncle Bob kept with the lonely man's recreation of nurturing certain romantic illusions. Even while raising a brood of five notoriously spoiled brats, my lawyering uncle continued to believe in the Nobility of the American Home. Further, that all who wore the gray of the Southland were gallant soldiers and gentlemen, that Southern womanhood is inevitably chaste, that Charles Dickens was the world's greatest author, and that the stages of the moon have a great deal to do with the fortunes of growing crops.

Like most of my kin, Uncle Bob never ceased to regard himself as a man of the land. For confirmation he had only to point to his back yard which he vowed was the longest damned back yard in all Arkansas. With the first coming of spring he dutifully planted a huge garden in the hard, rocky and astonishingly sterile plot directly behind his shabby old clapboarded house. He was a consistently bad gardener, and almost invariably by midsummer he would confide to my father, "My tender little crops are about all gone to naught . . ."

But at least he worked his crops. Having finished with his ritualistic early-morning hoeing, Uncle Bob would trudge to his law office above the undertaking shop. The office was a venerable twelve-by-fourteen boxlike space with a windowless anteroom piled shoulder-high with hard-used law books and miscellaneous papers. Uncle Bob would then settle himself to his plaintive easy chair, his flat-topped desk, and his fine steel pen that required spitting on before it would feed ink, and there wait the arrival of clients.

The latter eventually arrived in a slow-gaited caravan. They were luck-battered country folk in sad predicaments and in quest of happy solutions. Uncle Bob worked with and for them, frequently during hard times without bothering to collect fees. His first professional goal was to keep his country clients out of court, and next to keep them on their lands. As a land lawyer Uncle Bob knew and specialized in abstracts, titles, and land location. Land records were his vital literature, abstracts his particular documents of revealing biography. As a court lawyer Uncle Bob insisted, to quote his own words, that "the winds of the open court blow against the countryman's best interests." He therefore steered his clients away from courthouses, as well as from mortgage-dealing banks, and all other local Shylocks. He also urged his agrarian litigants to seek firsthand settlements, and, as he put it, to closet themselves with their consciences.

During his younger days, specifically until he reached seventy or thereabouts, Uncle Bob never wavered in his good belief that all people can "educate theirselves to honesty, honor and worthy lives." This conviction made him a sitting duck for the school politicians, particularly for the sock-wearing cluster of politicians who ruled and maneuvered the local state university.

While a young boy, the perennial good believer had plowed corn back of a wood-beam bulltongue plow and a white mule on the eighty acres which were to become the University of Arkansas campus, uphill west from the old Ozarks crossroads which Fayetteville, Arkansas, once was. Beginning in 1871 Uncle Bob had watched the building of the University's Old Main, five stories of home-kilned brick masoned in slavish reproduction of the then main building of the University of Illinois, which in turn was a slavish imitation of a French-Victorian government building at Versailles.

By 1871 Uncle Bob was ready married and possessed of a law license and a first offspring. He therefore never gave serious thought to attending the local college. Even so, throughout his two-generation membership in the Arkansas Legislature, Uncle Bob never ceased "standing" for the never too robust cause of the "collich." He felt true warmth for the school as long as it was headed by erstwhile generals of the erstwhile Confederate Army. Indeed, he trailed along with the cause even after a self-perpetuating covey of damn-yankees took it over. "Bettah we should strive to fill up this collich with stoodunts," he observed, "than with them blue-bellies which roosts there."

Through a score of sessions of the legislature, usually stormy, the believer continued to fight the university's war. It wasn't easy. Consider, for instance, the time when the university was seeking an appropriation of twenty thousand dollars for establishing a physics department. A fellow state senator roared, "Twenty thousand dollahs for physics. Holy blue-nosed bullfrog tadpoles! Twenty dollahs oughta buy enough physics to last them stuck-up teachahs and the whole stoodunt body for a yeah!"

Another time the sock-wearing professors and their shiny-breeched champion in the state legislature were beseeching books for the university's library.

"How many books they already got?" demanded a fellow legislator.

78

"Mebbe quartah-million," Uncle Bob hazarded.

"How many of them perfessers has read all them quartah-million books?"

Uncle Bob thought hard. "Ain't shore any has."

The downstate lawmaker was bristling. "Then why in Gawd's name be they a-hollerin' for more books when they ain't read through what they done got?"

My Uncle Robert continued to believe in causes, even to anticipate gratitude. Excepting some few of his country clients, he anticipated in vain. He was still expecting gratitude of the university's leadership even in his late eighties when the old man lost his memory and otherwise became as a little child. But my lawyer uncle appeared to enjoy being as a little child. He built and flew kites, collected walnuts and chased after cottontail rabbits. Occasionally he worried the local fire department by building wood fires in his daughter's gas range. But both the firemen and his daughter were understanding. From time to time, college youngsters brought the old man-turned-child bagfuls of shiny marbles. In reflective moments Uncle Bob confided, "I been a-tellin' you, them collich folks does have gratefulness!"

Otherwise the dean of the backwoods lawyers was soon enough forgotten. But some of his talents and lapses had made their marks. In part deliberately and in part by happenchance, Uncle Bob had served to link the far past with the near past, and folkish concepts of law with the more scholarly and arbitrary. Putteringly but determinedly, he had sought to translate the legal into the folkish, and interpret and serve the folkish in terms and contrivances of the law. While of sound mind Uncle Bob continued to believe that the best "crop of righteousness grows from the private or heartside moral reckonings of country people of self-proved good will."

During his maturing years, which began in his middle seventies,

79

Uncle Bob's doubts concerning the place and utility of courts of law in and for the rural places, or as he put it, "the breshy spaces," grew to giant dimensions. He came to believe that the utility of the formal court in the informal country communities should be that of the open forum set up to encourage moral self-examinations and neighborly discussions on right and wrong in terms of local reckonings.

As a backhill wanderer and novice reporter my own views tended to coincide with Uncle Bob's latter-day acceptances. For among myriads of background gleanings, I was noting that in most country communities the court of law, as a lingering hybrid of primitive politics and hardly less primitive application of procedural laws, appears unvaryingly alien to the agrarian concepts and moods. I was observing that in most Ozarks communities, "actin' like a judge," specifically an elected or appointed judge, still means behaving like a pompous jackass; the word *judge* is generally synonymous with *jackass*. It follows that when the judge asks, "What you got to say for yourself?" there is a thousand-to-one chance that the Ozarks countryman has something to say, something spang-out and pertinent, or impertinent, designed to change the unnatural and the imposed to the natural and the accepted.

On a drippy October day I wandered into a session of circuit court in Madison County, Arkansas, where a backbrush citizen was being tried on a charge of wife beating. After the clerk read the charge, the judge glared at the defendant and demanded, "You've heard the charge! What you got to say for yourself?" The defendant glared back at least twice as fiercely at the judge. "I ain't obliged to say nothin' for myself. . . . Why the hell should I be? She's my woman, ain't she? She done me wrong, lazied on her work; so I whupped her . . . wore out a hick'ry sapling acrost her shif'less bottom. And, by the way, what the hell business is that of yourn?"

The court dismissed the case without answering. On the way out the court confided, "I consent that silence is golden. And mebbe some sweet day at long last I'll begin to learn when to keep my big waggin' mouth shut . . ."

I began to note, too, that morally speaking the back-country Ozarker takes no part in or from the parable of Mohammed and the mountain. Mohammed does not come to him, and bedamned if he is going to or is going to move any mountain to get to any damn foreigner. By and large, the Ozarks countryman who "stays put" remains basically content with things as he finds them. His soul is not unconquerable and his morality is not *per se* invincible. He is, in truth, a relatively securely tethered son, or daughter, of an environment, of a parcel of earth which he owns with its sun, rain and seasons.

And no double-ply malarky about noble behavior! It follows, and for generations it has followed, that Ozarks crimes are likely to be whoppers, with manslaughter only the medium level. More recently in Madison County I studied twenty years of court dockets for this area which is about four times the size of Manhattan Island. The community has had only three larceny trials in the previous seventeen years. But it has had more than two hundred assault cases, forty-four occurrences of manslaughter and twenty-eight established murders, which include stabbings, meat-axing, and shotgun ambushes. In the backhills larceny is comparatively rare. When folk go wrong, they usually go really wrong in big, open, preponderantly bloody ways.

Appropriately or otherwise, backhill transgressors have an almost uncanny "feelin' fer the law" as regards court room crafts, including ways and means of turning state's evidence, frustrating

81

cross-examinations and causing practically any judge to wish he had chosen another trade.

However, there is a very real degree of compensation in the charm and carnival qualities which persist in the backcountry courts, which many country people continue to attend, if only to hear the court "set" and the lawyers "plead." The indigenous audiences almost invariably include ragged farmers come to wait out a change of the weather, farm wives come for escape from confining kitchens and wash tubs, youths and damsels come with yearnings not necessarily legal, and lonely youngsters come to look and listen and just possibly to learn the ways of successfulness.

It follows that the backhill courts, whether circuit, or justice (of the peace), live on with impressive folkishness. For color and humor values I early learned to seek out the Ozarkian justice courts. Including that one back in 1912 which was held under a sycamore tree on a bank of Leatherneck Creek back in Madison County.

A backbrush citizen was accused of stealing a hawg. The trial lasted three days, required sixteen witnesses and at least ten times that number of arguments. The court had only one law book, a copy of the Illinois Statutes of 1894. The justice's bench was a whisky barrel, originally full. At recurring intervals he would declare recess and dispense the intrepid moonshine, at a nickel a tin-cupful; on credit, of course, with names and amounts chalked on the side of the barrel. Late the third day of the trial, the justice rose laboriously and dismissed the case on grounds that the jury was in no "rightful shape" to try it.

Earlier, in the same community, there had been the justice court of Squire Amos Nottingham. The Squire was an over-length, red-headed countryman with an immense walrus-style mustache and an infallible craving for another drink. There came a day when some cattle broke from substantially fenceless pasture and ruined a neighbor's corn patch. Reportedly, one steer led the outbreak and committed a principal share of the damage. On complaint of the corn owner, Justice Nottingham resolved that the erring steer would have to stand trial for its misdoings. Accordingly, they unfastened a well rope and led the animal into court.

Found guilty of trespass, the transgressor was fined ten dollars and costs. Since the steer carried no wallet, the court ruled that the beast be butchered by the constable. The latter received a hindquarter for his fee, witnesses were paid off in steaks, and the justice took the rest of the beef and the hide.

Another of Squire Nottingham's epic decisions was administered in the case of a blacksmith and a preacher who had gone to law, each claiming ownership of a skewbald bull calf. After an entire summer's afternoon of deliberating, the jury reported itself hung up.

"What seems to be the argu-ment?"

The foreman scratched his head. "Wal, Squire, four of us thinks the calf belongs to the preacher. . . . Four of us thinks the calf belongs to the smith, and four of us don't think it belongs to either one of them punkin rollers."

In another case, after listening to all the testimony and all the arguments, Squire Nottingham wiped his mustache and took up his jug. "If I was to believe all the defense says," he mused, "I'd turn the feller loose. If I believed all the pros-ecution says, I'd hang 'im. But if things was jest as they be, me not believin' nary a word neither one of 'em says, I jest plain don't know what I'm gonna do."

Chances were that the Squire was at very least speaking a completely honest doubt. And that he was putting into hard-to-come-by words the hill man's concept of the court of law as a forum for outspoken statement of doubt and the will to evade what he could see only as un-natural procedures.

As my backhill wanderings expanded and as I continued to fill nickel writing tablets with scribblings, my father predicted that I was bound and beholden to get myself into trouble; somebody's troubles and not unlikely my own.

Papa punctuated his predictions with meaningful frowns and explosive discharges of tobacco spit. And he prophesied correctly as regards my getting into other people's troubles. During 1922, when I first graduated as a stringer, or the paid-by-the-column Ozarks correspondent for The St. Louis *Post-Dispatch*, I found myself being shuttled from one gutsy backhill crime story to the next.

From a functional standpoint the reporting came hard. For one thing, the mayhem recounting tended to push aside far better stories which, alas, could not compete for newspaper space. Also, the rural Ozarks were, and in considerable part still are, chronically lacking in peace officers. Many of the counties had no badge wearers except the sheriff and one, or at most two, deputies. During the 1920's no accredited crime statistics had been compiled except in Missouri, and even in Missouri the country court records were notoriously scarce and unreliable.

I had learned as a matter of course that the great majority of Ozarks communities are traditionally peaceful. But there were and still are an incorrigible handful of habituated scofflaws. When other news ebbed or refused to materialize I presently identified about a dozen communities, mostly in the Arkansas Ozarks, where one could count on overtaking a murder or stabbing, gang fight or some fairly good mayhem within a moderate lapse of time. A tramping reporter could take lodging in or near such a community reasonably secure in the confidence that if violent crime were not current or recent, it would shortly materialize. Entire counties, such as Newton and Madison in the Arkansas Ozarks (Madison is the homeland of Orval Faubus), were especially reliable hunting grounds for stories of homicides, whereas individual towns, such as Sulphur Springs and Eureka Springs were exceptionally good bets for on-the-scene viewing or at very least lively reminiscences of bank robberies.

But homicides were frequently the most ingenious as well as the most lurid of blackhill crimes. One of my first murder assignments took me into the far wilds of Newton County where two rustic thugs had shortly done away with a neighbor. Without any convincing motivation the two bad boys from Alabam township had decided to murder the money-lending storekeeper at Flat Crossin's.

The killers-to-be strolled into the store and sought a loan of two dollars. Since both had previously borrowed and repaid, the loan was readily granted. It happened that the storekeeper was nearsighted. While one of the thugs engaged him in conversation, the other tore off the day leaf of his calendar. When the storekeeper filled out the note form he glanced at the finagled calendar and accordingly dated the paper March 12 instead of March 11, the true date. Next day, while the storekeeper was in the county seat dickering for a wagonload of merchandise, the two yahoos slaughtered him.

Brought to trial, the thugs "sot on their alibi." How in tarnation could they have murdered old Reddy Leathers in the county seat which is a good day's drive away, when there was a signed debtor's note to prove that on that particular date they were at the Flat Crossin's store borrowing money? The conspicuously dated promissory note in the storekeeper's cash drawer proved the contention. The thugs went free. The folkish court accepted the alibi as invincible. The courtroom audience surmised accurately the identities of the killers even while predicting the cockeyed verdict.

85

Meanwhile, the country court lived on as folkish ritual and an intermittent social and entertainment center. To a surprising extent this is still the case.

The pattern of backhill crimes remains reasonably, or perhaps more accurately, unreasonably steadfast. They are revealing to a point, but by totals they remain baffling, even mystifying. And other kinds of Ozarks stories are far more engaging, even if less "newsworthy" than the crime stories.

Including the gospel saga of Old Repulsive Henry Boggs who "handled" chickens and other poultry for close to seventy years and carried home one live chicken every working day for more than thirty-eight years, and never tired of chicken. For this revealing and deeply significant heroica, the first item to demand clarification is that Henry Boggs was not really repulsive. Furthermore, he had not always been old. Those who insisted on referring to Henry Boggs as Old Repulsive Henry were speaking more for euphony than for factual exposition. Many Ozarkers are disposed to do so; no hurt intended.

From Bentonville, where Henry originated, to Fayetteville, where he kept a ramshackle poultry house down by the Frisco tracks, it was common knowledge that Henry Boggs was not repulsive at all. As chicken and miscellaneous poultry growers throughout the better part of a hundred square miles of Ozarks hillsides, valleys and prairie lands knew well, Henry Boggs was a gentle, slow moving, deeply thoughtful man who just naturally liked poultry. He began raising chickens when he was around five years old and he never ceased to cherish them. At fifteen he began working for a back-lot poultry buyer in his home countryside. After some thirteen years of helping to buy chickens, feeding and sheltering chickens, crating and uncrating chickens, even dousing home-churned buttermilk down their serpentine and not always trustful necks, Henry Boggs took on the post of managing partner in one of the most highly respected live-poultry firms in all the Ozarks. As an original term of employment and partnership, Henry was to receive for home use one live chicken every business day he worked.

And Henry Boggs was a man who respected agreements. He bought and sold fairly and on the generous side. When he gave his promise it was as good as any gold or currency ever minted; better than most. In the very rare instances of argument or misunderstanding, Henry had but one stock answer, "I keep my word and expect same of everybody."

That held for every practiced phase of his live-poultry handling —from advances of setting eggs and feed loans to hauling, crating and icing contracts. And for Henry's ever-personal selection and toting home of one live chicken for every business day he worked. As court records were presently to show, during the near thirty-eight-years-plus life of the agreement Henry Boggs carried home 11,678 live chickens. Included were occasional tender young broilers, lusty adolescent fryers, and on special occasions mature roosters which make the tastiest chicken salad. There were occasional stewing birds, fricasseers, and superannuated dumpling "stock." But above all others Henry Boggs preferred medium-fat hens for medium baking with old-fashioned giblet-and-cornbread stuffing.

When he was rounding seventy Henry Boggs met with a regrettable rash of court troubles, the first he had ever encountered. Heirs of his original partner began yammering about the continuation of the live-chicken-a-day take-home agreement. Henry's answer was preordained: "I keep my word and expect the same of everybody."

A sprucy young lawyer who had been retained by the protesting heirs began deluging Henry with "reasonability" letters. After all, so the license waver represented, no reasonable man should expect to eat or even have placed before him on a family board a whole chicken every working day. For Sunday's, yes. For Thanksgiving, Christmas, perchance New Year's and the Fourth of July, yes again. For church and family picnics, for entertaining the preacher, for birthdays and comparable ceremonial occasions, reasonable enough. But not for every living working day, by and for a man who was inclined to work and thereby change to business days all days except the Sabbaths and the extremely rare intervals when he was taken down by the shaking chills-and-fever. The procedure was neither natural nor reasonable. What of the heirs of his erst-while partner? What of their widows and orphans? What of their grandson who at forty-three was still waiting the money for attending barber college in Springfield, Missouri? Or of Fat Little Suzanne who had been waiting since 1927 for tuition money for the DeLuxe Beauty Parlor Training Academy at Little Rock?

Henry read, listened, said you know what, and kept right on carrying home a live chicken every night or very late afternoon. Then on a dismal day the protesters and their lawyer entered formal suit to recover the "graduated dollar worth" of 11,678 live chickens carried home by H. Boggs, one at a time, over a period of thirty-eight years, seven months and sixteen days. Though he lacked formal documentation, Henry took off just enough time from his live poultry business to appear in the local chancery court and say, "I keep my word and expect same of everybody." With that he went back to the clapboarded chicken house down by the railroad tracks and that night he carried home another medium-fat live hen.

The trial dragged along term after term as Henry kept right on doing what he was doing. The weary chancellor was heard exclaiming to his faithful clerk, "Creeping Jesus, it just can't be! No living man could eat chicken six days a week for thirty-eight years! I happen to personally know that quail is one hell of a lot tastier than chicken. Yet I couldn't eat quail six days a week for thirty-eight years." The Chancellor was heard to add in misty-eyed confidence, "Cousin Pat, I will tell you what I don't hardly every tell nobody else. . . . There was a time, back when I was just a free-growing fuzzy-faced boy . . . I wasn't but thirty-three years old . . . when I overran the absoluteness of statutes, as boys will do, and overshot my quail quota two days in a row.

"That was long before I taken on the judicial ermine, but I knowed I was doing wrong. I knowed it a lot better after I'd dressed off them twenty-eight pore dead lil quails and set out to eat 'em before they commenced to go bad. I ended up by giving the last fifteen to deserving relatives and to this very day I'd sooner eat a raw buzzard than a cooked quail."

The trial went on, and so did Henry Boggs. On a second brief courtroom appearance he said again, you know what, and added that the payment of the alleged claim value of the 11,678 live chickens exceeded his honest savings of a lifetime; that his payment of such an amount, even if possible, would put the partnership permanently out of business. The courthouse wrangling continued for additional months. Henry Boggs eventually triumphed. Meanwhile he kept right on running his live poultry establishment and carrying home one live chicken every business day he worked.

As to all men, death came to Henry Boggs. When his last illness was upon him, Henry spent painful days unable to take any substantial nourishment. When his nearest of kin and a few very special friends had gathered at his bedside, Henry roused and murmured that he was once more beginning to feel like himself. The assembled company was properly delighted by the confidence. Sister Lucy steadied her voice to reply, "I'm so very glad to hear that, Henry. And isn't there something, something you like, that I could bring you?"

As usual, Henry weighed his answer with great care. "Yes, Lucy, there is. I'd cherish it if you'd bring me a nice baked hen."

CHAPTER VIII

The Ozarks Storyteller

As a BACKHILL-TRAMPING country correspondent, I came to agree with a far more sagacious wanderer—name, Ralph Waldo Emerson—that the true tests of a civilization are not the census, nor the size of the cities nor the crops, but the kind of man the country turns out and the kind of stories he tells.

And the kind of stories he tells and lives. As no reporter could deny, or avoid learning, a great many of the more revealing Ozarks stories are the being-lived kind, with environment as catalyst and cause. I was learning, too, that both categories are very heavily dependent on very slight factors; the inflections, postures and tempos of speech, the subtle doings of nature, and the inevitable combinations or mergings thereof.

Such as and including the stray wind that touches the treetops; the spotted cow that munches roadside grass while dangling a copper bell; the line of buttercups that wave gallantly in a long-abandoned yardway; the country girl who sits on a cabin porch combing her hair in the sunlight; the lounging country man who whittles—not constructively in the sense of knifing a cedar stick into something useful, such as a churn dasher or a potato masher —but just whittling, to change a stick of wood into tiny slivers of wood.

It follows that the truly revealing Ozark stories are never exactly premolded. They change with time, moods and tellers. The great majority is not typebound because it never appears in type. But through the years and in their varied and oftentimes whimsical ways, Ozark stories tend to join or otherwise arrive in groups or arbors—stories of weather, deception, crime, sacrifice, love, hate, historic adventures, and so on. And stories of poverty, which the Ozarks cannot avoid and do not try to avoid, granted, of course, that some Ozarkian times and people are a great deal poorer than others. For example, there was that young neighbor couple who broke up when the shoeless groom found himself too poor to buy a nickel's worth of salt to season the final sack of potatoes he had dug on four-to-one shares for the tightest clodhopper on Greazy Creek.

And stories of weather, above all the drought. There was recently the deeply pathetic story of the harried rural child of the backwoods near Fayetteville overtaken and ensnared by a child psychologist who was spending the overheated summer as a visiting professor of education at the University of Arkansas.

The educator had contrived with the schoolteacher to produce a "problem child." The selection was an engaging nine-year-old boy, who was fat, freckled, confused, and extremely warm. The youngster's "problem" was one of "self expression." For many hard-bitten school terms he had been unable to make with "oral themes" or describe verbally any of the "impressive things" he had seen or otherwise encountered.

Recently the boy had been packed away to a week of vacation

Bible school in the backwoods of an adjoining county. The teacher was beseeching him to tell of impressive things he had seen, while the psychologist listened, took notes, and interpreted.

"Now Oliver," the teacher began, "please tell us about the most interesting thing, the most impressive thing . . . about the church house. Was it the tower? Or the trees outside? Or the pulpit?"

The child blinked warily and said, "Ulp!"

"Or was it the platform?"

The boy's lips show the faintest shadow of a smile.

"Ulp! Hit-was-the-stove."

The visiting authority smiled. The sweating teacher smiled. "Now Oliver, what was the most impressive thing about the church stove?"

After a prolonged and embarrassed silence the "Ulp" sounded again. And presently five words burbled out as one, "Hit-was-the-stove-pipe."

The greenish young eyes sparkled in glorious triumph.

The visiting authority pressed with the next question, "Now tell us, Oliver, what was the impressive thing about the stove pipe?"

The boy's eyes showed a wondrous light and his lips began to move with a strange and facile grace. "Ulp! Mister, I'm a tellin' you that there was the gadamndest longest, skinniest gadamn stove pipe you ever seed! Hit come pilin' and twisted out'n the top that great damn big monkey stove and went way high up onder the ceilin' and plum acrost that there church room. . . . I'm tellin' you, Mister, that there stove pipe was a long, skinny, scrimped up son of a bitch!" Breathlessly the youthful example added, "Ulp, my pappy says if they was ever anything any longer and scrimpier than that there stove pipe, hit is this here gadamn dry spell!"

Or take Ole Luke Kantz, who farmed the whole of a drought-tortured summer and raised nothing but a washtubful of corn, all of it little squirrel-headed nubbins that all hell couldn't shuck.

Luke managed to shell off enough of the harvest to fill a gallon sorghum bucket which he toted down to the pestle mill he had set up on Gully Branch down holler from his vacant cow pasture. As bad luck would have it, a big raccoon elected to raid the grinding basin just as the catch trough dumped its water and dropped down the big pestle block. That was bedrock hard on Uncle Luke; still worse on the pilfering coon which shortly became fragmentated, along with the shelled corn, into a watery mix for raccoon pancakes.

When Luke's wife found out about the ultimate mishap she cried and kept on crying until Luke went out and rounded in his two mules, hitched them to the sway-tongued wagon, loaded on his entire family, the three split-bottomed chairs, the cedar churn, the old white tomcat and the redbone hound, and so headed for the old Wire Road and the brand new state of Oklahomy.

The interdependence of weather and poverty is as perennial as it is potent. Ozark weather is whimsical, oftentimes violent, and usually protracted in moods. When rains come, the summers are likely to be quite comfortable. In droughty summers, which occur approximately two years in five, the heat can be and frequently is murderous. In successions of dry summers, which also occur and recur, the mercury soars to highs of 112° or thereabouts and leaves people to sweat and flounce through sweat-pouring nights.

Even as Ozarks summers can be witheringly hot, the winters can be bitingly cold. By averages, the excessively cold winters are fewer than the swinger summers. They can be blue-devil tinglers. But the burn-up Ozarks summers are the more prolific in terms of stories. Companion to people-torturing heat is crop-ruining drought. The latter is the first shaper of decisions. Drought is the all-commanding force which can and does upset the usually fine balance of subsistence farming and decide whether, and how many, hill country settlers stay with and on their land.

There was the drought-decided story of Tom and Elly Shrum and their exceptionally likable son Noah. Old Tom was a paralytic, a secondhand-wheelchair survivor of a firsthand accident in a thirdhand transient saw mill.

As usual, Tom had spent the summer days sitting under his front yard persimmon grove whittling and looking on. As he figured it, the summer was too man-heating hot to be used in any other way.

But Tom's boy Noah saw it otherwise. The nineteen-year-old was the up-and-comer sort. For four successive years Noah had plowed and planted and tilled the Shrum forty acres with almost startling diligence, aiming to take off for town and mechanics' school if ever he could make a paying crop. For three prior years the drought cycle had kept him from so much as a close look at that goal.

Old Tom was less than joyous about the underhanded weather. But he cherished his only son far too much to consent to losing him. Meanwhile, the crippled one was sitting and whittling his way through still another long summer, warpingly hot and cruelly dry; sitting and whittling and looking down on browning pastures and the valley fields which appeared to be praying, even grovelling for rain.

But there came an afternoon of omens. When Tom turned to reach for his tobacco bag he saw a raincrow, or yeller flicker, fly out of a dense congregation of roadside oaks and settle on the crest of the cabin roof. There the rain bird perched and swayed with lolling beak and droopy wings. After a time the feathered omen raised its snaky head and squawked its peculiar rain call, then flapped out of sight.

94

Shortly thereafter, Tom's wife Elly came swishing in from the garden patch lugging a basket of potatoes—to save them from being ground cooked by the summer sun. Elly seated herself on the forepart of the wheelbarrow, fanned her sweated brow with her sunbonnet while confiding her hopes for planting the snuff-dry potato land to late turnips. She granted it was a slim hope but perhaps a chance worth taking. At that point Tom Shrum saw their son heading his plow horse toward home.

Noah had finished laying off his corn crop. Tom reflected that one more week of the parching weather and young Noah wouldn't make enough corn to winter a lean red rooster. Tom spoke resolutely. "This be the decidin' week for the cawn crop. Hit's comin' into tassels. No rain, no crop." He paused for emphasis. "Speakin' candid and frank, I figger we're shore in for a dry spell."

Elly peered at him. "You keep sayin' that like mebbe you was wishin' it."

Noah tried to answer objectively. "Speakin' candid frank, I'm believin' hit'll come rain."

Tom sat alone and whittled until sunset and suppertime. He felt little interest in the sunset. He watched the yellowing west, oldest and surest of old-time rain signs. The cripple rammed his hands deep into his overall pockets. If rain should come—Sonny's corn would crop out. Sonny would sell the crop and he would be leaving. Resignedly Tom steered his wheelchair to the low tongue of the front porch where his son waited to lift him in.

Supper was a quarter-hour of comparative silence, with milk mush, corn bread and honey and the holdover from a blackberry cobbler. Noah was hungry, as boys will be, but he finished hurriedly, topped his bowl with knife and fork, and left the table, saying he had something to tinker about in the barn. That was what he said. But Tom knew that Sonny was going for a prowl in the early moonlight, likewise to check on rain signs. Elly finished

95

her purple remnant of cobbler, rested her elbows on the table, then began brushing the oilcloth. "Had a-plenty?"

Tom nodded. The old woman motioned aimlessly toward the door. "Hear that raincrow hollerin' soon after sundown?"

"Uh-huh."

"Old man Fiets done put his boys to haulin' in their oat hay . . . figgers hit'll rain."

Tom wheeled his chair from the lamp-heated table toward the side window. There he looked out on great throngs of fireflies rising from the valley, flashing their lights in more than ordinary fervor. Could be the lightnin' bugs were feeling the rain, too. On the gray ribbon of roadway, which was dusty dry even in early moonlight, Tom could make out what appeared to be the fast-moving shape of a grass snake. He recalled that snakes are disposed to get in some hurried scurryings for water-free shelter. The cripple reached for his cob pipe. At that moment he distinctly heard a frog croaking from the nearer grove of valley sycamores. Tom reflected that this was the first tree frog song he had listened to since middle May. And when a tree frog prays for rain, the good Lord is liable to listen.

Presently Tom heard Noah entering the back door and making for the loft ladder. He asked his son to help him into bed. As he lay looking out into the night, the old man heard a subdued murmur like the song of a far-off ocean. Coming storms have wondrous ways of putting hills to talking. Tom pulled the solitary sheet over his face and invited sleep. It was short lived. The cripple woke to find himself shivering. Wind was swooping down upon him and roaring through the woodlands. To the northwest he saw a peculiar blue-white recurrence of light. A whitish fluffery of clouds had covered the moon and the few remaining stars were strangely dim.

Tom sat upright and heard the first low roar of thunder. A

stray raindrop struck the windowpane. The aging man was certain there would be many of them soon—acres, miles and river feet of greedy rain, pillaging rain, come to rob a crippled old man of his only son. Rain . . .

A glarish pathway of lightning cut high into the sky, set off a hard-shaking blast of thunder. The big rain was on. Tom brushed the hair from his eyes, crowded toward the unraisable window. A repeat of lightning showed great silver needles of rain which appeared to be sewing earth and sky together. Then above the increasing roar he heard familiar voices, saw his wife and son at his bedside. Elly was holding a hand lamp; Noah pulled open the front door and standing on tiptoe peered out at the storm, even as he had once peered up at his first Christmas tree. When he turned, his red hair was blackened wet. And then the youth began to speak. The strength of his words carried even above the medley of the storm.

"How ye like it, Pap? Rain!" Noah's voice rose with joyous fervor. "Can't ye jest hear them cawn stalks gigglin'? Give 'em bare another ten minutes and they'll be haw-hawin' louder'n that thunder." The youth's words seemed to join in the drumming rhythm of the great rain.

"This time, by Jesus, we'll git cawn! This here will fill out the ears and fill up wagonbeds. Don't care if hit don't rain another drap after this 'un; we'll shore git plenty. . . . Comes mornin' I could sell off the whole field a-standin' to either Dave Hannum or Sef Connell. Dave would leave his hawgs eat hit down comes fattenin' time. Sef would have it plucked off and put to sprout for makin' moonshine licker. . . . I got twenty-two acre four-times plowed and proper laid by. Effen that don't give a thousand bushel I'll swaller my left hind leg."

Noah's words continued to carry above the abating tumult of the rain. "I'll leave for you and Ma all you'uns would be needin' for ten years. . . . Takin' two-bits a bushel for what's left, I'll still be takin' in all the cash money needed for takin' on that mee-chanic's trainin' down at Springdale. Ain't you proud about it, Pappy?"

Tom Shrum felt a mighty craving to pull his son into his arms and hold him there forever and ever. Instead, the old one just said, "Yeah, I'm reel proud!"

CHAPTER IX

It Gits Mighty Durn Cold

OZARK WEATHER STORIES keep on happening. Not everybody can swallow them, but nobody can squelch them. Granting that summer heat and drought comprise the most storied of weather combinations, cold weather also begets its own generations of stories, mostly true. As any long-time Ozarker can testify, cold weather likewise builds plenty of stories and decides a lot of lives. You take, for instance, the winter of 1917–18 when virtually the entire Ozark plateau suffered fourteen successive days of subzero weather; when town water works froze uniformly stiff and oak trees froze so hard that their trunks split—causing woodlands to pop and bang like old-time battlefields.

The Ozarks never were dressed or housed for extreme cold, nor, as my mother used to say, rightly spirited for it. But blizzards sometimes descend, from straight acrost the peach orchard, as my mother also stated the occurrence, and extreme cold has shaped a mighty fold of Ozark stories.

THE BODACIOUS OZARKS

Including the true chronicle of young Tint Barnes, the under-aged pistoleer from Wedington Gap—only the names have been changed to protect the not-excessively innocent. Tint was sixteen at the time (February, 1923) and abiding in a one-room-and-lean-to log cabin with his mother, the Widder Barnes, and now and then with Mul Sellers, his stepfather who was only now and then separated from the state penitentiary.

When I interviewed Tint, he opened with a double confidence. The first entry was that being treed by a wild hawg in a stiff-froze blackjack tree on the coldest night of winter ain't nobody's play party. Neither, for that matter, was the feat of living in a slaunchwise cabin with his in-again, out-again step-pappy.

Two years earlier Mul Sellers had set out anew at the forth-right vocation of robbing country stores. In the rapid progress of these stirring adventures, ill-tempered Mul had tapped Lyin' Johnny Wells' head a mite too hard. The court-housers called it murder and Mul found himself rewarded with a life sentence to what is discreetly termed the Tucker Prison Farm, down in the Pine Bluffs (Arkansas) mosquito bogs. After about nineteen un-cherished months Mul discovered an open gate with only one guard on duty. He slugged the guard, took to the hills and the little home he had earlier commandeered. There the violent individual-ist arrived sloshing mean with corn liquor and the sultry sus-picion that his wife, the erstwhile Widder Barnes, had been making too freely with Preacher Johnson and the latter's rather intimate techniques of soul restoring. Widder Barnes denied the charges. Mul started to work her over with a broom, including the handle thereof. The stepson heard the commotion, eased back up the lad-der to the bedloft, slipped the revolver from underneath his oat-straw mattress and emptied two cartridges into Mul Sellers' un-trustworthy head.

After that Tint remembered slipping the pistol gun into his

jacket belt and striking out into the bitter cold night. As he padded down the log road skirting Seamster's backhouses, a roving boar charged out from a grove of haw bushes and made after him. At the moment Tint didn't feel for another shooting and thoughtlessly elected to run for a cone-shaped blackjack tree which sentineled a turn of the road. As he shinnied up the rough-barked trunk the youth saw the pursuing hawg raising up behind him, tusks shining in the sickly moonlight, mouth wide open. Tint pushed on through the knife-sharp twigs and scrunched onto the first big branch. There he found himself treed, in the stinging cold of a February night, and able to identify nothing whatsoever between himself and the North Pole except perhaps a one-strand barbwire fence and certainly a man-eating wild hawg.

Even the sickly snow was frozen to a gray crisp. As well as Tint could see and feel, his hands were freezing to approximately the same color. Below him waited a more violent and painful death deliverable by the lank, winter-starved razorback hawg. In the hill country as elsewhere, a wild razorback gone mean is the most dreaded of all the free-roaming killers, even including mean step-pappies and murderously cold February nights. Tint was quite certain that he could not last out the hour, much less the night.

Accordingly, the backhill teen-ager lowered a stiffening hand to his belt and touched the butt of his pistol. He felt the skin of his fingertips sticking to the freezing metal and he recalled that the seven-shot revolver still held five bullets. Tint aimed with desperate care. When the foresights began wavering below a tier of stiff black bristles, he squeezed the trigger. The pistol spat cherry red and the hills roared with echoes. He aimed and fired a second shot, then a third.

But the wild hawg appeared not to move so much as a hair. As Tint slipped the revolver back into his belt, his gaze stayed with the line of stiff black bristles which reminded him deliriously of what was left of his step-pappy's hairline. Then the freezing youth reflected that the spectre of the pursuing hawg was nothing more or less than a froze-up nightmare. Otherwise, why didn't the shape move when he blasted it? Tint heard himself answering his own question. That there shape at the foot of the tree was the ghost, like as not the killer hant of Mul Sellers. From where Tint sat freezing stiffer than a well-digger's watch fob, he'd merely been banging away with common, ordinary lead bullets which for a ghoster are about as helpful as blowing kisses.

The youth sought to raise his free hand to his face. Judging by the feel of things he was already frozen as stiff as a constipated coon. Mayhaps this iron-hard shade of a blackjack tree was one of the fixin's of the other kind of a hell. Mayhaps he had already froze to death and got transformed to the cold hell which sets antigogglin' like to the hot hell. Parson Johnson had swore and be-damned there are lots of different kinds of hells. Tint was re-calling other gems of spiritual counsel with which Parson John-son had favored him—a 'tarnal sinner. "You ain't yet been saved, Tinty," the preacher man had vowed. "And onless you mend your ways, you're shore headed smackdab straight fer hell!"

"You mean I'd be stuck there with my step-pappy, Mul Sellers?"

Parson Johnson's reply had been obliterated by an unusually big mouthful of tobacco juice.

"Maybe another kind of hell?" Tint queried pleadingly. "In case I gets sended to hell I shore don't relish gettin' put up again with that no-good Mul Sellers." Parson Johnson at that point be-gan to shout "Hallelujah!"

Hell and hants notwithstanding, Tint yielded to the urge for a last try with gunplay. He had begun the evening with a seven-bullet pistol gun, full-loaded. He had let Mul Sellers have two bullets. He'd let the hawg shape have three. That left two. . . .

IT GITS MIGHTY DURN COLD

Tint managed to stand upright on both frosted clods which earlier had been his feet. With vast effort he lowered his right hand into his belt, took up the revolver, aimed shakily into the dimming moonlight and managed to close a stiffening forefinger on the trigger. An orange-red blaze tore into the night. The hawg spectre only waited—still as a dead oak stump. Tint fired once more, then permitted the empty pistol to slip from his hand. A surprising warmth came over him and an unreal flush which seemed to evaporate the blackjack tree.

As well as Tint Barnes could figure it, this time for sure he was waking up in hell. And just as certainly the cold hell was changing to the fiery sort. There an extremely hot fire burned directly before him. As Tint struggled back from it, he heard a voice which seemed quite alien to hell—his mother's—and certainly there wasn't any rightness about the Widder Barnes being in hell. She never killed, nor coveted, nor stole, nor worshipped brazen idols. Fact was, Tint's Ma had been saved more times at more meetin's than a cat has whiskers.

In time Tint made out another voice, a sort of sing-song which he eventually recognized as belonging to Sheriff Henry Walker from Jasper Town. Tint wasn't by any means surprised at finding the sheriff in hell; but to hear the sheriff making easy talk with his mother, and neither one seeming to feel pain . . . that was real peculiar.

Furthermore, Tint Barnes was surprised and a bit let down about finding hell such a pint-size, penny-whistle sort of a place. By gradual stages he had begun observing that this particular hell-fire looked a lot like a common fireplace fire, including the rock side walls and smoky cedar mantel boards. But when he recognized the maplewood clock that he had been raised by, Tint Barnes peered about less fearfully, first at the Widder Barnes, then at the sheriff. And though it hurt him to talk, he managed to shape a first question. "Was that really a wild hawg I was tryin' to shoot afore I come here?"

Sheriff Walker seemed to be grinning. "Sonny, it *was* a hawg . . . and you shore to hell blasted it. I found you piled down in the snow, square in front of the crittur. I walked up and gave the hawg a kick, and it toppled over like a daid rotten stump. I taken out my flashlight and counted five bullets put square between the hawg's eyes in a space about the size of a two-bit piece. So I fetched you in. Another ten minutes and you'd been stiff dead as that wild razorback was. . . . I drug in the hawg, too . . . left it on the porchway aside your dear dee-parted step-pappy."

The sheriff's puckered grin lingered. "You might say you done a right apt shootin' job on both them killers."

With immense effort Tint sat upright and scooted himself away from the fire. "But Mul Sellers wasn't edzactly a killer."

Sheriff Walker was fingering Tint's revolver. "You *might* say he was so, Sonny. Seems your dear dee-parted step-pa slew a penitent'ry guard whilst takin' off from Tucker Farm. . . ."

With great shakiness Tint got to his feet. "Meanin' I don't get hung?"

The Sheriff Walker's grin increased. "You *might* say it *could* mean that, Sonny." With great care the sheriff man again inspected Tint's pistol and slipped it into his jacket pocket. "I'll just keep this—for to save you from again gettin' led into temptation. . . . And you shore ain't got no need to stalk Mul Sellers no more . . . State wanted him took in . . . and you shore as hell took him in . . . same as that wild hawg. . . . I'm takin' along the hams and shoulders and tenderloin and bacon sides and spareribs and leavin' you all the rest . . . you might say as a ree-ward."

Widder Barnes almost smiled. "That there is mighty kindly of you, Sheriff. Hit leaves fer Tinty and me the makin's of headcheese." Her thin shoulders arched with unusual determination. "But, Sheriff, you was speakin' about a ree-ward. . . . While ago, while Mul was a-whalin' me with that there broomstick, he was yellin' that the state was offerin' three hundert dollars ree-ward for takin' him live or dead. Said he was cloutin' me so as I couldn't get to the preacher man. Said Parson Johnson would be ironin' onto the equal of five years of preacher pay for turnin' him in. . . . Suppose that there was so much silly talk?"

"You *might* say it was," the sheriff's grin remained extensive.

The Widder Barnes gulped determinedly. "Sheriff, so what comes of that three-hundert-dollar cash-money ree-ward? Does my Tint git it?"

For the moment Sheriff Walker's grin wavered. "You *might* say that ree-ward money has got lost in channels . . ."

The Widder Barnes peered closely at the law man. "Sheriff, I just don't seem to foller that lawyerin' talk. . . . When you'uns say that cash-money ree-ward for Mul Sellers musta got lost in channels, would you maybe be meanin' that somewhere between Jasper Town and here that there ree-ward got dropped into the river?"

The sheriff's grin returned and grew. "You *might* say that, Miz Barnes . . . you *might* say hit did."

CHAPTER X

It Can Git Spirited, Likewise

COMPANION TO THE Ozarks stories of weather and the excesses thereof are those of excessive religion. The latter were and still are demonstrated by the brush- (bresh) arbor meetin's. These are the recurrent and rather distinctive backhill equivalents of the tent revival or camp meetin'.

In earlier times, even in current times, the local faithful set up "coverin's of holiness" or "shades of grace" for temporary use as temples. Usually these remote structures are sided with upright sticks or poles and roofed with a loose thatching of brush. The arbors are disposed to rise on sun-parched hillsides or partly green valleys distant from tenanted farms or villages. As a rule the raisers and participants are the poorest of the poor of several communities or crossroads. They usually include more females than males, though the sick, the lame, the dim-witted, the fanatic and the intensely pious of both sexes are likely to be on hand and "praying through." Many of the arbors rely on itinerant "administers" or pastors who as a rule lack licenses, permanent churches, durable congregations, or distinguishable sects.

Some of the preacher men are notorious spellbinders. Some are obvious charlatans. Many are fanatically, even desperately sincere, even when in the throes of such primitive dramatics as whooping, bellowing, rolling on the ground ("holy rollin' "), or frenzied love-making.

Sometimes the meetin's are enlivened by a hymn singer or "holy chanter" who oftentimes emerges as a fat man who sings tenor. But the preacher man is rarely fat. He is more likely to be a slender little man with doll-blue eyes, spindly legs and a deep bullish voice. Pastor Luther Pennington, the bresh-arbor administer whom I knew best, had the latter characteristics. He also had a daughter named Mamie, who was about fifteen at the time and decidedly pretty. The Pastor was a widower and Mamie "kept home" for him.

None could deny that Mame was a devoted daughter and slavey. She washed, cooked and skimped, and meekly obeyed her father. The Pastor rewarded this devotion by dragging her from meetin' to meetin', displaying her in what he apocryphally termed honest rags, commanded her to lead in open confessions, and after services repeatedly whipped her black and blue as punishment for what she had or had not confessed.

Retribution came with and at the Tatt Arbor, one of the loudest and warmest in the holy-rolling history of Madison County, Arkansas. The new-built bresh arbor was about twice as long and close to half as wide as the Greazy Creek schoolhouse. Abner Tatt's sawmill had contributed smooth planks for the building of a preaching platform overlooking the "mourners." The meetin' opened on a Holy August Saturday. Pastor Pennington and Mame had been housed in a vacant branch-side cabin a mile or so downhill from the arbor.

Fully an hour before sunset Pastor Pennington had fetched a dusty jug from the maw of his rusty locker trunk, filled a porcelain mug and gulped down the contents. For many years this pious swigging had been one of the pastor's preparatory moves. He had explained to his daughter that it was a nectar of the Moving Spirits. Mame had observed that on the breath the nectar evidenced a rather commonplace and mortal smell, though she conceded that the ways of the Moving Spirit are wondrous strange.

By sundown country people were arriving from as far away as Mount Comfort, Goshen and Monkey Run. Among the worshippers were Uncle Billy Dye who drove up in his farm wagon with Aunt Martha Dye on the spring seat beside him, and their five sons followed afoot. The Dyes were a truly fervent family and it was common agreement that the Dye boys were the deepest-set seekers after the true Moving Spirit. One of the irrefutable evidences was that every springtime following the August bresh-arbor meetin' a flurry of infants would appear. They weren't named Dye, but they shore as hell looked like Dyes. However, as Mame Pennington kept reflecting, the ways of the Moving Spirit are wondrous strange.

By dusk the crowds were swarming into the bresh arbor. Pastor Pennington came spidering to the platform, raised his huge pale hands and opened the meeting: "Glory Hallelujah! Brethren! Leave us sing away our sins!" Fat Frank Grammer bellowed "Amen!" and opened stentoriously:

> *Some hippy-crits can look like saints, from men their idols*
> *hide,*
> *But what about the Judgement Day beyond death's monster*
> *tide?*
> *Will it pay? O, will it pay?*
> *At the last Great Judgement Day?*

As the great bellow subsided, Pastor Pennington leaped to his feet and cried out: "Hallelujah, Brethren. I can't speak nothin' but the words of God, so listen when I say Hallelujah! Lemme tell you, Brethren, God's a-gettin' tired a ye. Hallelujah! Hit's killin' me to do it, but I've got to tell—you're goin' to Hell, you're goin' to Hell—Glory, Hallelujah, you're goin' to Hell!"

For the time Pastor Pennington could say no more. The Moving Spirit was striking his feet. Mame reflected that the Moving Spirit almost invariably struck her pa's feet immediately after he partook of the Holy Cordial. The congregation began to grovel, and howl, and kick up dust and straw. The spirit was taking. But Mame sat stiffly in the outmost fringe of the crowd while the Dye boys strayed about wherever their presences seemed needed.

Outside, the katydids, crickets, screech owls and other night creatures remained strangely silent. The platform lantern burned low and the moon waned. The meeting ended at dawn. Arrived at his gift cabin, Pastor Pennington shed his free-flowing benevolence like a wet coat, commanded that his daughter shuck off to bed, and returned to his jug.

It was raining next day. Pastor Pennington had fallen victim to late-summer melancholy. He banged through the low-ceilinged cabin bellowing songs of salvation and dire prophecies. Long before noon he was paying addresses to the Holy Cordial. His eyes were acquiring reddish fringes and he was breathing noisily. Towards midafternoon he called Mame and commanded her to go tidy up the meeting house and to fetch him a bucket of cold drinking water, and that done to hie forth and tidy up the preachin' platform. Then he called her back and suffered her to stand before him.

"Mame, you've got till closin' time tonight to come prayin' through. Mame, your sinnin' flesh ain't yet been rightly humbled . . . if you don't come prayin' through tonight, I'm tellin' you it

109

will be . . . I'm warnin' you . . ." The Pastor stopped, for his tongue seemed uncontrollably thick. Had the minister not been unreasonably preoccupied with gulping cold water he might have noticed Mame leaving the cabin carrying half a broom, the cedar water bucket, and in her right hand a fruit jar full of bacon grease.

Fervor touched the second meeting early. Pastor Pennington was in no condition for speaking, but he was in great shape for shouting. So were most of the worshippers, including all five of the Dye boys who were looking more handsome and helpful than ever. Hoseah, the youngest of them, very personally greeted Mame Pennington and as one penitent to another, he kissed her.

Inside the meetin' house Brother Macy Harrison cupped his hands to his mouth and screamed somewhat like a freight whistle. Uncle Billy Dye bellowed like a morose bull. Pastor Pennington stumbled toward the platform. Mame watched him with hard, clear eyes. So after the show the Man of God would be all set to give her a licking that would make all the others sound and feel like love pats. What if she did pray through? Her Pa's mind was ready made up and his foot set down.

Beyond any possibility of doubt the Moving Spirit was striking Pastor Pennington's feet again. He bawled and danced, then leaped off the platform to shout exhortations into the ear of Lulu Horn. Then he patted an old woman's whitening head and hopped back to the platform. But his feet could not find anchorage. Abruptly they shot apart. The spidery little pastor came smashing to the floor. The small of his back appeared to strike the platform edge. He kicked spasmodically then rolled over. His little legs continued to jerk like those of a beheaded chicken.

Pastor Pennington began to scream as if in great pain. For a time no heed was paid him. The problems of salvation are too mighty for taking notice of a mere misstep. But Sister Andy Harrison, one to whom salvation came only by dribbles, looked

110

more closely; then she screamed for her husband. "Macey! Preacher's busted his back. Plum broke his silly spine. He won't never rise up no more. He's mortal ruint!"

A circling of penitents closed about the flouncing pastor. Brother Macey Harrison knelt to inspect. "His back looks like hit's broke all right. 'Bout the only thing left is to haul him to the hawspital in Fayette-ville . . ."

Lulu Horn shrilled an alternative. "Shorely Almighty Gawd will send down a golden chariot fer to carry the faithful up to Gawd's throne!"

Brother Macey Harrison was in no mood to argue. "Hope to goodness Gawd does jest that!"

Uncle Billy Dye knelt to reiterate, "Yas suh, he shore plum smacked his little tail!" The patriarch stroked the platform, then inspected his fingers in venerable astonishment. "Feel them floorboards, would ye! They've been oiled!"

"Bedurned if they ain't," Brother Harrison confirmed, "slicker'n owl lard. Somebody musta slicked hit over to stick down the splinters. Guess Mame done hit," the elder continued. "While ago she come over to git the arbor tidied up."

"Reckon that was the how of it," Uncle Billy Dye agreed. "Shore can't blame no young female for tryin' to purty up the preachin' platform. But whoever done the slickin' shore as hell overdone it."

"Ain't it awful about pore lil Mame," Sister Harrison squawled. "She'll be lefted all alone!"

But Mame was neither alone nor lamenting. Several minutes earlier she and young Hoseah Dye had gone for a conversion stroll in the moonlight.

CHAPTER XI

The Wonder of It

Believing is one of the finest attributes of Ozarks culture and one of its salient resources. The towns, such as they are, have largely lost their capacities truly to believe or honorably accept the indigenous talents of the region as a whole.

But in some remarkable part the wonderful talent for believing has lived on in the backhills and other far rural spaces. In substantial areas, mostly in the off-highway Ozarks, one still encounters it. This talent is not divorced from recognition or acceptance of truth. Actually, it is not only tolerant of truth, it is a living area of truth itself. Whether the perceiver is a searcher after Spanish treasure or mysterious tinkle bells or a demonstrator of the biophysics of inversion, his perceptive talents make him capable of factual appraisals and of interpretations, even if fragmentary, of elements and backgrounds of truth which are as important as life itself.

The last searcher after bells, or bell follower, I knew personally was an old man who lived on a crested hilltop near the crossroads of War Eagle, Arkansas. Uncle Luther explained the rudiments of his trade: "Bell follerin' leads a man to a mighty lot of mighty interesting things and places. Mebbe you'll be settin' in the shade or restin' in the sun and first thing you know you hear somethin' you take to be the tinker of an old brass bell on a strayin' cow . . . but you keep listenin' fine and careful and after while you hear the tinker of a whole flight of little tiny bells. You foller after 'em and d'rectly they'll lead you over the hilltop.

"So you trail on over the hilltop and then, by hicky, you look down and there you see a toy-size town all built of gold and alabaster and sparkly jeweled and peopled with purty little folks 'bout half the size of your lil finger . . . the whole town is small enough to lay in the circle of your right arm. And them towns to where the little bells leads is ever light and spritely and everlastin'. Winds can't topple 'em and age can't never rot 'em away . . ."

I believe Uncle Luther spoke more than fantasy. As Ozarks story-tellers come and go, they leave revelations of the land and its people which are far more reliable than anything any Chamber of Commerce will ever hand out. This is true even of backhill treasure stories.

The Ozarks abound in various denominations of yarns about the hunting and finding of all kinds of treasures. In principal part the stories are old, with roots reaching back into the dimly recorded times of Spain's exploring conquistadores, then to the years of Spain's treaty ownership of the region, to the times of bankless frontiers, then to the chaos of the Civil War and the hair-triggered and violent years of "reconstruction" which followed.

Most Ozark stories are based on fact, but the treasure yarns trend toward fantasy. In all my years of Ozarks reporting I have covered only one completely factual instance of an Ozark treasure find; only one which materialized before my very eyes and was

113

touchable by my curious hands. This recitation of Recorded Truth began during the gold-caching early years of the Civil War. The locale was far out in the hills of Madison County, within a few miles of Greazy Creek, the homeland of Orval Faubus.

In pre-Civil War times this backwoods lost land had been a hide-out arena for horse thieves and cattle rustlers and a stronghold for one prospering family of slave owners and Negro traders. These were the Hindsville Hawkinses. Grandpappy Jim took over and "brung in his niggers," beginning in 1836 while Arkansas was being admitted, rather begrudgingly, to the Union. Grandpappy Jim directed the building of a now historic grain mill and then used slave labor to plant peach and apple orchards, and in time to set up a long-enduring brandy works. The first settler labored hard, drove hard—using two giant Negresses as "whip swingers"—and for a quarter-century or so he prospered.

When the Civil War began, Grandpappy Hawkins traded half of his savings for Confederate currency (which he eventually used to warm up a side of fried catfish) and buried the rest as touchable Yankee coin gold which eventually provided the treasure find very personally witnessed by this rather personal writer.

Having rounded out his three-score years and ten, and thrown in twenty-one for good measure, Jim Hawkins died. His daughter, Sadie, took over the homestead. That was in 1888. By 1900 Miss Sadie had let the mammoth farms go back to brush and permitted the old orchards to die untended. But at the very least, the spinster daughter ironed onto the savin's. During 1925 Aunt Sadie died. After the services were spoken, some medium neighbors from Hindsville-way came down to do some clearing out about the old place which was being taken over by Aunt Sadie's widowed niece.

The usual brush grubbing, roof patching and fireplace and chimney mending required attention. I had been invited to the countryside "helpful party." When the helpful neighbors got around to the fireplace, they set in to replace the badly cracked flat rock hearth. The border rocks lifted easily, but the big center one held firm. When the do-gooders slipped a carpenter's iron under it, the rod bent like a strip of wax. They brought out heavy crowbars and tried again with three strong men stationed at the tips of the bars.

Bit by bit the big hearth rock surrendered. Inch by inch the near edge rose higher. When young Clyde Hawkins reached under to scoop aside a handful of soot, his fingers touched iron. He swept aside a layer of ashes and dug his fingers into an iron loop. He grasped it, pulled, and so drew out a time-battered strongbox. Others fetched hammers and chisels. They broke the lock and pried the lid. Inside there was gold—eagles, and double eagles, garnished with a mixed-up miscellany of old-time coins—in all close to nineteen thousand dollars worth.

Country people thereabouts keep on searching and probing for what they confidently term the balance of the Hawkins coin gold. In a leisurely off-and-on manner the treasure hunt continues. So far as anybody knows, for sure, not so much as a quarter eagle or a moldy penny has been turned up during the past third-century. But, as neighbor people keep pointing out, you can't never tell when the luck will change. Any day or any night may be the one when some well-meaning neighbor out in Madison County may find his fingers latched onto the low corner of a rusty chest grunting-heavy with a golden fortune—finders being keepers.

Particularly in the farther backhills where time runs especially plentiful and springs of imagination run strongest, treasure hunting comes as naturally as breathing and even more naturally than wash days. Hearsay of money buryings of the past century are supplemented rather gloriously by the "olden" legends of treasure caches. Even as lifetimes fade and generations follow, questers in patched blue overalls keep toting picks and shovels and appropriate hand tools to remote places. They keep finding and deciphering rock markings or prowling into caves that are heavy with the dank of dead centuries and the onetime lively hopes thereof.

"Spaniard gold" remains the most prevalent theme of Ozark treasure lore. The hardiest of these yarns deals with the Lost Louisiana Mine, supposedly buried by roving conquistadores somewhere along the cavernous banks of Little Mulberry River in the lower Arkansas Ozarks. I have followed these would-be treasure trails, noted and photographed the stone carvings allegedly left by the Spaniards, talked and visited with countrymen, including a country doctor and his son who spent their best years searching for the bountiful treasure of the Lost Louisiany Mine.

The background story is to be heard, with minor variations, in many other Ozark countrysides. The basis of the yarn is this:

Indians had mined precious metal in their own aboriginal ways; precise motives unexplained. Presently the Spanish conquistadores came a-thirsting for gold, took over the mines by main strength and musket ball (mustard ball, to quote literally). They enslaved the Indians, forced them to continue digging out the treasure metal. Then the conquistadores met disaster, such as fast-spreading pestilence or vengeful attack by still unconquered Indians. At any rate, the Spaniards fled or otherwise went away, having first buried their treasure and blazed marker trails and drawn maps of the hiding place.

But for one reason or the next the Spaniard fellers never came back. Maybe they got drowned, or massacred, or fever-killed while river rafting back to New Orleans. Anyway, they never came back. Years played on. Pioneers took out hillside homesteads. Then, in time, they noted that outlanders began to appear, men

116

from nowhere in particular, who strolled out among the back-hills, located carved rocks along river banks or blazed marker trails leading through mist-filled woods. In time, they, too, would go away. In due time the settlers took up the quest. Intermittently but ever hopefully their sons, grandsons, and great-grandsons carry on the quest.

Backhill treasure yarns are an engaging hybrid of vague possibility and fantasy. They lead, or tend to lead, into another story realm which is boundaried with the sheer spun gold of imaginative satire. Recording this backhill fantasia is on a level with collecting spider webs intact or photographing hummingbirds on the wing. Recording in type is almost ludicrously difficult. The prankish whimsy, the fragile satire, the pegging of witticism to local characters and situations, the reproduction of moods, and the oftentimes glorious illiteracy and inflections of the storytellers, all these and many other road blocks stand in the reporter's way.

For one example, there is the strange, much told but apparently never written story of the blind crows of Newton County, Arkansas. I first heard the yarn in a less than sober logging camp in the timbered wilds beyond the peculiar village of Boxley. I heard it again as told by a stuttering monk who was retreated to a monastery near Subiaco, on the southwestern fringe of the Ozarks.

The brother confided that prior to his conversion (he termed it "transformation") he had "follered white oak," specifically the surviving fringes of that epic timber, in the backhills of Madison and Newton Counties. The Ozarks were the last widespread stand of this finest of the oaks. The bulk of the stand was felled and shipped away as trestle timbers and crossties used for building railroads pretty much all over the world. Back in 1934, the death of the dismal National Prohibition revived demands for white-oak beer kegs. Those who fetched in the white oak were obliged to search very far back.

Two brothers were leaders in the backhill quest for the scarcening timber. One of them grew rich—not from white oak but rather from crows' eyes. Seems there was a real peculiar clan of cave-dwelling crows which had eyes made of them jewel stones—pearls, diamonds, emeralds and such as that. One day, the honest brother went tree searching among the far bluffs. Instead of white oaks he found a grounded covey of crows—all blind, all with bloody and festering wounds in place of what should have been their eyes. That night the forest prowler caught his brother viewing a veritable handful of sparkling though somewhat bloody gems. In horror the honest brother tossed the unholy loot into the fire. Shortly thereafter he changed to a graying, stuttering monk.

And there is the whimsy, recounted by a country storekeeper's jug-tilting brother-in-law, about a satyr who roamed the far hills with a giant-size axe which the peculiar little man used to free the tree spirits which become imprisoned in dead timber. Satyr performed other "magical slights." For example, when three particularly irksome louts from Cane Hill set out to break up a square dance, Satyr bade them better not. When the local louts sought to do him under, the tree sprite just up and snapped his fingers and changed all three of the punks to bullfrogs.

This happened late a Saturday night. Early Sunday morning the transformed hoodlums came leapfrogging down the mountainside, with eyes bulging and arms waving but otherwise unable to say anything except "ummbooah" like a paternal bullfrog which had just done away with a cruising delegation of tender and juicy water bugs.

Very early that Sunday morning the three louts went bouncing down the road past Tannehill's place. It just so happened that five or six of the young Tannehills were slipping out to do some perch fishing with redworms instead of going to Sunday school. Those

118

young'uns are still wondering what became of that bucket of worms they had dug for to use as fishing bait.

When next seen the three louts were splashing ever so happily in the horse watering trough. But when the church bell began ringing the transformed ones found themselves feeling natural again. They went leapfrogging right into the church, splashing with bilge water and mud and showing grass stains and all such as that. When Baptist Whitfield began dusting off the collection plate, meanwhile raising his free arm to bear down on his opening admonitions, the louts set back to chorus their customary approval. But somehow or other their "Amen" came out "ummbooah."

The young folks began to titter but the parson plowed into his sermon. All went along passably until a pair of big blue bottleflies began buzzing outside the big clear window. At that, Cato and Kink and Tola, the transformed ones, began lookin' all frog-eyed. And when the mornin' sun began showing those bottleflies as the beautiful plump, tasty morsels they truly are—to practically any bullfrog, that is—well sir, all three of those transformed lummoxes rose and went plumping out the open doors hot after the bottleflies which forthrightly took out cross-country with Cato, Kink and Tola leapfrogging after them.

Down in Henbest's Holler the three of them came smack on Satyr leanin' into a post oak tree.

"How's the frogs?" the little one asked.

"Ummbooah!" was all the answer he got.

Satyr stepped toward them, looked them over long and steady, snapped his little fingers. In half the time it takes to pucker to whistle, Satyr was gone and Cato and Kink and Tola were standing as upright and otherwise natural as ever, which, come to think of it, isn't saying such a hell of a lot in their favor.

119

CHAPTER XII

To Tell of Many Things

THE MILLRUN OF Ozarks "tellin' stories" are local recountings with tolerance for the trivial and a basis of factual happening. Practically any family in the course of practically any farming year can recount at least one true happening which not only makes a quotable story but sometimes a *bonne bouche* capable of enduring long after its principals have turned to dust.

For one humble instance, there was the true episode concerning Oscar who arrived at our farmplace for the summer just as the entire family and two helpful neighbors were setting out to get in the hay crop. Uncle Oscar loathed all work; he particularly loathed haying in the late and ruthless June sun. After lengthy and painful hesitation Great-Half-Uncle Oscar volunteered to drive the box wagon which we had lately provided with corner poles, thereby converting it to a hay wagon.

Uncle Oscar was a very bad horse handler. I harnessed the team and watched him take off up the oversize rock-strewn gully which served as a road to the hay field. Arrived there, Uncle Oscar permitted his team to wade ear deep in fencerow brush, then attempted to rein the team for a short turn. A forewheel encountered a high stump. Almost instantly the box wagon flipped over, completely upside down, with Uncle Oscar underneath it, unhurt but most audibly upset.

My great-half-uncle began to cry out for help. First he shrilled "halp" in his normal tenor. Then he bellowed "help" in his best Sunday preaching voice. Then in evident and high-pitched alarm, Uncle Oscar squealed "Help!" Finally, in his best hymn-leading baritone, he boomed out "Hal-l-l-p!"

My father, meanwhile, strolled to the inverted wagon, unhitched the scrambling team and continued walking ahead, even while listening to what sounded like an invincible chorus of "Helps." When my watery-eyed cousin Oliver asked him did he aim to raise up the turned-over wagon, my father pondered the question. I arrived in time to hear his verdict, which was, "Thunderation, no! If there is that many boxed underneath that wagonbed, I say, 'Let the bastards raise theirselves out!'"

My father's sentiments have durable counterparts in an unending harvest of yarns which are the essence of early Ozark history. These stories are not necessarily of pristine accuracy in terms of precise dates and names. But many are the vivid gist of living history, and they continue to raise theirselves out.

That holds for a number of backhill trades and characters, including the followers of honey hunting, an old-line Ozarks occupation which time cannot wholly destroy. It has been this reporter's good fortune to have known quite a number of backhill honey hunters, including another of my great-half-uncles, Ulley Deuteronomy Ellis, who grew up around my home town.

During his teens and early twenties, Ulley hunted wild honey in the far spaces of at least a dozen counties of northwest Arkansas

121

and so made a passable livelihood. In his mid-twenties Ulley set up his own bee farm. "It's not no apiary," my great-half-uncle confided, "on account I shore as hell ain't keepin' apes."

The bee farm failed, mostly because of man-made causes, including far-flung logging operations and successive forest fires which wiped out most of the flowering shrubs and many of the woodland flowers. There followed a cycle of dry summers which pretty well erased the common pasture and prairie flowers. Moreover, what Uncle Ulley called "them fancy, citified, silk-panty bees" which produced comparatively clear honey did not thrive in competition with the native bees. So Ulley gave up and carried the best of his queen bees in flannel bags to the then new and flowering Pacific Northwest. But the enterpriser and his bees shortly discovered that Washington and Oregon "territories" were nowhere near so flowery or as new as they were being pictured.

So Uncle Ulley took off for Central America with his insect queens. All flourished in those flowery lands. In the backlands of Guatemala, Honduras, and Costa Rica Ulley Ellis and his bees brought together tens of thousands of gallons of beautiful clean, clear honey which Ulley sold readily to the German traders. Ulley thrived so markedly that during 1937 he was robbed and massacred by frontier banditti down in Davìd, Panama. The swarthy ones ambushed Ulley among the bougainvillaea blossoms using embezzled Lend-Lease firearms and ammunition issued on behalf of the Good Neighbor policy which F.D.R. had earlier embezzled from H. Hoover. During that same year I was chasing bananas for United Fruit in the wilds of Panama. I got to Davìd in time to help bury Uncle Ulley. We found just about enough of him to fill a small shoe box. But that's another story with only indirect bearing on honey or any other sweetness.

In earlier times, and in lesser part even today, the Ozarks were among the more effective natural havens for honey bees. Prior to the mass destruction of white oak and other of the basic forest trees which served as knight defenders of the flowering under-growths, the quest for wild honey was a more or less classic back-hill pursuit. In my own youth many countrysides had their par-ticular honey hunters, usually men, sometimes boys, occasionally women. Their particular talent was that of studying the blooming sources of honey, then locating and following down the flight trails of the wild bees and thereby identifying the "honey bush"—as a rule the hollow trees or fallen logs in which the wild bees hive and store their honey. Having located the honey cache, the pay-off feat was to fell the tree or otherwise harvest the treasure with-out being grievously or fatally stung.

"Befriendin' the bees" is the decisive trick of the trade. So far as I know, the remarkable knack has never been explained, scien-tifically or otherwise. The wild bees appear to like certain people, to angrily detest others. The questers rarely use masks, smudge pots or other smoking devices. My Uncle Ulley used to recall that he had "worked" bees, wild, tame and intermediate, for more than half a century with only one severe stinging. Back in his late teens Ulley trailed down a honey tree, felled it, and thereby "laid open" several tubfuls of clear, firm honey. But instead of "gentle talkin'" the bees, which was his self-developed skill and advantage, Ulley decided to act big and to quiet down the little monsters by smok-ing a couple of store-bought stogies. My great-half-uncle had never smoked before (or ever did after). The cigars made him violently ill. While he grovelled and retched, the angered bees swarmed in and all but stang him to death.

That nearly fatal experience inspired my Uncle Ulley to com-pose his one lasting adage: "I'm fresh out of certainties and run-nin' mighty damn short of likelihoods."

The earliest "tellin' stories" which one encounters in the more remote Ozarks date back, like the treasure stories, to the four decades of Spain's treaty possession of what was presently to be designated as the Louisiana Territory. Spain's treaty ownership of La Louisiane began with the secret Treaty of Fontainebleau of 1762 and lingered through 1802. First baronial or "caretaker grants" of Louisiana lands were issued by the Spanish crown in 1776. Apparently the first land grant in the Ozark region was designated in 1791 with one Don Antonio de la Torre y Rameriz, an erstwhile Basque landowner, as recipient. The grant, a royal lease, included the valley of the Arkansas River, from a point near the present site of Fort Smith to a point near the present site of Dardanelle, Arkansas, and the rugged bulk of what is now termed Petit Jean "Mountain," some quarter-million acres of which is now the splendiferous estate of one Winthrop Rockefeller.

Here, as in many other places and instances, one is entitled to reflect that the U.S. royalty of great wealth is vastly more durable and secure, not to mention better press-agented, than any hereditary royalties of Spain or elsewhere. Apparently the Rameriz grant endured only eleven years. Old yarns of the Ozarks have it that the Don and his daughter, whose name is not agreed on, endured much longer. They tell that instead of searching for buried gold or plunging into the fur trade, such as it was, the Don and his daughter set out to change the far-flung glades of Petit Jean into a great cattle ranch which the swarthy and crotchety daughter continued to manage until the nineteenth century was half finished, by which time the octogenarian lady was at last finished herself.

Back in the 1870's my mother, then the early-rising belle of Hawg Eye, Arkansas, listened to, and in some part later remembered the extensive but entirely verbal anthology of the Petit Jean stories. Like a minority of contemporary Ozark settlers, the Spaniards of Petit Jean came into the highlands with considerable wealth; and the longer they kept cattle the poorer they grew, until at long last the frail old *señora* was found starving in a pole-built

124

barn which was the last of the farmstead buildings. One after another, lightning, feuding, arson, and bad luck had done away with the rest.

So, unlike Rockefeller of Petit Jean, the Ramerizes of Petit Jean did not remain wealthy. Old stories tell how rustlers, including maverick Indians, drove away great herds of jet-black Mexican cattle. According to these stories, even more of their cattle perished in lengthy succession of droughts. The same old-timers' yarns tell how the range hands recruited from the hot plains of Mexico perished in the bitter-cold Ozark winters. When the old Don died, his daughter mated temporarily with a he-man Texan named Tol Cross who presently emerged as a sort of backhill Paul Bunyan.

However mighty as a horseman and muscle man, Tol was no great shakes as a *mandador del ranchero*. He quarrelled alike with workmen, buyers and *la señora*. When he was no longer able to sell cattle to river-barge operators or anyone else, Tol blockaded the trails with giant trees. No good came of that either. Eventually, while swimming a cattle herd across the Arkansas River, the hot-tempered foreman was drowned. His rebellious rangers conspired to drive out the remaining herd and, in time, to burn the manor house.

The very old Petit Jean stories comprised the first cycle of tales about the dramatic frustrations which dogged the earlier beginnings of the white man's settlement of the Ozarks. Succeeding cycles of folkish yarns were rooted in the goings and comings of early clans or gangs.

As already noted, first settlers found the Ozarks difficult frontiers to take and to hold. Then as now, most of the fertile soil was in far-scattered "pockets." There were no gold stakes for easy panning or other bountiful outcrops of minerals. There were no particular bases for wealth-dealing or fast-growing industries.

Facing a greening and roughly tumbled wilderness, many of the settlers tended to join or flock together in what, for want of a better term, were listed as clans. Blood kinship was a principal factor in shaping the clans but in some instances outsiders or "lone takers" were permitted to join. It followed that the backhill clan was more a community than a family.

Clans helped with the settlement of farming valleys and timberlands which otherwise would have been extremely difficult or wholly unattainable for individuals. But colonizing by clans was not invariably successful; it was frequently far from peaceful. Most of the clans broke apart within a few years; none, so far as I know, endured for as long as a quarter-century. There were a few instances of interclan feuding, but the Ozarks as a whole never were much of a feuding country. There were family rows, of course, and neighborhood or community bickerings and occasionally "bad blood" between entire communities and townships. But ill will or twitchy trigger fingers only rarely gained fatal associations among families or groups. There are recitations about early clans which developed such strong dislikes for nearby clans that they just up and moved away. On a few occasions, particularly during the embittered and optimistically named Reconstruction Era which followed the Civil War, clan feuds actually flared as shooting skirmishes.

The one instance which I recall with some degree of clarity concerns the northwest Arkansas Reeds versus the northwest Arkansas Dyes. Both were huge families with reserve strength in in-laws and both were briefly disposed to the practice of highwaymanship as a self-help expedient. It is said that their first gang fight began when male members of the two clans became entangled while rustling the same herd of scrub cattle. In any case the opposing families, both top-heavy and larder-light with camp followers, opened a sort of comic-operetta war in which there were no fatal

126

casualties, but some bullet or minie-ball creases and a great many near misses. The Dyes presently took a family caucus and decided to go back to farming and ranging wild hogs in the white-oak acorn woods. The Reeds stayed with highway robbery until the pickings got so poor it wasn't hardly worth the toil and strain. So the family gradually shifted into politics and real estate, including a sucker trap line into St. Louis. But politics turned out to be the more dependable money-maker.

In the Ozarks at large the all-time champion of yarn makers was the Civil War. When that bloody Unpleasantry came storming in, the Ozarks, like most of the Border South, were overwhelmed with violent confusion and vacillation. The great majority of the people lacked any real feeling of belonging with either the Union or the Confederacy. Dependence on Federal jobs was exceptionally slight and the prevailing practice and ready-formed tradition of self-subsistence definitely thwarted the you-will-gain-by-fighting argument.

All the Ozarks were included in slave-owning territory; slavery continued in Missouri several years after the issuance of the Emancipation Proclamation which applied only to the "liberation" of slaves in states then engaged in rebellion against the Union. Politicians of the area, such as they were, had anticipated this turn of events; at least some had. In several instances slave owners in the Arkansas Ozarks moved their Negroes across the border into Missouri when Arkansas joined the Confederacy. Though Missouri adroitly by-passed the Confederacy and presently proved one of the more stalwart defenders of the Union, the Missouri Ozarks remained an area of "divided sympathies." Until well into 1862 the Confederacy recruited more successfully in south Missouri than the Union did.

The Ozarks were deeply confused regarding Civil War issues years before the actual outbreak of the war. Prior to 1860 sub-

127

stantial numbers of slaves had been brought into the Ozarks both from the North and the South—constituting in some counties as many as one-third of the entire population. But for the most part slavery had not proved profitable. The Ozarks have never been suited to commercial cotton growing, on which the basic economy of U.S. slavery then depended. It followed that local markets for slaves were weak to non-existent. Throughout the Ozarks slave ownership was already proved of doubtful profit and a trying obligation.

Politicians who were seeking berths on what many then hoped would become the gravy train of the New World, viz., the Confederate States of America, were counselling Ozarkers and other Border Southerners that the Brothers in Gray could and would arrange to take the unwanted Negroes off their hands, and presumably consciences.

Like multitudes of early promises from Birmingham and Richmond, these were not kept. But the Confederacy, certainly military planners thereof, recognized the strategic importance of garrisoning the Ozarks at the earliest possible date and using them as defensive bastions against invasion from the north and west. Even before the disastrous cave-in at Vicksburg, important land battles were fought in the Ozarks with the Confederates the usual losers.

Throughout the first year of the war the Men in Gray recruited diligently throughout the Ozarks area. Few statements of cause for recruiting have been more blunt or cynical than theirs. Confederate leadership tended to regard the Ozarks as alien lands lamentably afflicted with po' white trash. It said so, with minimum word mincing. It agreed that the Ozarks had no visible promise either of wealth or culture. But at least the Ozarks had men who could shoot straight and ride far and endure privation and ask little in return.

General B. L. Carpenter, who in 1861 signed himself as Adjutant for Recruitment, Western Command, Army of the Confederacy, delivered a public address at Little Rock on June 4, 1861, with particular reference to "borderlanders." The newly elevated General reminded his listeners that they were honored by being offered the opportunity to fight beside distinguished gentlemen. He reminded the hill-country riffraff that by joining the Army of the Confederacy they could prove their worthiness by defending "unto the death" the most "genteel mode of life and privilege yet attained by members of the Anglo-Saxon race." Indeed, in many ways the explorative reader will find remarkable similarities between the earlier "literature" of Germany's National Socialist Party of the early 1930's and that of the Confederate States of America in the very early 1860's. Jefferson Davis was not Hitler, but on occasions A. Hitler talked remarkably as J. Davis had talked some seventy years previously.

In any case the Confederacy coveted the Ozarks and set out to get there first with the most men. It succeeded in recruiting far better than in fighting. Eleven volunteer regiments, averaging somewhere near 360 men each, were mustered by Confederate forces in the Ozarks of Arkansas; at least five more in Missouri. In addition scores of volunteers rode forth as plainclothes raiders or guerrilla troops locally assigned.

As the loquacious war got under way, Confederate recruiting squads, rarely uniformed and sometimes without accredited leadership, began series after series of "round-ups" to the end of filling in volunteer companies or regiments already under command of prominent citizens who were at least theoretically the "right people." In some part at least, the ethics of recruiting were sub-Queensberry; liquor, ropes, threats, derision and violent shanghais were employed on occasion. But after all, suh, the hillside white trash were being given the chance to help save the Southern Genleman.

My great-half-uncle Oscar was among the many who never gave a whoop whether the Southern Gentleman got saved or not. When the Rebel recruiting squad came for him, Uncle Oscar took to the hills. When the man catchers rode after him, Uncle Oscar found his way into the debris of a burned farm home and burrowed under. The Rebels never caught him. The following year, when Union victors of the nearby Prairie Grove Battle came forth to encourage enlistments, Uncle Oscar headed for his pre-established hiding place. When the Gallant Preservers of the Union rode by to the north, Uncle Oscar looked on from the south side of the remaining pillar of fireplace chimney. When the Heroes in Blue circled, so did Uncle Oscar. But not quite soon enough. For that one time the recruiters caught him. They gave him the Oath and a musket so rusty that nothing short of a holocaust could conceivably cause it to fire.

The following night the recruiting officer assigned Oscar to picket duty. That was a mistake. When another dawn came Uncle Oscar was again gone over the hill, that time permanently. The fact that he had X-ed the recruiting papers, however, established him as an enlistee in the Grand Army of the Republic and therefore pension-eligible. As age came upon him Uncle Oscar behaved reasonably and took the Federal pension. Some three years later when the State of Arkansas enacted a Confederate pension obtainable by any male citizen who could give proof of Military Association with the Heroic Arms of the Confederacy, Uncle Oscar, who certainly had military associations, was available to sign on the state pension roster. He first figured to stay with the State of Arkansas pension which paid the better. Then after long reflection and examination of conscience, my great-half-uncle stayed on both pensions. After all, he was an American, wasn't he?

Not all Americans were anywhere near so fortunate. Civil War casualties were shockingly high on both sides and by 1863 Confederate casualties were in the brackets of mass slaughter. Even earlier the fiery baptism had swept across the Ozarks. Before the end of 1863 all Ozarks places deemed worthy of holding were in Federal hands. One of the final Confederate group surrenders occurred on New Year's, 1864, in the area of Harrison, Arkansas, when a half-starved Confederate detachment of four men and eleven teenagers surrendered to a midget Federal garrison on rather special terms. The Rebels agreed to cease fighting, go home peaceably and mind their crops, hunting, trot lines (for absentee fish catching) and manners, and within thirty days to deliver to the conquerors fifteen steers properly butchered and dressed off. The specific motivation for the surrender was rather typical. Throughout the first long winter of the war, both fighting forces had shared the springs, brushwood and protection of Hawg Scald Holler (near the present site of Eureka Springs) for butchering and dressing off their respective requirements of pork. But there came a wretched day when a high-struttin' Yankee officer man, who spluttered half in German and came from St. Louis, ordered the ready ragged Confederates to get the hell out of Hawg Scald. It just wasn't neighborly. The Rebs were upsot and onsteadied, and otherwise of a mind to leave Abe Lincoln take his war and he knew what he could do with it. At the outbreak of the war the same blabber-mouth of a Yankee colonel had acted mighty unneighborlike up in Springfield, Missouri. He had marched his company down the main street on a Sunday morning, surrounded the Lutheran church and forced every last worshiper to sign an oath to support the Constitution of the United States and to take a pledge never to aid any cause of secession. The run of Ozarkers agreed such doings as that were truly low-down onery.

During the wintry shank of 1861 and throughout 1862 the Ozarks were the scene of numerous skirmishes, at least sixty, and five full-scale battles. The two fiercest battles, which saw the initial

131

collapse of the Confederacy's "Western Theatre," took place at Prairie Grove and Pea Ridge, both in northwest Arkansas. Southern commentators listed both as "draws," whereas Union Army "historians" listed both as victories for Union forces. Casualties on both sides were heavy. In the Battle of Pea Ridge the Confederates lost nine field-grade officers, including four generals.

For the most part the Union forces were better led and far better provisioned than their opponents. Hardly more than one-fourth of the locally recruited Confederate troops were ever issued uniforms. Most of them brought along their own firearms and all mounted troops, including field officers, supplied their own horses. Despite amateurish and sometimes tragically incompetent leadership, the Confederate forces usually knew the homeland terrain better than their foes and for that reason effected some amazing tactical feats.

One instance intrigued me. Directly before the Battle of Pea Ridge, Confederate troop leaders successfully bivouacked a combat force of approximately 12,000 men, 700 horses, and more than 100 supply wagons in a cave about seven miles from the battle site. They halted the enemy force with a few dozen guerrilla-style cavalrymen and presently "fed out" their foot soldiers with such subtlety that the Union forces did not locate the cave until weeks later. The Confederates did not triumph, but they did effect one of the most remarkable operations in Civil War history.

The end of the second year of the war saw the remaining combat forces of the South reduced to guerrilla squads which roamed the more remote countrysides as "bushwhackers," conducting surprise raids on Federal supply depots or caches and wagon trains. The resulting adventures changed rather abruptly to folk stories of banditry.

All in all there is a wonderful dunderheadedness about many of the Ozarkian stories of the War between the States, including abject tragedy and hilarious comedy. Time and time again fighting men from rival armies battled each other during the week, frolicked together on Saturday nights, worshipped together Sunday, then went back to fighting the following Monday morning.

For better or worse the soldiering showed invincible individualism and a great deal of carefree picnicking spirit. Crop-making furloughs were routine and many became as indefinite in length as they were spontaneous in origin. Ardent recruiters for the Confederacy repeatedly joined the Union forces because the food was better. My grandfather recalled that his outfit's "cookin' chores" were customarily rotated among men who had never purposefully cooked a meal before. He told how rival foraging or raiding parties used to join in the common assassination of a freely roaming steer or bull, then draw straws for the steaks and tallow. He told, too, of a bitter winter day when he and his fellow Confederates raided and captured a Union commissary wagon and thankfully replaced their tatters of one-time Gray with spanking new Union Blues.

Beginning in 1862 Indians began straggling out of the generally somber Indian Territory, which included the greater part of the present state of Oklahoma, to join the Confederates. The entire Cherokee Nation, then the strongest of the coppery-skinned transplants, "went Southern." The nation saw one of its most brilliant chiefs, Stan Waite, become the first Indian to wear the stars of an American general.

For the most part the oncoming generation of outlaws likewise sided with the Boys in Gray. Both Frank and Jesse James, for example, served with the writer's grandfather. Grandpa Alf remembered Captain Frank as a likable and generally able soldier, and "Lil Jess" as a "spoiled, surly, unreliable little twerp."

As the war bumbled toward its end, the tales grew taller and the documentation sparser. Many months before Lee's formal surrender at Appomattox Court House, Ozarks fighting men continued straggling back to brush-grown farms, unplowed and un-planted fields, wrecked, burned or sorely tried homes. The tradi-tionally dim structures of law enforcement had moldered away. The commonplace poverty had grown acute and oftentimes des-perate, even in rural communities. One expression of aftermath were the family-led robber gangs which presently came to include such eventual headline makers as the James boys, the Dalton brothers and Belle Starr and spouses. There were other more nu-merous and temporary bandits who joined together in raiding and robbery primarily as a defense against hunger and abject want. The usual crime pattern was to mount horses, proceed over the hills to the first sizable town or the second or third country crossroad with a store, and there loot, lift and divide the usually scant properties of the haves with some few of the have-nots. Particularly during the remainder of the 1860's law enforcement had faded like Rebel Yells in the second Battle of Bull Run. It was each human animal to himself and his conscience and there weren't quite as many consciences as human animals.

My Uncle George Wilson, who later became the shooting deputy sheriff of Benton County, Arkansas, used to recount some of the bizarre choices of goods which the amateur raiders made in evi-dent haste and after courage-building tippling. There were, for example, the Proud Poindexters from acrost Avocy-way who set forth to heist a dowry for their Little Elly who was getting mar-ried off. They polled down the back door of Delliner's Store and loaded a long wagon with the most accessible merchandises. The theft list included a cedar coffin, a rack of buggy whips, a barrel of block salt and a case containing twenty-five heavy porcelain chamber pots. I used to lie awake at night picturing sweet little Elly and her happy groom moving the impromptu dowery into their own little pole shack on their own little hillside clearing.

There were other storied outgrowths of the Reconstruction Era which lingered excessively in much of the Ozarks. Among these were the mysterious birth and whimsical antics of a localized secret society called the Bald Knobbers. This group was an Ozarkian version of the Ku Klux Klan which had risen like a very bad smell from points south.

Actually the Kluxers took no widespread hold on or in the Ozarks during Reconstruction times, though they later did come bedsheeting in by way of a strange and distinctly bastardly resurrection shortly after the First World War and flapped around throughout the early 1920's. But the original Ku Klux Klan made only sporadic appearances in the Ozarks, and those were principally confined to a few fringe settlements in the Arkansas counties. Even so, as my local-historian father used to point out, Arkansas never was extensively spooked by the Kluxers until well into the present century. Little Rock was the one principal town and state capital of the erstwhile Confederacy which never had a Klan. My father vowed that the nauseating if generally harmless re-emergence of the Klan circa 1920 was living proof that all too many Sensible People had moved out of Arkansas while all too many Mush-Brained Idiots, including folklore compilers, were moving in.

The Bald Knobbers at least were indigenous. The "order" seems to have been born during 1866 in Stone County, Missouri, still an intriguing area of Ozarks backhills. During the following year the self-alleged "brotherhood" spread into nearby Taney County, but little if any farther. The name signifies the group's practice of holding meetings on the bare tops of hills where signal or call fires could be seen and "read" for many miles.

The order was not only secret, it appears to have been almost completely illiterate. The alleged grandson of one of the alleged founders told me with Doric directness, "No wonder they didn't make no written records; none of them old roosters knowed how to write." The chronicle of the Bald Knobbers is now in the realm of folklore, for the most part unwritten. Accordingly, and also because of the intense prejudices of its times, the facts are very much blurred.

It seems probable that there never were more than about three hundred of the Knobbers, and that the count included a majority of well-intentioned countrymen with some inevitable bad apples. Reputedly the primary goal was to put an end to a then alarming prevalence of horse stealing, cattle rustling and comparable larcenies, and to supplement or as need be replace the immigrant or carpetbagger sheriffs. The merits of the Bald Knobbers apparently included great agility in climbing steep hills and building bonfires atop them, the development of fire signals for transmitting messages to fellow Knobbers and other perceptive onlookers, and a veritable genius for staging out-of-doors barbecues.

Indeed, even as with the present-day Chamber of Commerce, board of trade or "service club," the particular talents of the Bald Knobbers seems to have been for eating, or better say gulping oversize snacks. Folksay has it that there was practically never a meetin' without eatin'. Back-creek gossip still insists that no small part of the eatin' involved the consummated coveting of thine neighbor's ox, or perchance his fatted calf, or lacking that, even his lank, stringy old steer.

The civic works of the Bald Knobbers are likewise somewhat subject to folkish doubts. Some of the contemporary tellers vow that the Knobbers put the fear of the Lord into the lawless rabble. Others recount that in addition to picking off prime cattle, farranging bacon hawgs, and perchance an occasional hen roost, the Knobbers went out for such dubiously disciplinary pursuits as shaking down duress loans from local Shylocks and reasonably honest storekeepers, also whipping women and girls for reasons more personal than reasonable. A far gulch recounter once told me,

"Ever when one of them thugs would git told off by his own wife or mebbe couldn't make no time with mebbe the school teacher or tavern gal, he'd apt as not git a whole passel of them bums together and whale the hide off'n her."

This writer simply isn't reliably informed concerning the Knobbers and has never located anybody whom he regards as reliably informed. But at least I have learned that the inherited estimates of the Bald Knobbers are warm, even if vehemently contradictory. When I was much younger and infinitely more beautiful and eking a living such as it was by helping run a farm magazine called *Farm and Fireside,* known by its hired help as *Barn and Bedside,* I once made an after-hours plunge into writing short fiction, God forbid, for women's magazines, God forbid.

Being an Ozarker, and visibly malnourished, I undertook to "spot" the would-be stories in my homeland. In one sudsy outpouring I included a brief but less than flattering reference to the Bald Knobbers as "men of dark and stealthy ways." The story, to use a term loosely, was eventually published in *The Woman's Home Companion,* now scuttled but then the most widely circulated medium for muffin recipes and counsel on how to subdue a husband. I had never seriously suspected that any great numbers of *Companion* subscribers knew how to read, much less write. But my simple crack brought home a deluge of protesting or condemning letters from the erstwhile homeland of Bald Knobbers. Practically all the letter writers represented themselves as being granddaughters, grandnieces or other blood descendants of Bald Knobbers and practically all agreed that the latter-named were unblemished patriots and gentlemen whereas I was an insolent and abusive rat; "dumb sap" was a designation which actually appeared in the kindly Letters from Readers page.

About a year later I sold another would-be short story to another inevitable female monthly, *The Ladies' Home Journal.* In this

137

dishout of lifeless prose I made a kindly, even complimentary reference to the might-have-been better side of the Bald Knobbers. And guess what! In came another sluice of letters, mostly pencil scrawled, and likewise from lower Missouri. Again the sentiments were of an almost identical shrill soprano. "What's the big idea of handing boquets to that bunch of smelly thugs?" "They were thieves and murderers and worse." "Those big bold hill men you yap about came on a dark night and ransacked my widowed grandmother's home and almost whipped my sweet little Aunt Imogine to death . . ." And so on. I gave up. Apparently after about ten years the Bald Knobbers gave up too.

The Civil War story crop remains far and away the biggest yet known in the much-storied Ozarks. The war yarns were gradually succeeded by other stories of crises and poverty. Crime, railroad building, floods, fires, famines, and many other substantially factual events took places in the slow-spoken run of story material.

During the 1880's and '90's politics and spellbinding gained repeated entries. The turn of the century saw the advent of many "tellin' stories" which dealt with facts and forces beyond home boundaries. These included the opening of nearby mining centers, such as those in the "Joplin country," the pioneering of the great Kansas wheat fields, and the muscle-happy opening of Oklahoma to the immediate west. For the first time in two generations the backhills began losing people. And for the first time in a century the dependability of Ozarks land ownership became less than absolute.

The duress purchase, repeatedly the free-handed grab, of privately owned lands by builders and promoters of railroads had served as overture to the even more swashbuckling and upsetting grab of valley and hillside lands for use as water-impoundment basins for hydroelectric dams. The stories of power dams and dam sites began sprouting during the years immediately preceding the First World War, and they have kept on sprouting, flowering, seeding and resprouting.

The persistency and vitality of the stories of land grabbing to make room for power dams (whether as bona fide developments or fronts for defrauding stockholders) took vividness from two sources: the yeoman's love of his land, and the influencing importance of the pioneer mill sites which the earlier power dams frequently usurped and replaced.

For at least three-quarters of a century the country mill had kept its place for countryside neighbors. Ozark mills are still important to Ozark people. By and large, the country mills no longer grind by means of water power alone. Some are powered by diesel engines, a few by turbines, and a majority by electricity duly bought from power corporations—of outside ownership. But a significant few of the old mills still "water grind" an important share of the local grains, particularly corn. Water-ground corn meal remains a rightfully coveted foodstuff, and old-style water-wheels built of cedar, cypress or other durable hardwoods are still excellent processing equipment. In the way of time and geography and mortal perceptiveness, mill sites continue to mark the basic "water points" which remain fundamental to Ozarks survival.

As years follow, the reach of Ozarks stories grows wider; their impacts and insight show a tendency to increase. More contemporary themes include the great and touching exodus of Arkies during the bitter depression of the 1930's; the regional impacts of the magnificent Rooseveltian boondoggles; the personalized chronicles of World War II and the Korean War, in which Ozarkers participated most actively; the steadily increasing influx of tourists and tourist catering; the conversion of abandoned lime kilns to commercial cold storages and many other contemporary pragmatics.

All told, if they ever are, Ozark stories are a far-flung fold and

139

THE BODACIOUS OZARKS

harvest in which the human, the trivial and the whimsical persist in doing most to enrich, sustain, and perhaps immortalize. Like other sustaining crops of the land, Ozark stories continue to rise from the age-old firm of soil, rain, sun and circumstance.

CHAPTER XIII

Way Folks Say It

As a PERENNIAL backhills tramper I learned that the Ozarks, off and beyond the highways, are an excelling school for learning the ever surprising English language and the related and even more astounding institution of American speech. The living language of the Ozark backhills was once and still is basically the country and village speech of a much earlier England which, more than any other nation, supplied the original crop of Ozark settlers.

Living instances keep oozing, dripping, and otherwise pouring through the backhills and presently cropping out like wild violets on a woodland edge or native daisies in failing hillside pastures. Like Piers the Plowman, a back-country Ozarker still carries a *budget* on his back and *tarries* now and then to *spend* an opinion, even as Hamlet did. So common a backwoodsism as *tetchous* directs the listener back to Richard the Third and his mother's recollection that *"tetchous* and wayward was thy infancy . . ."

Gower told of a *"sight of flowers"* and a *"soon start."* So do a great many Ozark people today. Like Gower's yeoman, the contemporary Ozark yeoman may continue to own a *scope* of land and *prank* with his young 'uns while his crops *go to naught*. In the backhills a *sorry feller* continues to be a good-for-nothing, but not a sorrowful or worried fellow. A *turn of meal* is still what one gets at a country mill, and the *toddick* is the portion of grain paid for the grinding, a backwoods survival of the toll dish of feudal days.

Such Ozark speech entries as *afore* for before, and *ax* for ask, go back to the times of Lagamon. *Dauncy,* meaning "under the weather" or below par of health, reaches back through the centuries to the times of Towneley and his plays. Such usages as *usen* for used, *perk up, aver, atwixt, afeard,* and *I dare ye* are at least as old as Chaucer's *Canterbury Tales;* perhaps considerably older. The rural Ozarker still uses the Old English *stark* in such phrases as *stark wild* or *stark foolishment;* also the Middle English suffix, *like* or *lik* in *suchlike, familiarlike, pertlike,* etc.; and the distinctly Shakespearean *afeard* and *writ,* and *straddle* (for mount). Like Milton, he may speak of pastures *trim* with daisies *pied,* and like Hamlet take on an "antick disposition." Like Spenser, the rural Ozarker is still predisposed to use *sleight* to signify skill and to employ such completely reputable Spenserian pronunciations as *sech, sence, agin, ventur, nater, yit, yander,* and *Scriptur.* Like Hakluyt, he uses *allow* for assume or take for granted. As with Piers, a *heap* of people still mean a great many people. When the hillside testifier terms a salad a *sallet,* or a bag a *poke,* or a kiss a *buss,* he is rarely if ever aware of Elizabethan precedents, which nevertheless are as real as can be.

Quite inevitably, the Ozarks language continues to change, and its channel-flow continues to tap a deep and peculiarly perceptive illiteracy and the vital spontaneity thereof. But this does not preclude its use of comparatively big words, including *dilatory, caterwaul, beleaguer, understanding, deliberate,* and so on. The back-

142

hills commentator is usually astutely aware of place, occasion and company, and his habituated inconsistency of appropriate word choices is frequently a veritable bagful of surprises. Thus he may replace the Anglo-Saxon *hit* with *it,* and with almost startling lack of precedence *hit* and *it* may follow one another in the same sentence or clause. Furthermore, the same speaker, as the occasions move him, may use either *saw, seen* or *seed; fotch* or *bring; set* or *sot; ain't, hain't, isn't, aren't*—all completely interchangeable. He may *lug, tote, shoulder, heft, pick up* or *iron onto a parcel;* he may *fling a rock* or *throw a stone.*

With this rare treasury of free and open choices, the hillsider is seldom at a loss for a word. And when he finds himself in or near a verbal tight, he is quite likely to produce *spang out'n the free air* an original coinage or a spontaneous interchange of nouns, verbs, adjectives and adverbs

He shines brightly at making adjectives of verbs—the *travellin'-est, workin'est, preachin'est, lovin'est.* He employs adverbs and adjectives interchangeably—"I shore hope all your folks is gayly" —and with carefree abandon changes adjectives to verbs: "I wouldn't *contrary* nobody"; "He tumbled down and *nastied* hisself"; and adjectives to nouns—*old hatefuls, young braggies,* and so on. He delights in changing nouns to verbs, viz., "Henry don't *faculty* the workin' of them town telephones"; "Eddy Dodd can't even *muscle* lil Kimealie"; "Colonel Bullteeters couldn't never *confidence* no Republican"; "Dickey Dye can't *sweetheart* nobody that ain't a proper footwashin' Baptist."

The ever impressive emphasis of Ozark speech is partly cerebral and partly composed of significant survivals, including the "strong" preterites such as *rung, shrunk, stunk, drunk, begun, holped, cotched,* (for caught), *ruck* (for raked), *saunt* (for sent), and *het* (for heated). There are also the double and sometimes triple negatives which can be powerful even if not grammatical, as, "He never

143

done nothin' nohow." Emphasis devices gambol freely among the double-barreled pronouns, such as *we-all, you-all, they-all, we-uns, you-uns*.

Though watered and fed on illiteracy, the back-country speech of the Ozarks is remarkably rich in accuracy of pronunciations, particularly of the vowels. In this respect the Ozarker remains one of the very few Americans, including radioers and televisioners, who can be counted on to say *dew* instead of *doo*; *new* rather than *noo*; *in*, not *en*; *humor*, not *hoomur*; *spoon*, not *spun*; *drink*, not *dreenk*; *apple*, not *epple* or *oupul*; *error*, not *er-r*; and so on. A glimpse into the Oxford Dictionary will show, too, that the Ozarkian *et* is an accredited pronunciation for *ate*; and that the *narry* is *ne'er a* pronounced correctly.

Despite its oftentimes distinguished accuracy, the backhill speech is consistently inconsistent. The spontaneous omission or addition of the letter *r* is a case in point. The *r*'s come in and go out with the fanciful unpredictability of thrown (and non-loaded) dice. So do the largely unpredictable alterations of vowels as in *hed* for had, *chist* for chest, *upsot* for upset, *sarve* for serve, *raffle* for rifle, *turrible* for terrible; or of other consonants, as *seben* for seven, *brickle* for brittle, *atter* for after, *tejus* for tedious, and their surprise insertions, as *warsh* for wash, *gyarden* for garden, etc. Thus, also, with the largely spontaneous substitutions, such as *memorize* for remember; *disfurnish* for inconvenience, *damify* for damage, *unthoughtedly* for unthinkingly.

The truest glory of Ozark speech, at least as I have heard it and lived it, is in its spirited improvisations and the picnicking mood thereof. There is a sort of happy game involved in renaming a woodpecker a *peckerwood*, in changing a cow to a *cow-brute*, renaming nervousness *the all-over fidges*, speaking *frank and back-actual* instead of just truthfully, or in designating the out-of-kilter homestead roof not merely as slanty or slopey but as *wauper-jawed, catawampus, hip-sheltered* or *antegogglin'*.

Ozarks town names demonstrate the same quality of inventiveness. At very best the feat of naming Boston, Massachusetts, after Boston, England, or Putney, Vermont, after Putney, London, or New York after Old York, is dismally unimaginative. Not so with Ozark town names, past or present. Monkey Run, Red Star, Ginger Blue, Calico, Stand Around, None Such, Far Ply, Alabam, Panther Scald, Nellie's Apron, Hell for Sartain, War Eagle, Greazy Creek, Dove Nest, Hard Times, Gizzard District, Hawg Eye, Blue Eye, Red Ball, and Shingle Bottom are pertinent examples.

Through the years the living speech of the far rural Ozarks has kept pristine word qualities, engaging oral values, and a peculiar but ever refreshing distinction. The backhill speech stays forceful and pertinent. Though it changes quite inevitably with the times, its vitality and epigrammatic force live on. Through my years of roaming the Ozarks I have had good opportunity to ponder the changes of speech and of many other facilities. Back in the middle 1920's, Ellery Sedgwick, then editor-publisher of *The Atlantic Monthly,* assigned me the task of compiling what he presently captioned an Itinerant Report on the Ozarks Language. In the course of compiling I called on a storekeeper, a first-line Ozarker whose language had long intrigued me. Pappy Satterfield, yielding to the changing times, had lately installed beside the porch of his store a manual gasoline pump and an explosively loud air pump. The latter was attracting a dusty uproar of business. A local farmer came sputtering along in his spanking-new Model-A Ford with two almost flat tires.

The storekeeper asked the driver's appraisal of the gas buggy. The answer was indicative of lingual mutation. "Pappy, I'm

145

standin' here to tell you hit's the costin' of the *awl* and *ges* that's ruint me." A moment later Pappy Satterfield called out to his helper grandson: "Orvall, are them tars!" (Translation: "Orvall, put air in those tires!")

Yet despite such appalling intrusions, the speech in the main has kept remarkably well to olden furrows. I ponder this as I write this page far out in the backhills of Newton County, Arkansas, which is the most remote county of all the Ozarks. Here I note again that the peony flower is still a *piney*, that a circumstance is still a *sarcumstance*, that a keg is still a *kaig*, a terrapin remains a *tarpin*, that wire is till *war* and fire is still *far*. Directly remains *dreckly*, resin remains *rosum*, and heathens are still *heatherns*. Somewhere is *summers* and drowned is *drowneded;* a saucer is still a *sasser* and the past of pour is usually *pourn*. A curiosity is still a *wonderment*. Whoever stays *ever-who;* however is usually *ever-how*, and behind, more likely than not, is *in back of*.

One still hears remarkable and sometimes habitual insertions, such as: "I'll have you-all under-godamm-stan' I'm the super-by-Jesus-intendunt of this meetin' ground, and I won't be pushed go-to-hell around by nobody . . ."

Feather into 'em still means to attack with vehemence. *Funk* still means stench. *Tree* keeps its revered place as a transitive verb; one *trees* a 'coon or wildcat. *Bait* frequently means a meal and *carry* oftentimes means to lead. A *stopper* is a short drink, a *rench* is a chaser. *House* frequently means only the main room. A carbuncle usually emerges as an *arbuckle*, and the choir singer is rather more likely to sing like a *martingale* (the wooden back brace for a plow harness) than a nightingale, thus signalizing the change-over from the unknown to the known.

A running fire is still a *burn-out*. To remember is to *call* or *call by name*. A necktie is recurrently a *choke rag*. To beat up or punish severely or conquer a person is to *clean his plow* or *grease*

146

his wagon. To make an embarrassing mistake is to *cut a gut.* A covered passage connecting farm buildings is usually designated as a *dawg run.* A monster is still listable as a *gally wampus,* or a *golly wogger,* or even a *gowrow. Peach-tree tea* or *hickory oil* still mean a whipping. Minding one's own business is *weeding your own row, killing your own snakes.* One's character and/or self-respect is still his *name.*

In a great many instances the pertinence of the spoken word is based on the specific and the local. Thus, when a man or woman is *pushin' the collar,* he is working very hard, or like a plow horse. A hard-driving leader or boss is still designated as a *ramrodder.* To live as a renegade is still *to ride,* like the James boys and the Daltons, the Starrs and others among the more notorious Ozarkers. A *strawberry friend* is an amiable moocher, such as those who come to visit just as one's strawberries begin ripening.

Suckin' the hind tit remains a vivid and literal metaphor which designates holding an unfavorable position. *Whitenin'* is a good old Ozark term for them newfangled face powders. *Blackberry winter,* referring to the mid-springtime period when the black berries blossom, is a designation for a late cold snap. So is *blackbird storm.* To *bedpost a feller,* is to tie him down, like tethering a toddling child to a bedpost.

A great deal of the charm and effectiveness of Ozark speech stays in its spontaneous similes: *hotter'n homade hell, cold as a froze-up frog* (or *a witch's tit*); or *hot as a firecracker,* or *a bothered monkey,* or *fire in a peppermill* or *a banty* (bantam) *pullet laying a squar' goose egg.* One moves fast *like a shot cat,* or *slower'n molasses in Janawery,* or *like a stump-tailed cow in fly time.* One can be *busy as a buzz saw in a pine knot, ugly as a mud fence,* or *pretty as a bug's ear.* Or *sharp as a green briar* or *sorrier than a sheep tick in a tar barrel.*

One's troubles may be *thicker than carter's oats* (which were so thick there wasn't room enough for them to fall on the ground) or *thick as warts on a cowcumber pickle,* and still one may be *as happy as a lost pig in a corncrib.* By offhand recollection, here is a sampling of other favorites collected during my not completely lost youth: *Prissy as a wet tomcat walkin' in wet grass. So high-collared he can't see the sun exceptin' at high noon. Struttin' like a rooster in tall oats. Walkin' like she was belly deep in ice water. Women is after me like lean hens chasin' a fat June bug. Swelled up like a pizened pup. Blinkin' like a toad frog cotched out in a hail storm. This here is wors'n smellin' whisky through a jailhouse winder. This road is so crooked a feller can't tell goin' out when he passes hisself comin' back. I was so froze-up cold I knowed there wasn't nothin' between me and the North Pole 'cept a one-strand bobwar fence.*

And so on, by the page, the hour, year and lifetime. Ozark speech is a living river which pours on through the generations and, indeed, the centuries, intermittently rising and falling and occasionally overflowing, but never changing any principal portion of its channel. From time to time the river adapts, muddies, clarifies, and filters its own water, and continues to fill its own ever particular needs.

Outcomes are remarkably individualistic. A previous chapter notes the admission of Sammy Blankhall, the honest dwarf, who had built a brush fence about part of his clearin' and appraisingly remarked, "It's not such a bodaciously good fence, but it's a heap better than no fence atall."

I first jotted down this gem of verbal exposition approximately forty years before I write this page. Sammy used the word *bodaciously* to mean *particularly, very,* or *extremely.* During an intervening generation I have heard *bodaciously* many times in many Ozark places—with no fewer than half a dozen other meanings, including brave, brazen or insolent, big or gigantic, cruel or hard, complete or in toto, and wicked or evil. The connotation varies by place, person and dramatic circumstance.

Many other Ozark words and phrases have acquired unique meanings which have now become comparatively steadfast. For example, to *beat work* is to avoid manual labor; *begouge* means to stab; *blanny* is presumably a mis-hearing of blarney; *boggle* means to bungle or botch; *bounden* is a legal obligation; *clabber* frequently means cloudy or threatening weather; to *juber* is to caper wildly; a *dido* is a rowdy act; *disremember* or *disrecollect* is to forget, *edzact* is accurate; *flowsy* is untidy: *foreparents* are ancestors; *gallynippers* are any large flying insect; *to hate* is to regret or deplore; *hip-swinny* is a pain or atrophy of the back (*sweeny* means a shoulder ailment or injury of horses); *holly eve* is Hallowe'en; *hornscriggle* means to hornswoggle or cheat; *inkle* is an inkling or hunch; a *joky* is a harmless imbecile; to *jower* is to quarrel; *juleper* is meat juices; *lavish* is a large quantity of; *laid out to* means intended to or prepared to do; *let on* is to pretend.

Light a shuck means to depart in great haste. *Mammy* means to pass along one's likeness to an offspring. Narrate is *norate*, newness is *novel*, and castoffs are *offcasts*. Furthermore, a pair is not necessarily two; more frequently it is a set of—as of spoons, saws, knives or pistols. Jive talkers who still refer to *scads* and *oodles* are decades behind the Ozarkian *scadoodles*, meaning great numbers of. *Starve* means to become extinct, rather than to die of hunger.

This recounting could go on and on; in terms of living Ozarks speech it does just that, growing out of the land with vital directness which does not diminish, and growing up as a living part of the stories which it serves to tell.

CHAPTER XIV

Way Folks Serve It

USED TO BE THAT Ozarks food and cookery grew as directly from the land and told its stories almost as pertinently as the living Ozarks language. Used to be that Ozarks food and cookery perpetuated comparable outcrops of the original and the adopted, the traditional and the inventive, the tough and the tender, the sweet and the salty. Anyway one viewed it, or chewed it, this very vital parallel was fitting and reasonable. Just as language is the stuff with which stories are built, and story builders sustained, so are food and cookery.

This statement appears to be about as unchanging as it is unoriginal. But such is not entirely true of Ozarks foods and cookery which have changed far more extensively than the Ozarks language. The latter changes, of course; any living language is bound to. But the food and cookery have changed far more markedly. In great part, the reasons are economic. During the present decade and the three or four preceding it, Ozarks farming, though still the majority and most decisive occupation of the region, has tended to shift from total subsistence to what Department of Agriculture pamphleteers term "diversified agriculture."

More or less inevitably, as the variety of home-grown crops has diminished and as part-time or seasonal employment in various industries (mostly small or small-unit) has become the principal money crop of the region, more and more commercial or store-bought foods keep pouring into homes, country homes as well as town or village homes. But whether slurped or otherwise eaten in Hawg Scald Holler, Arkansas, or the Waldorf Towers, Campbell's Tomato Soup tastes a great deal like Campbell's Tomato Soup, even as Spam tastes a great deal like Spam.

To this sparkling revelation one might add the less gladsome clairvoyance that the store-bought foods consumed in the Ozarks tend to be more stabilized, more monotonous and, let's admit it, lower in quality as well as price, than those ordinarily consumed along New York's lower Park Avenue. One cause, of course, is what Mr. Winthrop Rockefeller ingeniously describes as the basic economy, or what my long-time Ozarks neighbor, Bill Coldiron, used to term the jangles in the right-hand breeches pocket. Another is foundationed by those horrid Madison Avenue video gags about Time & Convenience.

Venison shinbone soup happens to be one of the most delicious soups that ever warmed mortal palate. But in order to produce it one must first have the deer, the know-how for salvaging the shins of same, the time (at least forty hours of cooking time), and the correct kind and size of fire. When one works mornings plucking chickens for Campbell's TV Dinner Branch Plant at Hoxie, Arkansas, or turning plow handles at Senator J. William Fulbright's Hardwood Plant at Nastyville on Mondays, Wednesdays and Fridays, one rarely has the time to pursue the nimble deer or to keep a three-day watch on the simmering kettle. Heinz's Beef and Vegetable, available as a Safeway Special, is not as tasty and perhaps not quite as nutritious as homemade Venison Shinbone. But it fits the time budget, and at a very special, special mark-down it does not wholly annihilate the part-time paycheck. Similarly Spam, or Blam, or Wham, may not be nearly so epicurean as Aunt Narcissa's six-week sage headcheese with pork tenderloin. But it doesn't take six weeks and the home butchering of a special six-month shoat to devise.

One of my own particular blessings was Divine permission to grow up on an Ozarks farm in an era when the utilization of the home-grown and the home-picked, plucked or otherwise recovered, was in prime. Throughout my boyhood my mother did most of the cooking in our home. Much of the time I was her willing but not always helpful helper. Mamma was not an excelling cook and made no pretenses of being such. Quite accurately she described herself as a "thoughted cooker." Throughout her forty years of homemaking she succeeded in putting home-grown fruits, vege-tables, greens, meats and berries to noble ends with noble consist-ency. The latter lapsed only during her recurrent late-summer "take-down" with malaria, which usually lasted about two weeks.

During these emergency intervals I did the cooking, with some able bedside counsel. Also with the free access to Mamma's "re-ceipt books," which were ancient issues of *Munsey's Monthly Magazine,* flour-pasted with recipes clipped from all manner of rival publications, from *Youth's Companion* to *The Arkansas Farmer.* I never actually bothered with the hallowed receipt books. Neither, for that matter, did Mamma. Instead, she stayed with the indigenous and "memory receipts" rarely, if ever, found in print.

During the past forty years or so there has been a sizable crop of Ozark cook books. At one time or another this writer has glanced through at least seven. I find some of them edifying and many of them bewildering because they keep mentioning foods which as a born-and-raised, third-generation Ozarker I never personally encountered. The multitude of ground beef dishes provides one pertinent example. I cannot recall having tasted ground beef more than half a dozen times during all my Ozarks youth. We regularly ground pork into sausage, occasionally we ground suckers, even catfish, into fish patties. Many country families, including ours, used hand mills or countryside water mills to home-grind meal and flour. But we didn't grind beef. We pickled beef, smoked it into jerky, corned it in vinegar water, canned it in glass fruit jars or "tallowed it down," precooked, in earthen crocks. Except for preparing nourishment for the toothless, I simply cannot recall having participated in grinding beef. At least in the Arkansas Ozarks the multinamed ground-beef recipes did not come into widespread use until after the First World War when "burger" stands began gracing or disgracing the public fair and picnic grounds. Even so, for many years fillets or boneless slabs of fried catfish remained the most popular of sandwich fillers. When a youth could flash a dime and command, "Sandwich me a slab of that there catfish!" he was really living.

In several of the would-be Ozark recipe books I note oyster recipes. This also bothers me. We never had oysters other than the dismal gray corpses which come in cans. But even these were rare-occasion entrées and almost invariably struck the table either fried or in stew or soups. I never tasted a fresh oyster until I went newspapering in St. Louis in 1925; I never appreciated half shells until I went newspapering to New Orleans in 1927.

For the most part the cakes, nut breads, fruit pies and short-cakes which one encounters in the Ozarks are findable just about anywhere. The exceptions or near exceptions include dried fruit pies, with filling prefabricated by soaking dried peaches, pears or apples in water many hours prior to baking. Another older Ozarks tradition is the use of ordinary pie crust—crisply baked—as the base or cake for fresh-fruit shortcakes; for one reason or another we tended to call strawberry shortcake "short strawberry cake."

Bran bread used to be one of the more distinctive breads; wheat bran was obtainable virtually for free at any country mill. As I recall, the recipe called for mixing three cups of wheat bran with a like quantity of whole-wheat fiour. Then one pours in one-half a teacupful of sorghum molasses or honey, then adds a cupful of hot water containing about two teaspoons of sugar, one of baking powder and one of salt. One mixes the ingredients in a sizable bowl, wets them down with sour milk to batter consistency, then bakes the mixture in a medium oven for about three-quarters of an hour. Served hot and well topped with homemade butter, this bran bread is truly recommended.

Our household, like a great many others, was addicted to hot biscuits. The prime reason was that my father had survived all four years of the Civil War on cornbread or Johnny cakes and very little else, with the result that he reacted violently to the sight of any kind of cornbread. I rather doubt that the biscuits were distinctive. As a habituated biscuit maker I used to "lay out" half a dozen cups of sifted flour, about six teaspoonfuls of baking powder, one or two of baking soda, three of salt, a full teacup of cold lard, and three cups of cold buttermilk. This conglomerate made approximately thirty biscuits, each near the size of a railroad fireman's pocket watch or the heel of a plow shoe.

Following Mamma's directions I would sift together all the dry ingredients, "cut in" the lard—a feat involving about five minutes or more of aggressive chopping with a table knife in each hand. Then I poured on the buttermilk and kneaded the mess with a great deal of finger squirting. Next I rolled out the dough on a floured board, used a jelly glass as cutter, hoisted the spongy discs to a greased pan, fired up the wood stove until its oven was very

154

hot—probably 450 to 500 degrees. The resulting biscuits were richly flavored, enormously fattening, and profoundly habit forming.

My own favorite bread was my father's particular nemesis— Johnny cake—crisp, clean-tasting, epicure-challenging. There are two indispensable ingredients. One is well-churned, fresh and otherwise honest buttermilk. The other is white meal, best flavored when ground directly and fairly coarsely by a water mill, or by a hand-operated and adjustable grist mill. To produce a medium-size pone, I used to mix two brimming cupfuls of such meal with three tablespoons of sugar, and a teaspoon each of salt, baking soda and baking powder. The next step was to beat three whole eggs in a separate bowl, melt three tablespoons of lard and pour it into the beaten eggs, then add about one and a half cups of pristine buttermilk. That done, one combined the liquid with the mixed dry ingredients, beat well, poured into a greased pan, and baked in a medium oven 20 to 25 minutes. The flavor was and will ever be, rich with subdued nobility and virtuous simplicity.

The most primitive of the more or less indigenous Ozark breads is the corn dodger. Its ingredients are severely limited to white corn meal, salt, lard or butter, and water. To make a dozen dodgers or stick rolls, one sifts together four cupfuls of white meal and one and a half teaspoons of salt, then mixes in enough cold water to form a stiff dough. You dip your hands in cold water, shape the dough into rolls or dodgers, place them in a hot greased pan, put a lump of butter on each dodger and bake until crisp and well browned. What results excels as chawpin' fare—good alike for teeth, belly and spirits, particularly good as accompaniment for a glass or mug of cold buttermilk.

Comparatively few distinctively Ozark meat recipes remain in widespread use. Granting that because of better pastures, livestock, butchery and refrigeration, Ozarks-grown beef is very much better in flavor than it used to be, its routines of cooking are no longer exceptional.

The pork story is different. Since the passing of the free-roaming, ridge-spined razorback hog, Ozark pork has lost much of its flavorful distinction. The lean, long-flanked, bacon-glorifying wild hog is virtually extinct. There are fragments, more or less accidental remainders, of the race of open-range swine, but the boar hunts and the countryside man-and-dawg roundup of free-roamin' hawgs are substantially finished. Standard swine breeds, particularly Duroc Jersey, Tamworth, Chester White, Hampshire and Berkshire, have made widespread entry. Porkwise, as beefwise, the Ozarks remain crossbreed or mixed-breed country. But mongrel or "sheer" scrub livestock is extremely scarce.

Even so, Ozark pork, more than pork cookery, keeps distinctive ways. The widespread substitution of grass and legumes for corn feeding tends to maintain leaner and more than averagely flavorful pork. The flavor advantages are also in the curing. In these times, when commercial pork curing is so grimly synthetic, Ozark farm homes continue to produce and provide as delicious lodes of cured pork as the roaming epicure is likely to find or even imagine. Despite the comparatively widespread use of commercial curing mixes, many Ozark farmers still devise and apply special cures for hams, bacon, jowls, and joints, using sorghum molasses, wild-growing mint leaf, sage, maple sugar and various other sweeteners—also, very special smoke cures of green hickory wood, sassafras, or rock maple. Otherwise, many, perhaps most Ozarks pork dishes are not markedly different from those of other sections. Pork scrapple is a tasteful exception. Study of family diaries shows that my Ozarks forebears have been making and eating scrapple since the 1840's and perhaps long before. The fact that Ozark-style scrapple is outstandingly good rises from the fact that it employs better ingredients, including prime cooked pork instead of head, tails, feet, and other scraps or castaways.

My mother made scrapple by stirring finely minced roasted pork into boiling mush, a pound of pork to a pound of meal. She seasoned it boldly with ham drippings, sage leaf (about three heaped teaspoons), plus two teaspoons of salt and one of black pepper per pound of minced pork. She added the seasoning after the meat-and-mush mixture was partly cooled. She "firmed" and molded the end product in butter molds, fried it in flour-coated slices and served it with sorghum molasses.

Well-cooked, home-cured pork provided noble stuffing for baked green peppers. Chopped ham, mixed with equal parts of chopped onion, eggplant innards, well-salted and buttered, and baked in the handsome purple shells of the eggplant, provided another magnificent stuffed dish. My mother used to improvise hashes with virtually any available meat: pork, beef, mutton, chicken or turkey. The outcomes were usually delicious not from knack or wizardry, but because the meats were prime instead of scrap and because the accompanying vegetables, usually beets, potatoes, carrots, or parsnips, and onions were also prime. Not necessarily in terms of size, since all our vegetables grew naturally under sun and rain and in real soil, rather than in outshovelings or overpourings of chemical fertilizers and the accrued sludges thereof.

Hog jowls and whippoorwill or cowpeas are another distinctive Ozark fare. Its creation is simple enough once one has the ingredients. First you shell the hard, brown-splotched peas and soak them overnight in water. Next you take a couple of hog jowls, with a generous retainer of the meat, preferably fairly lean. You cook the jowls in boiling water for an hour or so, drain the peas and sprinkle them with one teaspoon of salt per pound of peas, and permit the peas and jowls to simmer along for two to three hours

157

more, or until both the meat and peas are tender. Smoked jowls are recommended.

Injun spareribs were another distinctive pork dish of the old-time Ozarks. Indians might have been the originators, but the generation of sparerib revelers with whom I grew up was preponderantly non-Indian. In any case, to create Indian spareribs, one begins by selecting and laying by one medium-size sweet potato, half a medium-size onion, half a teacup of diced salt pork, a big roasting ear of corn, a smallish green pepper and about one pound of fresh and well-meated spareribs for each person to be served. Use a stout knife to shave off the meat and fat from the bones, pour the cuttings into a stewing pan or kettle and heat to a lusty simmer. Then dice the green pepper and add to the stewing meat, and as it becomes tender, clip the sweet corn from the ears, pour it directly into the stew and, if you see fit, sprinkle lightly with salt.

One uses the finely chopped salt pork as a gravy base. Fry it until the fat runs free and the cracklings are crisp and brown, then add flour and liquid from the stewing meat to make a thick gravy. Place the meat in a baking dish, dice the onions and pour them on and then cover with the gravy. Then cut the boiled sweet potatoes into small-sized chunks and place over the meat. Dot the potatoes with butter, place the baking dish under the broiler, and cook and brown for about fifteen minutes.

Sweet potatoes are another standby of Ozark cooking, with favors going to the golden-fleshed Nancy Hall type of true sweet potatoes, rather than to the more commonplace African-born yam. Sweet-potato puddings and pies are among the more palate-coaxing developments. Both require the collandering of well-baked potatoes, the generous use of homemade butter, egg yolks and whites beaten in separately, also sugar and mace and candied citron.

Pumpkin pies and sauces or custards are among other distin-guished items of Ozarks eating. It isn't that this king of the squashes is an exclusive or indigenous Ozark crop. It's mostly the neighborly and cherishing view of pumpkin which decides the status and stature of the beautiful red-golden blobs in backhill cookery.

In too many places pumpkin means the figurative meat of the squash, with some sugar or syrup put in and the living hell boiled out. But Ozarks style in pumpkin cooking involves the deft se-lection of the more flavorful sizes and "grains" of pumpkins, plus the generous use of fresh cream, eggs, ginger and cinnamon. My mother used to begin the filling of each pie crust with two teacups full of strained pumpkin—cooked and simmered for days rather than hours and mostly on the back of the stove. Into this mellow measuring she stirred a cup of sugar, half a cup of sorghum molas-ses, a teaspoon of ginger, another of cinnamon, a tablespoon of but-ter and a pinch of salt.

Then she would stir in the stiff-beaten eggs and a cupful of rich sweet cream, beating constantly and diligently. She poured the total into the raw crust, baked the pies in an oven kept very hot the first ten minutes, and low medium for the next half hour. I still believe those were the best pies I ever ate.

We had country neighbors who painstakingly "cured off" their pumpkins. To do this, some would take the best of the first ripened whoppers and cut them into crescent-shaped slices which they dried, flesh up, in the open under the usually moderate autumn sun. Others sliced their pumpkins big, hammocked the slices to the roofs of the smokehouse and cured them off with the green hickory, sassafras, or other "special smokes" being applied to the home treasury of ham and bacon. The smoked pumpkin, when eventually changed to pie filling or sauces, delivered some truly exciting flavors.

159

Today, even as a century ago, greens provide the greatest amalgamation of freely-growing Ozarks foodstuffs. Among cultivated vegetables, turnip greens with pot licker remain the most used green vegetables. By old-time Ozarks custom, this creation began with fresh picking a gallon or so of young turnip leaves, with a maximum of leaf and a minimum of stems. One "supports" with half a pound of salt pork, dribbles of salt and pepper and a quart of cold water. First put the salt pork into the cold water, heat gradually and keep boiling for about three-quarters of an hour. Next you wash the greens, not hesitating to leave an occasional tender turnip a-clinging, place the total in the pot and cook steadily for another hour. Then you employ a long-handled knife and fork to chop up, virtually decimate, the pot's contents. Salt and pepper to taste, and serve with corn pone, hot, cold or medium, depending on personal liking.

Pot licker is a strongly traditional food-drink of the backhill Ozarks. Its flavor qualities range from barely tolerable to near heavenly, granting that what one Ozarker may declare the most larripin of all pot licker, the next may rate as under-par hawg slop.

There is a glorious, arbitrary quality about Ozarkian appraisals of foods. This critical virtue applies with particular aptness to home-grown garden vegetables and to greens, whether garden-grown or wild. I reiterate "garden-grown" because in general Ozarkers have never surrendered to the onslaughts of field-grown leaf crops such as spinach and collards. The Ozarks just never took to spinach, perhaps in some measure because so-called wild spinach is one of the area's most noxious weed pests.

For still better reasons the Ozarks have never cowtowed to the Southland collard, that strong-flavored, frost-resisting round leaf which endures as one of the gastronomic plagues of nearby Dixie. I grant that collards taste tolerably at the moment they are swallowed. But the horrible truth is that for hours, even days thereafter they continue to plague the taste buds. It is this continuation that ruins one. For years I have suspected collards of adding most hurtfully to the toils of integration in the South. I am practically certain that no digestive tract ever integrated a plateful or even a forkful of collards; I submit that very few ever really digested a mess of collards.

But Ozarks greens, thank goodness, are something else again. Even the garden greens are enjoyable as well as edible, beginning of course with turnip greens. So long as they are plucked in tender youth and cooked immediately, turnip greens can be delicious, quite regardless of place or season and with or without meat-strengthened pot licker, though I for one recommend the latter.

But wild greens of the Ozarks are the truly creative filler of the land and its people. They are as one with the Ozarks springtime. Their absoluteness of excellence is attainable only by the experienced alertness, poetic understanding and imaginative courage of the picker. Wild or "wile" greens are to be taken from the unmarred open country like any other true treasure. There are some basic elements, including the curly-leafed dandelions, the narrow-leafed sour dock and the new-sprouted polk plant, a deep-rooted perennial with crisp emerald leaves and wine-red stalks. All three grow abundantly in most Ozarks landscapes, and any one alone is capable of providing a firstrate "mess" of greens. Wild mustard is another fairly available staple. So are native water cresses, lamb's quarter, old sage, wild lettuce, hen pepper, and several more.

Proportions are the distinguishing factor of these inventive harvests. The picker of wild greens requires no equipment save a bag or basket and a knife, which need not be sharp. But the picker's eyesight must be. For she or he must not only be able to recognize the edible greens; they must be mixed with propriety and

161

sagacity. If one mixes in too much polk leaf, the greens will be too slippery; too much wild mustard and they will be too strong; excessive quantities of dock leaf makes them too sour. But a wise and democratic mixture is proof of true art.

Unquestionably early morning is the best time for greens picking, for then the leaves are not only the most recognizable, but the most succulent. Gentle cooking is indispensable, slow simmering in an iron pot is recommended. The greens should not be "drowned" in water, and certainly not in grease. The "curin' meat," hog jowls, ham hocks, or whatever, used for seasoning, usually requires precooking. The recommended side dishes for wild greens include crisp corn pone, cold buttermilk, young onions or scallions.

In looking back to my lost youth, lost calendarwise that is, I recall that game also provided an important share of the more distinctive Ozark fare. Take squirrel pie, for example, with plump gray squirrel meat within crusts or "wrappin's" made of the dough of hot biscuits as earlier mentioned. By old-time precedents, two gray squirrels (red squirrels are not first rate, and chipmunks and flying squirrels are not acceptable) make a pie. Understandably, the first step is to get the squirrels. My country-doctor uncle used to slay them with rocks, hurled unerringly at close range. A light shotgun loaded with single shells is usually the best weapon. Spreading shot damages the meat and imperils the diner's teeth. Buckshot, as my father used to use, tends to pulverize the meat and reduce it to gray slop.

Having "clean killed" the gray squirrels, one skins them, discards the shot-torn areas, cuts the good into pieces about the size of a man's wristwatch. Next, one cleans the meat with a damp cloth and chills it until the body heat is gone, preferably overnight. Place the meat in a baking pan with a generous slice of salt pork, the leaner the better, for each squirrel. Pour in water and let simmer for about half an hour. Then pour off part of the liquid and make it into fairly heavy flour gravy. Then one moves the partly cooked meat—two squirrels and two pork slices, to a dough-lined deep dish, pours on the thickened gravy, covers with a topping of biscuit dough and bakes for another half-hour in a medium oven. Variations are optional. The foregoing is at least a promising beginning.

Salt pork remains a steadfast accessory to many game recipes, including venison. This is noteworthy because Ozark deer population is very strongly on the increase as the proportion of forest lands, including state and national forests, continues to increase. As with beef, Ozark venison cookery relies on roasts. The best venison roast this reporter ever encountered in the Ozarks, or anywhere else, is devised along the following lines: Take a sizable crosscut, say five pounds, of fresh venison. Clean the meat with a damp cloth, then "side it" with about half a pound of tangy, thinly sliced salt pork. Rub the rest of the surface with flour, salt and black pepper. Fry another half pound of salt pork in a heavy iron kettle, then surface-brown the venison in the fat. Add about two teacups of water and a few leaves of wild mint. Cover the pot and cook until the meat begins to tender. Then fortify it with freshly peeled carrots, turnips and onions, at least half a dozen of each. Continue cooking for another hour, or until both the vegetables and the venison are unanimously tender but still intact. Once more, "larripin" is the old-time Ozark word for what results.

There are a great many Ozarks recipes which have long since passed out of general or widespread use. These include erstwhile game animals such as the possum, racoon, and groundhog or woodchuck. Nowadays these are usually spurned as food, only rarely used as roasting meats. The traditional cooking routines are almost identical. Having skinned and dressed off the carcasses, one parboils the halves or sides, using a bag of charcoal to draw off

163

the rank flavor or juices. The old-time recipe directs that as soon as the meat is tender, one places the sides in a baking pan, surrounds the meat with sweet potatoes, covers the pan and bakes until the potatoes are tender. Then remove the cover and brown well.

But the marginal or less orthodox game animals are rarely eaten nowadays. Unfortunately, the same holds for the special flavored vinegar, seasoned with honey, onion, garlic and "mixed herbs," including fennel, basil, and sweet marjoram, none of which are duly cherished by enough contemporary Ozarkers. The gatherable Ozarks herbs include an extensive list—thyme, burnet, native chives, borage, caraway, coriander, rosemary, catnip, sage and horehound, to name only a few. These "yarbs," incidentally, are traditional ingredients for a number of homemade remedies as well as flavors or homemade seasonings. There are great numbers, too, of raw salad ingredients. My personal favorite is garden lettuce mixed with native water cress and narrow-leaved dock. One washes about two quarts of the greens, chops them into small pieces, and slices two hard-boiled eggs and half a dozen green onions over the greens. Then one takes half a teacup of browned bacon, adds a little salt and a quarter cup of vinegar, heats the mixture and pours it—sizzling hot—over the top of the salad.

There is a stubborn futility about trying to tell about Ozarks cookery and foods. The fare is essentially plain. But its flavors and combinations are oftentimes subtle and complex. There is no substitute for experience in the actual growing or gathering, cooking and eating of the foodstuffs. This is usually true of regional cookery and eating habits. It stays particularly true in the rural Ozarks where many of the most distinguished and delectable dishes were born directly of poverty and isolation. Both of the latter-named phenomena are now on the wane. So is at least some part of the charm of Ozarks cookery.

But this is not inevitable. The culinary distinction can be restored and maintained to the extent that people are willing to experiment, to propagate both new and old varieties of edible plants in fields, gardens, orchards and berry beds, and even more definitely to take food materials directly from the open fields, ranges, woods and creeks or rivers. Perhaps nowhere in the nation is the attainable variety of foodstuffs so great. And nowhere can one attain a finer correlation between native fare and prevailing season.

As a lifelong student of Ozarks people, their stories, confidences and histories, this writer remains convinced that people came to the Ozarks in great part because good food was available or readily attainable there. It is difficult, or impossible, to name a better reason for coming or for staying.

CHAPTER XV

The Thoughted Change-Over

DURING MY EARLIER years of roaming the backwoods, I became aware of changes and mutations which were considerably more evident in what the college English teachers call "folk" stories than in any other kinds. I blundered on occasional yarns of witchcrafts and spell castings, of good men changed to destroying werewolves and other pattern stories. I was aware of the strong survival of numerous folk beliefs, some of real distinction. But for the most part folk beliefs and the more fragile and exotic wildflowers were thriving only in the more remote and shady Ozark places.

Common beliefs and adages showed numerous changes, not invariably for the better, but tending to link the remote past with the isolated present. My mother termed them "thoughted changeovers." Her phrase was based on firsthand experience. Mamma was the folk believer of the family and she came by it honestly. She was raised in Hawg Eye, Arkansas, still one of the most brushly and remote crossroads in all the lower Ozarks. As a child she had been immersed in veritable tides or fogs of folklore which had filtered or swept into the Ozarks from all sides, indeed from many nations. Here are some examples of the then prevailing folk beliefs to which my mother very sincerely subscribed, at least during her childhood:

Plants of darkness (root crops and tubers) should be set out in the dark of the moon; above-ground crops in the light of the moon. Trees should be deadened and fencerows cleared in the dark of an August moon. A dream told before breakfast, or one dreamed on Friday and told on Saturday, will come true. If the sun sets behind a bank of clouds on Thursday, it will rain before Sunday. Lightning in the south foretells dry weather. A red sunset means clearing weather; a yellow sunset, rain or worry. Thunder in February means frost in May. If a chicken's tail feathers spread in the wind, that is a sign of rain. A whitish halo around the moon foretells rain or snow; the number of stars within that circle indicates the number of days before the falling weather begins.

Mamma quoted and in considerable part revered many other Ozarks "sayin's" which would associate the visible with the eventual. For example, in order to grow hot peppers, one should get mad while planting them. Or to make a watchdog fierce, feed him gun powder. Wool which is washed and warped while the moon is waxing will stretch; while the moon is waning, will shrink. Or the arrival of the big black turkey buzzards tells that spring has come, whereas the coming of big brown butterflies assures one that it is time to shed one's shoes and start going barefoot.

The luck adages were legion, but as I recall the bringers of bad luck were considerably more numerous than those of good luck. It is bad luck to shake hands across a gate, or sweep a floor after sunset, or get out of bed left foot first, or carry a hoe or an ax

167

through the house, or to move brooms or cats from one house to another. It is bad luck for a girl or woman to walk across a room with her bottom bare. It is bad luck to whirl a chair on a single leg, or spill salt, or look at the moon through bushes. On the other hand, it is good luck for a woman to shake her dress at the new moon; by doing so she is sure to get another.

A great many of the adages which my mother cherished were flagrantly unreliable and easily proved as such. The old saying that fruit crops are never killed in moonlight, for example, just isn't true, as any observant Ozarker knows. The same holds for the old-timer about eggs set on Sunday will hatch all roosters, or eggs carried in a woman's bonnet will hatch pullets. Or a snake cannot die until the sun goes down. Or catch a butterfly, bite its head off, and you will get a dress of the same color. Or to set the color of an unborn colt, drape a cloth of the desired color in front of the mare's stall; the colt will be colored like the cloth. Or, if you have money in your pocket when you first see the new moon, be sure to turn the money over; that way you will have money all the rest of the year.

All these and many more of the fringe-line credo can be disproved at will and oftentimes unavoidably. Mamma granted as much. She merely noted gently and with evident respect that she had known some fine people who truly believed many or all of the list. Her estimates of many of the folklorish remedies implied a similar respect for age and whimsy. I refer to such backhill gems as:

To cure foot cramps, turn your shoes bottom side up before going to bed. To cure fits, tear the sick one's shirt or blouse off and burn it. To cure sterility in a wife, spank her with a split shingle. If you have a sty on your eye, touch it with the tip of a black cat's tail. Mare's milk cures whooping cough. Gold beads worn about

168

the throat cure a sore throat. Wearing red beads cures nose bleed. For curing chapped lips, kiss the middle rail of a rail fence.

When my father would inquire how anybody could go along with such unswallowable hog slop, my mother would reiterate gently that what good people have believed for a long time, whether right or wrong, is not hog slop.

Mamma had still another catalog of earlier backhill sayin's which dealt with marriage and feminine approaches thereto. She never confided this particular list to her peculiar son, but I used to overhear from time to time, sometimes legitimately and sometimes sneakily. Here are, or were, some typical gleanings:

Burnt corn bread portends that a girl's sweetheart is or will be angry at her.

Marriage consummated in rainy or snowy weather ends badly. Therefore it is advisable to postpone the more athletic love-making until a clear day or night.

A bright-burning kitchen fire signifies that one's suitor can be depended on; a slow, balky fire suggests he will bear watching.

If a girl keeps leaving cobwebs on her kitchen door, her suitor just won't come back.

One auguring test for true love can be made with apple seeds. You take two apple seeds and name them for the couple in question. Then place the two seeds on an ash shovel and hold them over a hot fire. If the heated seeds jump apart, all is not well with the set-to. If the two apple seeds jump together that's real peachy. But when the boy seed moves away and the girl seed is left forlorn, or vice versa, that's just too bad and real pitiful besides.

If a sparking girl sits on a table she won't be married for another year. If she clips her fingernails on nine successive Sundays, her sweetheart will come and dine with her. When a briar gets attached to a girl's skirt, she should name it. If the briar sticks or

169

otherwise clings, her lover is dependable. If it drops off, well, he wasn't no bargain no-how. If a girl wets her apron while washing, she will have a drunken husband. A naturally wondering young girl can give her swain the old mullein treatment. She bends a mullein stalk in the direction of her lover's home. If he loves her, the stalk will grow up again. If he doesn't, it won't. If he loves somebody else, the stalk will die.

Hanging the breastbone of a turkey over the front door has an amorous effect on eligibles who may be passing through. If a redbird flies across a girl's path, it means she will be kissed before the night is over. If a girl accidentally stubs her toe, and straightaway kisses her thumb, a sweetheart will surely appear. When a damsel's skirt flies up, her lover is thinking of her. A girl may expedite the progress of the courtship by putting a drop of her menstrual fluid in her swain's drinking liquor.

And so the recitations go or went by the unhurried hour, the old and unsure whimsies and vagaries of a remote and ever imaginative people. Unquestionably, during parts and intervals of her Ozarks-spent lifetime, Mamma believed a great many folk sayings of one kind or another. She likewise banked heavily and perhaps not always irrationally on specific folkish remedies, including catnip tea for colic, horehound tea for coughs, mullein-leaf tea for asthma, the inner bark of post oaks as a reliable laxative, and so on.

But on approaching middle age, Mamma began discarding much or most of what my sister had so archly termed silly superstitions. She described the process of reviewing and discarding as a phase of "the thoughted change-over." But with gentle insistence she pointed out that modern times (she referred to the beginning 1920's) were producing a far sillier cycle of folklore than any of the old-timers would have begun to tolerate.

She insisted that whereas the old or "true-blue" folk beliefs had earned or proved their right to life and dependence, most of the new folklore was too silly and frothy to bear serious repetition. She pointed out the then near-idiotic popularity of flagpole sittings, marathon dances, Cal Coolidge garbed in Indian war feathers, and flush toilets being installed in Baptist churches as appropriate examples. She pointed to the newly revived Ku Klux Klan, in which her plumber brother had turned out to be a local Kleagle, or Klazer, or Klaptrap, or some such a fool thing, as an evil example.

Mamma believed that Ozark stories which reflect and depict the inner beliefs and sentiments of the real Ozark people are the most precious resources of the place, or of any other. In this connection my mother also contended that Ozark stories are particularly revealing of their countrysides and the people and life thereof because they are the heritage of a "thoughted" people—of creative thinkers.

Here again I agreed with her. From time to time I encountered the living exhibits of creative thinking. The exhibits were not always conspicuous; in several instances they were but remnants or echoes of heroic or otherwise attractive phrases. One such phrase which I had noted many years before was "Social Justice," the more or less magic trademark of what was to eventualize a dozen years later as the Administration of Franklin Delano Roosevelt.

As I presently learned, Social Justice had been a crusading phrase in the rural Ozarks more than half a century before F.D.R. became President. The reasons were potent and convincing. The 1880's were hard times throughout the United States. In the overwhelmingly rural Ozarks the 'eighties were almost unbelievably depressed, so much so that a dollar looked at least as big as the moon and was only slightly easier to lay hands on. By 1890 the entire Ozarks area had only fourteen national banks, nine on the Missouri side.

At the close of the Civil War the total circulating currency of the United States was approximately two billion dollars. Between 1865 and 1890, the U.S. population had almost doubled. Its consumption of goods had more than trebled. Yet the total of circulating currency was a fifth of a billion dollars less than it had been in 1865. Year after year the farmer's plight had worsened. Year after year the Ozarks, where farm population was above eighty percent of the total, remained one of the most nearly moneyless regions in all the thin-pursed U.S.A.

Rural Ozarkers had begun thinking out solutions and striving to change their thoughts to deeds. The most noticed of the protest groups called itself the National Farmers' Alliance. By 1890 the Northern, Southern, and colored "departments" claimed a combined membership of three million voters. The Alliance was strongly rooted in the Ozarks. The second largest and perhaps the most lucid of the protest groups was the Agricultural Wheel, founded during 1882 at McBee's Schoolhouse in the far fringes of the Arkansas Ozarks. It began as a neighborhood debating society.

By 1890 Agricultural Wheel membership had spread into nine states for a claimed total of three million members, of whom two million or thereabouts were voters. The Farmers' Alliance and the Agricultural Wheel presently merged into the Populists, or Peoples' Party of America, which survived longest and planned most inventively in the rural Ozarks. The Party's final convention was held in 1936 in the peculiar lost village of Monte Ne, Arkansas.

The motivation of the protest parties was substantially bona fide and doggedly recorded by news developments. During 1890 farm prices of wheat, corn, and cotton ranged from a third to a half of their 1870 levels. With desperate seriousness the Populists "preached" and otherwise pointed out that the makers of clothes were underfed even while the makers of foods were underclad, and pled for a remedy for the tragic malady of farm foreclosures.

It followed that, from the southern Ozarks foothills all the way to St. Louis and beyond, there arose a distinctly folkish philosophy of agricultural planning which in very basic part and about a half a century later re-emerged as "The New Deal for Agriculture." The latter's gospel of "domestic allotment" and the ever theoretical "Ever Normal Granary" grew from the thinning Ozarks earth. It was originally named the Sub-Treasury Plan for the Relief of Agriculture. The latter's birth year was 1891; apparently its first published statement was drafted by "Libertarian" Charles W. Macune, who published a little magazine, *The National Economist.* The June, 1892, convention of the Southern Farm Alliance was first to adopt the Sub-Treasury Plan as a basis for its official platform. Earlier the plan had won the blessings of a succession of eleven local farmers' conventions held in five lower-tier counties of the Missouri Ozarks.

The Sub-Treasury Plan of 1892 proposed specifically that each state of the Union have its quota of federally owned warehouses or other storages for wheat, corn, oats, rice, tobacco, cotton, wool, and sugar. Farmers were to bring their crops to their local warehouses where they would receive storage certificates redeemable in United States currency to the extent of eighty percent of the market value of the crop. Farmers were to pay the government interest at the rate of one percent a year and, if they failed to redeem the goods within twelve months, the government would have the right to sell the produces in storage.

In his campaign of 1896, William Jennings Bryan, the perennial Democrat candidate for President, officially approved the Sub-Treasury Plan with this pronouncement: ". . . It harmonizes with and carries out the currency system in vogue on a really safer plane because the products of the country that must be consumed every year are the best security in the world, and with more *social justice* . . ."

Thus, forty-one years before first federal enactment of the

Agricultural Adjustment Administration, the key principles of "domestic allotment," government storage of basic harvests, including "Ever Normal Granaries" and the principle of rigid price support and acreage limitation for farm crops were being devised, extolled and believed in, in the poorland Ozarks and many adjoined farmlands. Then as now, devotees of the Sub-Treasury Plan were pestered by hecklers. Political bosses in Philadelphia and New York snarled about the "hayseed Socialists" and "potato bankers." A Missouri farmer with exceptional talent for plowing up rattlesnake nests requested a government storage for baby rattlesnakes, and other snake eggs. A self-styled poet reported markets poor and recommended that the government warehouses for crops be provided with bins for unsold poetry.

But the imaginative Ozarkers kept on thinking in social and economic concepts which were many decades ahead of their times. In the area of Joplin, Missouri, Jacob S. Coxey began forthright planning for nationwide unemployment relief based on government-sponsored works in line with lasting public good—the concerted building of dams, levees, bridges, roads and public schoolhouses. Coxey's Army of Unemployed, which presently marched vainly on Washington, was manned in great part by Ozarkers. Joplin, Missouri, was its primary recruiting base.

Interestingly, the Sub-Treasury Plan for federal assistance for agriculture meticulously avoided any and all boondoggles or loose talk about the avoidance of alleged surpluses. Mary Elizabeth Lease, who spent several of her best and most vocal years stumping the Ozarks as a self-professed philosopher in petticoats, clarified this stand with typical directness: ". . . Politicians," she vowed, "said we suffer from 'Over-production' . . . Overproduction! When ten thousand little children, so statistics tell us, starve to death in these United States each year. And over

100,000 shop girls in New York alone are forced to sell their virtue for the bread their niggardly wages deny them!"

So far as I am able to discover, Mary Elizabeth did not disclose the source of her statistics. But the petticoated spellbinder, with fervor and courage as well as imagination, found in the rural Ozarks her most appreciative audiences and beyond possible doubt the cerebral sources of her crusading words.

Ozark thinking added richness and depths and inevitable change of viewpoint to the living and self-perpetuating stories of the land and its people. There were other story-changing forces. The most powerful of all was the determined if bouncy infiltration of the auto era. Bad and sparse as the back roads were (and in some areas still are), the incorrigible Model-T Fords were coming a-bouncing and a-banging into the backhills. The clutterings of gasoline cans which had previously harrassed the front porches of the country stores were being replaced by manual pumps and in more sizable villages and towns with newfangled fillin' stations. The latter began appearing in the Ozarks during 1912–13.

But the automotive age was not being welcomed with open arms. Persisting lack of roads still blocked its access to scores and hundreds of the farther-back communities. Depressed buying power, intrenched conservatism of view, and a powerful and long-proved dependence on horses and mules for draft power served additionally to delay the conquest by the gasoline buggy. Furthermore, a great portion of the rustic population aggressively resented and detested automobiles. Speaking and acting as a fairly typical Ozark countryman, my father was disposed to scowl and swear at every damn fool gas buggy he saw and to mix pertinent discussions of eternal damnations with such classic quotations as "What fools them mortals be!"

But the automobile came in anyway—changing the life and

175

stories thereof, even in the farthest backhills. By contrast to the railroads, which had begun jabbing into the region half a century earlier, the auto was to succeed in destroying or powerfully undermining even the most stalwart breastworks of isolation.

In earlier times the railroads had likewise encountered embittered opposition. For one example among thousands, when the Frisco came pushing down from St. Louis, my grandfather opposed it with vehemence even if not with ingenuity. When the track builders began digging a great cut through his property in order to get into the town of Fayetteville, Old Legal repeatedly chased off the surveying crews with his shotguns. Even after the trains began "hell-roarin'" through, my grandpa used to stand at the brink of the deep cut and throw rocks at the locomotives. Railroad officials countered by formally naming the mighty ditch Wilson's Cut. That foul deed foreshadowed a succession of peculiar accidents. Time and time again when section crews were at work in the steel-railed maw of the cut, wheelbarrowloads, even wagonloads of rotten potatoes and other refuse would come catapulting down on their Gaelic heads.

The steel rails and the wood-burning and eventually coal-burning locomotives that rode them striated the borderlands and pushed into substantial areas of the hill country. But they never came within whistle distance of more than one-fifth of the rural homes and they failed to reach many hundreds of the villages and scores of the smaller towns. Inevitably the railroads brought and perpetuated great numbers of stories, many even more gospel than the train-robbery sagas of Frank and Jesse James and companies.

But, as noted, the railroads never came anywhere near saturating the land. My mother, who spent her childhood and teens in the backhill village of Hawg Eye, never saw a railroad train until her nineteenth birthday. Her father, who ran the Hawg Eye mill and store (he lost the mill to flood and the store to bankruptcy), never saw a railroad track until he was past fifty.

But Ozarks stories and folksay had been influenced quite markedly by still another historic phenomenon which regional scholars or historians are strongly disposed to overlook. This was the remarkable birth and lusty growth of the Great Kansas Wheat Belt. By 1910 the golden oceans of Kansas wheat and the all-necessary wheat harvest had set up one of the largest and more dependable labor markets within easy reach of the Ozarks. The Kansas wheat fields were bigger and more prolific than the saw-mills, migratory logging camps, mines, apple orchards, strawberry fields and various other available industries of the times.

Comparatively speaking, the big wheat harvests were bonanzas for hardy job followers. During an overlength era when Ozarks wages sagged to averages ranging from fifty cents to a dollar per long, hard day, an able bundler and stacker of new-mown wheat or a threshing-rig jockey could earn as much as four dollars a day. It followed that when Kansas wheat ripened, beginning in June, thousands of Ozarkian males began hopping freight trains, pooling resources to rent wagons and teams, or hiking afoot to the great grain fields to the not too distant northwest. Some returned in late August or early September, pockets a-jingle with wheat money. One of my cousins "wheat harvested" his way through college. Along with the remnants of comparatively robust wages, thousands of Ozarkers brought home veritable wagonloads of tellin' stories which poured on throughout most of a century.

Some of the tall yarns about the Kansas wheat harvests were so incredible that one quickly forgot them. But there were some memorable aftermaths. There was young Jim Barger, for example, whose mother, Little Suzie (she was considerably shorter than five feet, whereas Jim was considerably taller than six) vowed that her

177

baby boy just wasn't of rightful age to be treking away to such far-off foreign places as Kansas. Jim, who was barely twenty-nine at the time, vowed to his ma that if only she would permit him to go to the wheat harvest, he would bring her home an ostrich plume as long as she was, or maybe longer. (Those were the days of feather plumes when bird populations were being all but exterminated for the savage adornment of women's hats.) Little Jimmy hiked away to the harvest and sure enough, he returned bearing a bright purple ostrich plume of truly gigantic proportions. When Little Suzie anchored the plume to the side wall of her sailor hat, she appeared from the stern to breeze along like a Tennysonian argosy.

My cousin Oliver, already mentioned, regularly came home from the harvest fields bearing a roll of currency sized to choke a large cow or a small elephant. True, the inner layers or first couple of hundred thousand dollars were Confederate bills. But the twenty-dollar greenback which comprised the outer coating of the roll was profoundly impressive per se. Cousin Oliver was a giver as well as an endearing show-off. The time he poured kerosene in his father's whisky jug, he assured me that if I would keep still about it he would buy me a beefsteak supper the very day he got home from wheat harvest. He kept his word. We tramped in to Hodge's Café where Oliver ordered the best steak in the ice box. It was so good that he ordered another. But that third rounder was one too many. It made us both woefully sick.

My cousin and I agreed there was a moral to this story. But we never could agree about what the moral was. I perceived it as a parable of excess. The Ozarks just never were a three-beefsteak country. Very practically speaking, one fairly thin haggle of beef was about their repeatable limit. Oliver more optimistically viewed the sorry-ending episode as a parable of the folly of resisting inevitable change. Just as the kerosene had changed his pappy's drinkin' liquor, so gasoline would certainly change all his pappy was drinking for—and intermittently shooting at. Oliver was, of course, referring to the inevitable infiltration of that gasoline buggy, which town upstarts were already renaming the autymobile. It was bound to bring in new ways and, God forbid, new stories, but one's capacity for steak would, too, adjust to changing times.

CHAPTER XVI

Roads of Destiny

THROUGHOUT MY BOYHOOD, 1905–15, Arkansas law directed that citizens had the choice of paying the road taxes—two dollars per year—in cash, or of "working it out" with one day of labor, usually in June. At nine I first went along as water carrier for my father and an affable mob of about thirty other symbolic taxpayers, all assigned and duly beseeched to work the old Mount Comfort Stage Road.

By midmorning I was being directed to pour cold water on pick and shovel handles. "They got so ga-damned hot we're fearful to swing 'em . . ." Shortly after the basket lunch of fried pork propped between huge slices of home-baked bread, a deputy sheriff appeared with a six-gallon keg of confiscated moonshine licker. The afternoon was spent appropriately, and shortly before sundown the sloshy facsimiles of taxpayers were headed home afoot, and finding it still a mighty rough road to stagger.

Fifteen years later, as a highly temporary employee of the Arkansas Highway Department, I was helping to locate first roads into various stretches of Ozark backhills, and noting with alarm and penitence that livestock and people alike had still not learned to respect the deadliness of the automotive age. In numerous hill and valley communities autos and trucks were getting in and out for the first time. By and large the chickens, guinea fowl, cats, hounds, hogs, horses, and mules had not learned to get out of their way.

Since long before the stuttery beginnings of the internal combustion engine, the open or occasionally open road has been an often repeated subject of the folk literature of the Ozarks. It can be argued, of course, that this is merely another repetitive characteristic of many lands and peoples; that since the times of the Odyssey, the pastoral travels of Abraham, or significant interims such as *The Canterbury Tales*, the traveled throughway has been the most storied way and the traveler has been the premier storyteller.

The lower Ozarks of a hundred years ago already had their pint-sized Aeneas. He was that affable straight man, The Arkansas Traveler. His loose-jointed but revealing epic begins and ends on or beside the ragged or mirey shapes of country roads, where the incorrigible Traveler plays fiddles, saunters with fellow wanderers, seeks lodging at wayside taverns, and otherwise talks and gets talked to. In the process, the rural Ozarks come alive and stay alive.

Somewhere in the southern Ozark foothills the Traveler, riding an aging saddle horse, gets lost. As he follows an unfamiliar backhill road, he sees the Squatter perched on a whisky barrel set next the doorway of a ramshackle log cabin. The Squatter saws away on a battered old fiddle, playing the same snatch of tune over and over again:

181

Traveler: Hello, Stranger!

Squatter: Hello, yourse'f!

T.: Can I get to stay all night with you?

S.: You can git to go to hell!

T.: Do you have any spirits here?

S.: Lots of 'em. Sal seen one last night by the ole holler gum. Hit like to skeert her to death.

T.: You mistake my meaning. Do you have any liquor?

S.: Had some yisstedy, but Boss, my ole houn' dawg got in and lapped hit out'n the pot.

T.: I don't mean pot licker. I'm wet and cold, and want some whisky. Have you got any?

S.: Yeah, I drunk the last this mornin'.

T.: I'm hungry, haven't had a thing since morning. Can't you give me something to eat?

S.: Hain't a damm thing in the house, not a mouthful a meat, nor a dust a meal here.

T.: How far is it to the next house?

S.: Stranger, I don't know. I never been thar.

T.: Well, do you know who lives here?

S.: I shore do.

T.: As I'm so bold then, what might your name be?

S.: Hit might be Dick, and it might be Tom, but it ain't.

T.: Sir, will you tell me where this road goes?

S.: Never went nowhar since I come here. Ev'ry mornin' when I wake up hit's still thar.

T.: As I'm not likely to get to any other house tonight, can't you let me sleep in yours? I'll tie my horse to a tree and do without anything to eat or drink.

S.: My house leaks. Thar's only one dry spot in hit, and me and Sal sleeps on that spot. And that thar tree is the ole woman's persimmon tree. You can't tie to hit 'case she don't want the persimmons shuk off. She 'lows to make beer out'n 'em.

T.: Why don't you finish covering your house, and stop the leaks?

S.: It's been rainin' all day.

T.: Well, why don't you do it in dry weather?

S.: It don't leak then.

T.: As there seems to be nothing alive about your place but children, how do you do here, anyhow?

S.: Putty well, I thank you. How do you do yourse'f?

T.: I mean what do you do for a living here?

S.: Keep tavern and sell whisky.

T.: Well, I already told you I wanted some whisky.

S.: Stranger, I bought a bar'l mor'n a week ago. Me and my wife Sal went shares. After we got it here, we only had a bit 'tweenst us. Sal, she didn't want to use hern fust, nor me mine . . . I had a spiggin' in one end, and she in t'other. So she takes a drink out'n my end, and pays me the bit for hit; and then I'd take one out'n hern, and give her the bit. Well, we's getting along fustrate till Dick, the damn skulkin' skunk, he bourn a hole in the bottom to suck at. The next time I went to buy a drink they wurn't none thar.

T.: I'm sorry your whisky's all gone; but my friend why don't you play the balance of that tune?

S.: Hit's got no balance.

T.: I mean you don't play the whole of it.

S.: Stranger, can you play the fiddle?

T.: Yes, a little sometimes.

S.: You don't look like a fiddlur, but ef you think you can play any more onto that thar tune, you can just git down and try. (The traveler dismounts, takes the fiddle and bow, plays the entire tune.)

S.: Stranger, take a half dozen cheers and sot down! Sal, stir yourse'f around like a six-hoss team in a mudhole. Go around in the holler where I kilt that buck this mornin', cut off some of the best pieces and fotch it and cook it for me and this gem'man directly. Raise up the board under the head of the bed and git the ole black jug I hid from Dick, carry the gem'-man's hoss round the shed, give him all the fodder and corn he can eat. . . . Play away, stranger! You kin sleep on the dry spot tonight.

We are told that when the Traveler finally slept, the contents of the black jug caused him to dream peculiar dreams. But apparently none was as "quare" as the coming of the greatest of enforcers of change, the internal combustion engine.

But for another half century after the fiddle-addicted Traveler had gone his way, most of the Ozarks remained off bounds for the auto. By 1910, when one of the writer's more distant cousins and the latter's new bride became "teched with the autymobile crazies," the couple was obliged to travel by train all the way to St. Louis in order to buy one of the gas buggies. Roads being what they were, the newlyweds headed north instead of south, solely because the driving was better up that way. Cousin LeRoy never really liked the North. And he never approved of supporting a woman; after all, women were made to fend for themselves. But he felt duty bound to support the auto. The only way he could accomplish that was to take to barbering in Cleveland.

Meanwhile Ozarks roads and lack of roads were producing other historic consequences. As recently as 1912–15, the principal Ozarks mileages were of erratic, largely undependable and bridgeless farm roads. Potential auto roads linked only some of the larger towns. For the most part the rural communities fell in one of three list-ings, the On-roaders, the Off-roaders, and the Trail Settlements.

Obviously most of the first settlers had been more concerned about selecting well-watered and comfortably located home sites than with locating possible road sites. Indeed, many Ozarks settlers appeared to have placed remoteness as a first requirement for their new homes. Early township maps show cabins and other farm homes scattered like fine birdshot fired into a tornado. Land abstracts and other sources of local history also indicate that, whatever else they may have known, a great many of the first homesteaders did not know how to recognize fertile or "lasty" farm lands. By 1880 the abandonment of first holdings of land was so commonplace that ghost countrysides were appearing even ahead of the era of ghost mining towns farther west.

The second generation of Ozarks settlers was strongly disposed to homestead, buy, or otherwise acquire valley farms. Their establishment of bridle trails and largely hypothetical wagon roads to connect the various valleys resulted in an extremely eccentric pattern for road building. For the sake of convenience, most farm roads were routed either along or near river banks or across the occasional flats or prairies. This tended to destroy any logic of direct access between any two given points, and to place communication at the mercy of recurrent floods, overflows and washouts. Thus the first generation of Ozarks roads tended to twist, backtrack and meander like a punch-drunk fighter groping his way to the shower room.

When the auto era finally began puttering and honking in, many towns sought to build new roads to link themselves with other towns. To attain this, many of the farm and county roads were grouped into district or "bond-bearing unit" roads which, at least theoretically, would draw trade to all towns on the new routes, even while enabling traffic to materialize.

In many instances the road districts were poorly organized by bad planners. Presently great numbers of towns and villages began

185

to learn that the new dirt or gravel throughways were bringing trade through rather than to their intermittently dusty and muddy main streets. I recall one astute country neighbor who predicted eloquently that them road boosters were "chawin' dynamite caps in place of honest terbaccer." It presently came to pass, even as Squire Crump had forecast, that many a road booster figuratively "got his head blowed plum off."

While the "district" road building did score some noteworthy victories over remoteness, the intercounty road was adding to remoteness in many areas by literally obliterating established villages, crossroads and small towns which simply were not needed by an auto-owning public. Among the many who recounted the latter casualties was old Cato Fietz who had served and thrived as a crossroads merchant until that "pesky big road come pushin' through."

"You're askin' me what that through road done for me?" Cato roared. "Wal, so I'm tellin' you, hit ruint me!" He continued through a browning fog of tobacco spit, "Them greazed-up booster monkeys vowed as how that high road would bring the country trade straight to my store door. Fact is, the fool thing fotched the trade past my door and taken it all the hell acrost the county. Main trouble with them high roads is they make big towns bigger, and leave the rest either to rot away or freeze to size."

Time has continued to prove that Storekeeper Fietz was right as the rain, which at least as this page is written, again falls on the Ozarks. The era of building auto roads served to enlarge some of the principal towns, presently to erase scores of villages and hundreds of crossroads stores, and to thwart the growth of somewhere near two hundred established small towns, including some twenty-five county seats, by freezing their respective censuses at between 1,000 and 2,500.

The lengthening of auto roads and the evolution of interconnecting systems of highways was destined to yield other baffling after-maths. Here is one significant instance:

Throughout the third of a century between 1890 and 1923, the Ozarks were well forward among the nation's most productive fruit-growing regions. Between 1910 and 1923, for example, two counties in the Arkansas Ozarks, Washington and Benton, repeatedly led all counties of the United States in apple production. The quality of the harvests easily matched the quantity.

Though the market tallies slipped markedly during the middle 1920's, the Ozarks apple carts kept rolling happily until paved highways came in. During the closing 1920's, the completion of U.S. 71, which was the first paved highway to link this area with the Midwest and West-South, brought about the decline and collapse of commercial apple growing in this especially productive sector. Substantially the same fate befell the lesser fruit crops such as peaches, pears and, presently, strawberries.

Before the coming of Highway 71 and other long pavements, practically all fruits grown commercially in the Ozarks went to market by rail. This was not easy, nor entirely adequate. Because so much of the Ozarks never had accessible railroads, backwoods growers of fruits and berries were either barred from taking part in the trade, or put to the great toil and expense incident to wagon hauling their produces to railside, a dozen or more miles from the place of harvest.

But, in order to endure rail shipment, all the fruits, berries, and other home-grown perishables required exacting standards of grading, sorting and inspection. To be marketable, all produces had to be picked and packed correctly and handled with very special care. The necessary enforcement of high standards for railroad shipping increased the market range of the Ozarks harvests. As a rule, the carefully loaded rail cars would be dispatched to the nearer "brokerage points," such as St. Louis, Kansas City, Dallas or Memphis.

187

With the development and improvement of iced freight cars early in the present century, the market ranges were greatly expanded. Meticulously sorted, graded and packed carloads or even train-loads of perishables could be highballed or "throughed" to farther and larger market centers. When nearer markets became saturated or otherwise dulled, the rail cars could be and frequently were dispatched all the way to New York, Boston, Chicago, Detroit, Denver, or San Francisco. Actually, the Ozarks helped substantially in introducing the practice of long rail hauls of premium-quality fruits and vegetables.

But the coming of the paved highway and its chugging and gaseous parade of trucks changed this sound procedure. The individual truck shipments did not require uniform sorting or grading standards and tended to dispense with packing. Individual truckers or fleet owners with low-wage hired help came bumbling along the new pavement and began buying fruits and other produce directly from the growers. In many instances, the truck drivers or other employees picked the fruit and poured it loose or roughly boxed into their vans.

That done, the wheeling opportunists would head for the nearest markets, usually those within a day's drive or less. But the roughed and tumbled perishables could rarely be counted on to endure more than a few hours of haulage. Almost instantly the nearer markets would become glutted with ungraded produce. Area markets would sag dismally or collapse entirely.

Harvest after harvest foundered or failed to profit either grower or dealer. Ozarks fruits, berries, and fresh vegetables began losing the market support and grade prestige which their flavors and other merits justified. Grade markets were replaced by snatch-grab buying and selling, or, too frequently, dumping. Interstate shipments dwindled rapidly. Neither the ungraded or bulk markets of the local canneries were able to reward adequately the principal orchards and berry farms. There were fortunate exceptions but, for the Ozarks as a whole, a once eminent horticulture began dimming and dying like a failing flashlight.

For other Ozarks harvests, including milk and poultry, highways proved of strong advantage. But, in general, easy-way exploitation via paved highway and motor truck joined in doing for the market orchards and berry and vegetables farms what the same inpushing pavements had already done for so many country stores, crossroads and villages: They blame near ruint 'em. Like so many other highway calamities, this didn't have to happen. It just happened.

CHAPTER XVII

Ballets and Play Parties

THE OZARKS CASUALTIES or near casualties of through roads include other distinguished resources. Among these are communications and the peoples' own uses thereof. The early "wire roads," actually the first interstate roads to pass through the Ozarks, brought together the stagecoach routes and the first telegraph lines. Then the retarded but inevitable construction of auto roads opened the way for a series of closely interrelated means of communication, including rural mail delivery, the telephone, local newspapers, and an array of published materials, from patent-medicine leaflets to dictionaries.

It followed that the advent of roads into the Ozarks, and the various communication devices which the roads facilitated, proceeded to reduce or replace completely various phases of indigenous communications. The latter included such folkish expediencies as signal fires, blazed tree trunks, methodically broken twigs, rock markings, and others.

But the greater loss included the unwritten and individually remembered, inventively recounted chronicles of local people and places. I am thinking particularly of the Ozarkian ballads, commonly pronounced "ballets," which in great numbers could not survive auto fumes and the singing wires of commercial communications.

Throughout most of the nineteenth century, the Ozarks were one of the nation's most fertile seed beds of what we now call the folk ballad. Some of the latter were transplants from the British Isles. Many more came directly from earlier U.S. settlements, particularly the hill countries of Carolina, Kentucky and Tennessee. In great part these carry-ins were adapted to local people, places and happenings. Some of the ballets were obviously invented by Negro slaves; they show clearly the virile and inventive African talent for the merry recitation. But perhaps the greatest number was of indigenous improvisation by backhill singers and verse makers who were generally innocent of literacy.

During recent years several able scholars have sought to search down and record available remnants of the once immense ballad treasures of the Ozarks. At best the compilations are short of being adequate, though one must grant that some of the pursuing scholars have worked competently and well. Quite inevitably their works have been ransacked extensively by commercial exploiters, including, alas, quite a number of resident pretenders. One sometimes glimpses the pretenders at college-sponsored folk festivals and similar shindigs.

They usually come garbed in what they seem to consider quaint costumes. These are almost invariably climaxed by oversize red bandanna handkerchiefs twisted about the singer's neck or draped over his or her head. A listener is oftentimes disposed to suspect overly direct influence by Burl Ives and perchance the Grand Ole Opry radio broadcasts. However, this is not invariably the case, and the fact that the word "ballad" has been pirated by the popular-music industry and assigned an essentially alien meaning serves to indicate the multitudes of temptations which are being strewn before even the best-intentioned of contemporary balladeers.

Looking on as another student of the present-day Ozarks, I find the performances of the usually non-indigenous ballad singers generally commendable and at times quite brilliant. What I personally regret is that the quasi-professional renderers rarely select ballad material which is actually born of the Ozarks. Rather, they are strongly disposed to repeat such textbook stand-bys as "Barbara Allen," "King Edard," and "Daemon Lover."

I would pick no crows as regards these interstate and international classics, and certainly do not deny that all have places in the balladry of the Ozarks. But there happen to be many other "singin' stories" which are far more distinctively Ozarkian.

In my childhood, most of the ballet singers whom I knew were female. Most of them were old ladies who "remembert" the singin' stories they learned from their grandmothers or great aunts. Others were young wives or younger girls with inborn likings for song, who sang or chanted what they had earlier learned from their own grandmothers or great-grandmothers. Practically all lipped the ballets from sheer love of singing and many improvised tunes or melodies or adapted their tunes from church hymns or then-popular songs, such as "In the Shade of the Old Apple Tree" and "Darling, We Are Growing Old."

My present Ozarks wanderings are leaving me with the less than happy assurance that the unassuming and spontaneous ballet singers are growing fewer as well as older and that, with the exception of the farthest backhills, the noble breed is now all but extinct.

Granting this, as I fear one must, Ozarks ballets are still an engaging subject and a particularly attractive field of memories. Those which this white-thatched reporter is able to remember best and most fondly are in three recurring categories. The first includes the random ditty or whimsy adapted to virtually any known tune. The second is the eternal child's story in ballad meter. The third is the sentimental narrative adapted to or invented in a given community and dealing with present or past residents and occurrences.

The first-mentioned listing, I strongly suspect, originated with the Negroes who were first brought into the Ozarks more than a century ago. Both the vigor and the humor of the improvisations seem strongly African. My father recalled one ballet which he learned as a very young child from his slave "mammy" or governess. It deals with the fate of a summer-loving grasshopper:

> *Grasshopper settin' on a sweet-potato vine,*
> *Sweet-potato vine, sweet-potato vine*
> *On a summer day.*
>
> *Big turkey gobbler come a-slippin' up behind,*
> *Slippin' up behind, slippin' up behind*
> *On a summer day.*
>
> *He yanked that grasshopper off the sweet-potato vine*
> *Off the sweet-potato vine, sweet-potato vine*
> *On a summer day.*
>
> *He et that hopper off the sweet-potato vine*
> *On a summer day . . .*

The whimsy ballad, usually fantastic and ludicrous, takes special delight in courting and love-making. An old-time favorite,

193

THE BODACIOUS OZARKS

which Old Miz Jennie Demott used to produce with bestirring enthusiasm, dealt with the adventurous courtship of Froggie:

> Froggie went a-courtin', he did ride, uh-huh
> Froggie went a-courtin', he did ride,
> Sword and a pistol by his side, uh-huh.

> He went into Miss Mouse's den, uh-huh
> He went into Miss Mouse's den,
> And says, "Miss Mouse, are you within?" Uh-huh.

> He set Miss Mouse upon his knee, uh-huh
> He set Miss Mouse upon his knee,
> And says, "Miss Mouse, will you marry me?" Uh-huh.

> Mouse girl says, "Not without my Pa's consent," uh-huh
> Says, "Not without my Pa's consent,
> Would I marry the Pres-i-dent." Uh-huh.

The romance carries on with delightful disregard of natural history:

> Ole Mister Rat laughed till he shook his fat sides, uh-huh
> Mister Rat laughed till he shuck his fat sides,
> Thinkin' of his daughter be-in' a bride, uh-huh.

> Where will the weddin' supper be? Uh-huh
> Where will the weddin' supper be?
> Way down yabder in a holler tree, uh-huh.

> And what shall the weddin' supper be? Uh-huh
> What shall the weddin' supper be?
> Two green bugs and a black-eyed pea, uh-huh.

194

First come in Ole Mister Bee, uh-huh
First come in Ole Mister Bee,
Bringin' a fiddle on his knee, uh-huh.

Next come Mister Snake, uh-huh
Next come in Ole Mister Snake,
Passin' around the weddin' cake, uh-huh.

Next come in Ole Mister Bug, uh-huh
Next come in Ole Mister Bug,
A-passin' around the weddin' jug, uh-huh.

This was the end of the weddin' day, uh-huh
This was the end of the weddin' day,
And I ain't got no more to say, uh-huh.

The ballads of dilemma and sentimental adventure were disposed to burrow into the contrivances and daydreams of a greatly and distinctively daydreaming people. The local or individual variances of an identical narration prove baffling to the listener, bring graying hairs to any diligent editor, and reinforce the ballet's inherent opposition to literal recording. Incessant remouldings to fit specific persons, places and situations are, indeed, the qualities which permitted the singin' story to survive and remain appealing.

But in seeking to remember or track down Ozarks ballets, one is hard put to decipher accurately either the exact time or the exact place of origin. All the more so because so many of the dramatic situations are essentially timeless and omnipresent. The sad chronicle of Pore Lil Omy Wise is fairly typical:

I'll tell you the story of Lil Omy Wise
How she was kilt off by John Lewis' lies.

THE BODACIOUS OZARKS

He told her to meet him at Adam's Spring
Where he'd fotch her some money and other fine things.

He fotched her no money to set up the case;
But says, "We'll go and git marriet so hit won't be no dis-
grace."

So she hopped up behind him and away they did go,
Down to the river where the deep water flowed.

"John Lewis, John Lewis, do tell me your mind.
Do you figger to marry me or leave me behind?"

"Lil Omy, Lil Omy, I'll tell you my mind;
My mind is to marry you and leave you behind."

"John Lewis, John Lewis, I beg for my life,
I'll go around beggin', and won't need be your wife."

Then he up and he kissed her and turned her around
And throwed her in the river where he knowned she would
drownd.

More typical and more numerous are the remorseful-lover ballets. The lyrical decision of a swain to up and leave Sweet Willie
is a tender instance:

Willie, sweet Willie,
Willie, farewell;
I'm 'bliged to leave you
I love you so well.

BALLETS AND PLAY PARTIES

My foot's in my stirrup,
My rein's in my hand;
I'm goin' to leave you
For some far-off land.

Your Pappy don't like me;
He says I'm too pore,
Says I'm downright on-worthy
To enter your door,

Some says I drink whisky,
But my money's my own;
And them as don't like it
Can leave me alone.

Willie, sweet Willie,
O Willie, farewell;
I'm 'bliged to leave you
I love you so well.

The ballad as an indigenous and folkish medium for entertainment and recall has run its course. In the Ozarks it is not entirely dead but it is dormant. However, the ballad or ballet has a folkish companion which is distinctly alive and in many instances and places is meeting with active restoration. This is the eminently Ozarkian "play party."

My mother was a perceptive play-party enthusiast and in her younger years a capable and carefree participant. Even when age and enfeeblement came upon her, Mamma would sometimes join me on auto junkets to various backhill communities which she had known when young. The list included an invincible play-party

197

community far out on War Eagle River in Benton County, Arkansas.

Following my mother's death, I spent a dazed week re-exploring old back roads which we had traveled together many years before. This lonely but comforting pursuit led me back to War Eagle Valley and the countryside of the old Frost Mill, formerly kept by a couple of Mamma's girlhood friends.

The mill had burned in the interim, but the Frost family and several of their in-laws continued to keep riverside farms. I called on Miz Janey Frost, found her chair-bound, almost blind, yet with her usual lightheartedness. She chatted merrily about old times, told of how she and my mother, when they were fifteen or thereabouts, once attended a play party over at Cane Hill where both "ketched" their first beaus.

"We still keep with play parties hereabouts," Miz Janey assured me. "One is set fer tomorry night up at Hansard's School. Shore would be proud if you'd wait over and go . . ."

I waited over and I went. Miz Janey explained that for most of forty years the countryside had kept with square dances, usually the first Saturday night of each month. But lately they'd run fresh out of fiddle players. Pressy Drake had up and moved away to Californy. Gab Hines had crippled his arm by falling off a hay wagon. Uncle Tolly Ladd had banjoed off to heaven. Except for the radio and funnygraph, which don't scarcely ever make rightful music for country dancing, there weren't no more proper jig players. But the neighbor people still kept with play parties.

A play party is substantially a square dance without music. It is the oldest of Ozarkian socials and in terms of group participation the most inventive. I had straggled along to play parties as a very young child, but without actively participating. This time I began with the determination merely to look on and remember earlier times. I set out at twilight. Miz Janey's housekeeper-nurse had left earlier with her new boyfriend from Ball Creek. Accordingly, I walked alone and kept my distance. Long before the white flint road circled into the schoolhouse clearing, I could hear voices, laughter and the stomping of feet on bare boards.

As I stepped toward the open door I was dazzled by an electric torch being aimed squarely at my eyes. "Evenin', Preacher Man!" A strong hand clasped mine and began pumping it violently. I presently focused my eyes on a barrel-shaped form garbed in shiny green. The man had wildly tousled white hair, apple-red cheeks and a truly enormous smile. As soon as I had made certain that my hand and forearm were still attached, I explained that I am not a preacher. "So what *is* your line?" he whooped.

"Fry cook for the White Tower Hamburger System."

He grasped my other hand. "Put it there, Doc! We'll be needin' hamburgers comes the first dozen sets. We'll leave you fry cook 'em." For the moment his laughter drowned out the cicadas and the many other sounds of the early autumn night. "Mighty pleased you come by. We're runnin' short of menfolks."

When I explained that I didn't know the sets, he bellowed the assurance, "We'll shore as hell learn you, then." He flashed off the light and hustled me into the oversize schoolroom where three overhead lanterns shed a strange golden light on a ready-formed circle of country people. Otherwise the room was almost bare save for a corner pile-up of desks and chairs.

The barrel-dimensioned host shoved me into the circle, between a barefooted little girl in a gorily red dress and a skinny and towering young man garbed in skin-tight dungarees and a completely buttonless shirt. A frail, elderly man with a poet's face and a bull's voice stood in the middle of the circle. Unquestionably he was the caller. As I joined the circle he grinned in my direction, stamped heavily booted feet and boomed, "Take up hands and circle right!" As the participants obeyed, a pretty gray-haired woman in a bright yellow dress pressed her way into the circle and grasped my hand. With my free hand I reached for the very small hand of the very little girl in the blood-red dress.

The caller turned with the moving circle, then dashed toward the tall young man who had been at my right and grasped his buttonless shirt front. "Git to the middle, Orvull. I'm a namin' you Ole Dan!" There was a great deal of laughter. The chosen youth blushed and mumbled but quickly subsided as the moving circle, on command of the caller, broke into song. It was the ancient and ever silly recounting of Ole Dan Tucker:

> Ole Dan Tucker he got drunk,
> Fell in the far and kicked up a chunk;
> Coal a far it burnt through his shoe
> And O by Golly, how the ashes flew!

> Ole Dan Tucker's a good ole man,
> Washed his face in a fryin' pan,
> Combed his hair with a wagon wheel
> And died with a toothache in his heel.

> Ole Dan Tucker down in town,
> Ridin' a goat and leadin' a hound,
> The hound give a howl and the goat give a jump
> And throwed ole Dan'l a-straddle a stump.

At this point I began to sense dramatic tension. As the moving circle chanted or yelled the final stanza, the drama began materializing.

BALLETS AND PLAY PARTIES

Ole Dan Tucker's down in town,
Swingin' the ladies all around;
First to the right and then to the left,
Then to the one that you love best.

At the call of "first to the right," Old Dan grabbed for the right hand of the most accessible girl (she may have been a deliberate choice), pulled her into the ring, swung her about with tremendous acceleration and returned her to her place in the circling line. At "then to the left," he dashed for another girl, grasped her left hand, swung her about and returned her to the line. At "then to the one that you love best" a rollicking pandemonium broke. Every male in the circle hurried to swing his partner to the right; every one except myself, that is. The center man, Ole Dan, plunged laterally to take a girl for himself. More or less inevitably he made off with the pretty grayhead in the yellow dress.

That left me as Ole Dan, or the man in the middle. The singing, swinging and chanting continued for at least four more rounds before I was able to attach myself to the very little girl in the extremely red dress and thereby get free of the middle. In the course of my repeated bumblings I noted that the chanted ballad of Ole Dan Tucker seems to have a virtually infinite number of stanzas which all participants except myself seemed to know by heart. Some of the verses are extremely funny, at least they seemed so at the time. A few sounded to be hilariously ribald, though the actual words were comparatively discreet.

I resolved to institute a compilation session the instant the party closed. As things turned out, by closing time I was much too dizzy and winded to take part in any form of cerebration. All the more so because the jingling ballad of Ole Dan was presently succeeded by at least half a dozen other "singin' rounds" and a

201

couple of "line sets," all requiring stamina and concentration. Ole Dan was followed directly by several rounds of "Juniper Tree." In this the "middle man" is a girl who sits sedately on the floor and waits for things to happen. The singing circle forms again. A male member throws his own or somebody else's hat in the air. At a common urge, all the menfolk jump or dive for the hat, while the female participants do their best to keep out of the way. Whoever comes up or down with the hat, or the largest piece of it, gets to kiss the girl in the center.

Having effected the warm-up, the girl who has been kissed appoints her successor, which of course is a distinct challenge to feminine stratagem. She may elect to pick the ugliest girl present, or the prettiest, or the youngest or oldest, or her best friend, or cattiest competitor, depending on her mood or the male contender who is likely to be the fleetest snatch grabber.

In any case, when the successor is duly seated and braced, the participants resume their marching in a circle and singing. Here again many different ditties may be used, including improvisations and revisions. The one which I partly remember is entitled "State of Arkansaw":

> *Rise up my pretty dear,*
> *Present me to your Paw*
> *And we'll go off together*
> *To the State of Arkansaw.*

> *So keep your hat orn,*
> *Hit'll keep your head warm,*
> *And take a sweet kiss*
> *You wont never miss,*
> *Hit'll do you good, I'm shore, I'm shore,*
> *Hit'll do you good, I'm shore.*

At the lyric command "keep your hat orn," the swain who has held on to the tossed hat or the biggest part of it (a lot of Ozarks hats get everlastingly ruint this way) places what is left of the headgear on the head of the center girl and claims his kiss. The girl names her successor and the lucky man makes ready to throw the hat again, come the next musical cue.

There are also marchin' games. One of the more athletic of these is called "The Needle's Eye." A boy and girl, or man and woman, preferably tall if stiff backs are to be considered, stand facing one another with arms raised and hands locked to form an arch. The players romp, sneak or bow under the arch single file.

The needle's eye that doth supply
The thread that runs so true;
O, many a lass have I let pass
Because I wanted you.

I don't want him, I don't want her,
The thread that tells so true;
O, many a lass have I let pass
Because I wanted you.

At the stipulation, "Because I wanted you," the arch couple drop their arch at a quick and common impulse and so capture the player who happens to be passing under. When a girl is caught she takes a place behind the catching girl and a captured man falls in rear of the masculine captor. Then each captive puts arms around the midparts of the arch couple and strives to pull them apart. In case they fail, the arch couple traps another victim couple who join in the abdominal tug of war. And so the merriment goes. Arch couples have been known to break grips abruptly and thereby seat themselves rather violently on the midsectors of their pullers-aparters. "The Needle's Eye" is far more exciting than most college football games and only slightly less energetic.

Another fine old Ozarkian line game which I had encountered many times before is called "Sugar and Tea." Players form in parallel lines, boys on one side, girls on the other, partners facing. The beau at the head of the line leads his lady down the aisle and the singing begins:

> *Lead her up to sugar and tea,*
> *Lead her up to candy,*
> *You swing around that sugar and tea,*
> *While I swing around that dandy.*
>
> *Hi ho, that sugar and tea,*
> *Hi ho, that candy,*
> *You swing around that sugar and tea,*
> *While I swing around that dandy.*

The boy leads his girl back to the starting point, swings her about. The assembled party sings again. Then the boy takes the next girl in line, the girl takes the next boy, and so on until everyone is properly swung.

They also played a double-ring game at the War Eagle play party, another fine old stand-by called "Jingle at the Winder." Here again the ditty varies with time, place, singers and shouters, and here again I list the words which I happen to remember from the somewhat long ago. The sense of the game, to use the word rather playfully, is to get all participants very personally introduced.

Players choose partners and form a double ring, womenfolks in the inner circle, each one standing in front of her partner. The menfolks "sashay" or short-step about in single file. The women wait in place, and all sing:

> *Jingle at the winder, to-de-O*
> *Jingle at the winder, to-de-O*
> *Jingle at the winder, jingle-O*
> *Jingle at the winder!*

When the festive males have circumnavigated the entire circle, each returns to his partner, swings her once. Then they begin another "sally" to the same tune, or a fairly reasonable facsimile thereof, but with words purposefully changed:

> *Pass one winder, to-de-O*
> *Pass one winder, to-de-O*
> *Pass one winder, to-de-O*
> *Jingle at the winder!*

During the foregoing each swain passes his partner and swings the girl next to her, and so on until the entire inner circle is thoroughly swung. There are further variations, "Pass two winders," "Pass three winders," and so on. When the men and boys are pretty well worn out, the more durable sex may take the outer circle and do the swinging.

Ozarks play-party games are practically without limits of number and completely beyond prediction, as regards improvisations. They have lived and cavorted through generations past. They could and most certainly should provide merry evenings and robust exercise for generations still unborn.

I cannot speak as a scholar. But it is my deduction that play-party games and songs have been brought together from a great many older settlements and countries to renewed life and delightful spontaniety in the backhill or backroad Ozarks. I left the play party from up past War Eagle Crossing with a wonderful glow of festive exhaustion and a soul-restoring liking for the people.

CHAPTER XVIII

A Ballet Singer Bears a Son

ODDLY BUT TRULY, the writer's most recent discussion of old-time backhill ballets was with the most controversial of contemporary Ozarkers—Arkansas's continuing governor, Orval Eugene Faubus, born and raised in the area of Greazy Creek in the true backhill Ozarks of Madison County, Arkansas.

Addie Joslin, daughter of the local book peddler, was sixteen when she married Sammy Faubus who had lately homesteaded a rocky and forested quarter-section in the farther backhills beyond Greazy and Ball creeks. Addie was seventeen when she bore Orval, the first of her seven. She was also one of the better-known ballet singers of the countryside. She sang ballets to her firstborn and to each of her successive two sons and four daughters. She continued singing ballets until the day of her death at forty-three.

Few living men are more authentically informed regarding backhill balladry than Orval Faubus. Curious, intelligent, aggres-

207

sive and talented in expression, he could have proved himself one of the most capable folk scholars of our times. But Orval chose a more dramatic folkish course, that of politics. As a result, the Ozarks may well have lost the services of an engaging balladeer. In any case, the backhill Ozarks have produced another profoundly revealing phenomenon. For better or worse, Orval Eugene Faubus has been one of the most pertinent Ozarkers on nationwide and worldwide exhibit.

The man personifies in depths and shallowness, in nobility and depravity, in honesty and dishonesty, a very real regional heritage. The most-noticed Ozarker of the present generation is a fire handler, a wind feeler, a living echo of the backhill man, who would burn his bridges before he reaches them.

Orval's paternal antecedents, who fought with Andrew Jackson in the Battle of New Orleans, spelled their name Forbis. His great grandfather, who emigrated into the Ozarks following briefer stops in the Kentucky mountains, spelled his name Forbes. Abe Forbes' son, who stayed put in the hills of Arkansas, intermittently X-ed his name or spelled it Forbus. Sam and all his young-'uns took Faubus and stuck with it; in many respects, all are the sticking kind.

Pappy Sam, who is past seventy as this is written, stays with his quarter-section homestead, raises chickens and, with the help of $33 a month in Social Security, remains entirely self-supporting. Sam stays an individualist and a habituated independent. In political matters he has been a Socialist, a La Follette Progressive, a Bull Mooser, a Free-Silver man, a Republican and a Democrat. His black-haired, medium-sized (five feet, eleven), cat-muscled and deeply reflective son, Orval, continues to describe himself as a Lincoln-style Democrat. Professional Democrats and qualified students of Lincoln might very well challenge this description. But Orval is an experienced recipient of challenges and is one of a large family which is almost peculiarly uninterested in exact political definitions as such.

Pappy Sam designates himself as a live-and-let-liver. Orval's next-younger brother is a log trucker out in Washington State. Elvis, his "baby brother" is currently a farmer in Arkansas. One of his sisters is a cook, another a waitress, another a store clerk, the fourth a farm wife. Orval describes them as good, self-tending people. "Not one's a harpie"—the Ozarker's old-line word meaning any kind of a no-good woman. Pappy Sam adds a few words about his eldest and "helpin'est son." "Orval never liked to be looked down on. Never asked nobody to hoe his row, nor sharp his ax nor light his far (fire)."

Above all other tangible pursuits, Orval Faubus enjoys lighting fires. To intimates he recalls that his crowning glory to date was being chosen as a boss brush burner in a big logging camp where Orval used to labor as a "squirrel chaser" or utility woodsman. The self-described Burn Man from Greazy Creek has started fires from virtually every known source—from fireplace coals carried in a gourd dipper to flammable words.

A reasonably typical example of the latter is: "We are all now party to a life-or-death struggle between those who would live by Constitutional democracy and those who would build up an all-powerful central government to make our decisions for us from afar. . . . If Democracy is to live, the duly voted will of the citizens of a given state and community thereof must and will transcend the self-assumed powers of Federal courts and the Congress . . ."

Reminded that the latter sentence paraphrases one which Abraham Lincoln spoke almost exactly a century earlier while protesting the Dred Scott Decision of the Supreme Court, Faubus nods enthusiastically. "Lincoln is my all-time hero, my chosen philosopher. He was the greatest burn man of all. He planted fires

209

in the understandin' hearts of the real and common people he loved and was one of."

When standing, even sitting, Orval Faubus frequently gives the impression of hovering—like a cagey woodsman waiting for a large "ninepin" tree to decide which way it will fall. When he mentions Lincoln, he straightens and his peculiarly light brown eyes show a surprising fire. He can and repeatedly does deluge one with documentary facts and textbook details, which are usually correct, and "spang-out" interpretations of Lincoln, which are frequently debatable or suspect.

When fronted by an oblique query, such as: How do you reconcile Lincoln's leadership in emancipation of Negroes and your own opposition to permitting their children the advantages of integrated public schools? Faubus tends to answer: "I'm not a segregationist, never was, don't plan to be. Like Lincoln, I believe in government by the people, of the people and for the people. . . . Therefore I'm opposed to integration by Federal decrees and political connivances. . . . Here in Arkansas, some of my people, Negroes and white alike, have already accepted integration by local choice and democratic vote, which is the only American way to accept or reject any issue. The majority of my people is still against integration of public schools. . . . This would be so if I'd never been born. . . . The point is simply that my state and its people are making a last stand for states rights, as approved by the U.S. Constitution. . . . Like Lincoln, I stand with the people and their right to decide for themselves, God directing. In this view I believe I'm right with Lincoln."

Right or wrong, Faubus is unquestionably an environmental prototype of Lincoln. His homeland, still one of the backwoodsiest counties of the Ozarks, was settled during Lincoln's lifetime, probably reached its population peak during the 1850's, perhaps Lincoln's most formative decade, and a century later remains astonishingly little changed. Orval, in turn, was "cabin-borned" in a slab-board shack with jail-dimensioned windows. When he was seven, the backhill Ozarker began "axin' alongside" his pappy, helping take out ash blocks and hickory splits for sale to a nearby handle factory, oak blocks for the local stave mills, and presently white-oak crossties to sell to the railroads. At fourteen, in about that number of hours of work, Orval was accustomed to fell and hew one good tie, saleable "on the ground" for about sixty cents. He also split rails. The enduring "stagger fences" suggest that O. Faubus may have split many more rails than A. Lincoln.

In scouting and felling a far-back whiteoak, the governor of Arkansas recalls that he used to drink up to three gallons of spring water a day. "Can't recollect ever urinating . . . just sweated it out. But I sure feathered into that stave oak . . ."

He feathered into other backwoods enterprises which tended to out-Lincoln Lincoln. Consider for example the Faubus adventures as a country schoolteacher. Orval was eighteen when he finished the eighth grade in the one-room, one-teacher, all-grades district school at Combs, Arkansas. Like other "all-graders" of the area, school "kept" until the money ran out, which was usually within four months. Faubus was twenty-seven when he finally drew his diploma from the county's only four-year high school. As soon as he had "hatched out" of grade school, he tramped into the county seat and stood the open examination for a third-grade teacher's license, led the fifty other applicants by scoring 100 in arithmetic and American history.

When midsummer school opening came around, the eighteen-year-old kept the Ball Creek District School, taught all eight of its grades, memorized all the lessons. In the best Lincoln tradition, the local school director "homed" Orval, simply by opening the spare room, butchering another pig, and loading on an extra

211

bag of wheat for water-grinding at Hawkins Mill. When the Ball Creek School petered out for the year, Orval took his "pay savin's," rarely more than $50, returned to Huntsville (present census, 1010), and attended the shank end of the high-school term. Orval came of age in 1931, still remembered as the Ozarks famine winter. He celebrated by "teacherin'" a roomful of eighty-three youngsters and marrying the preacher's daughter.

Like Orval, Alta Haskins of the midcounty Jasper community, is one of a brood of seven. Her farmer father also "preached Baptist"; less than mysteriously, Orval was "converted Baptist" and remains so, although Alta has changed over to the Church of Christ. When April came and high school was out, the bride and groom joined in the principal exodus of the times—fruit tramping. For the first season they "took to" strawberries, "peckin'" their way north through Missouri, roughing it in pickers' shacks, brush camps or the rained-on open. But the bride was game. Next spring the couple expanded their circuit to include the Rio Grande Valley vegetables, Louisiana, Arkansas and Missouri strawberries, then followed melons, raspberries, cherries and apples north to Michigan. Alta recalls that however lean the larder or thin the wallet, Orval "stood up" to any cheaty employer; also for the first time the Faubuses found themselves working with and liking Negroes.

The newlyweds made still another prolonged fruit tramping. Alta stayed game all the way, even when their first baby died; indeed, even after their second died. Farrell, their surviving son, who was born while Orval was feathering into politics, is now grown to a robust two hundred pounds and is "real helpful around home." In 1936 Orval returned to the Ozarks, "felt of the air and wind," and announced for the state legislature. In one of Arkansas's three traditionally Republican counties (the rest of the seventy-two are steadfastly Democrat), Orval listed himself as a "Lincoln-style Democrat." With five in the race, he lost by four votes. His disappointment was deep. But he figured he had lost because he had not fully heeded the "natural and proper sovereignty" of the stubbornly opinionated local communities—such as Alabam Township (current census 694), or Kentucky Township (290), where pioneers have perpetuated the literal names as well as general beliefs of their places of origin. (Venus Township (196) is not so readily explainable.)

In 1938 and home from a stint in the Washington State woods, Faubus announced his candidacy for county recorder and headed for the hills, seeking to view each community as a distinct "commonwealth." This time he won. He had also formulated a political commandment: Keep with the Local Vote. Duly "roosted" in the old Huntsville Court House, which is a pleasantly folkish combination of countywide social center and cuspidored Mecca of backhills viewpoint, the dungarees-wearing recorder found himself liking even more the deep-rooted independence of his backhills constituents. He noted that many still use the word "judge" as a synonym for "jackass," and that a man "naturally" owns his wife. Faubus does not invariably accept the local credos as gospel, but he became entirely convinced that "people can't be changed by writ or transformed by court decree."

Orval's next adventure involved a great deal of fire, but it wasn't altogether the spiritual or even the brush-burning kind. Early in 1942 he volunteered for Army duty, abandoning public officials' immunity to draft. At sizzling Fort Benning, Georgia, the Arkansas primitive reported for officers' candidate school and found himself "pecked" as one of 208 officer candidates, all but three college graduates, for a very special Intellectual Competence Test. Faubus took first place among the 208—and began feeling himself a man of destiny.

Assigned to the 35th Infantry, a rough-and-ready Border West

213

national-guard outfit, Second-Lieutenant Faubus was promptly marked as one of the sloppiest platoon leaders of the outfit and as one who clearly lacked the "ring of command." But on field maneuvers Orval stood out as the most able scout and woodsman to be found in all the division. This led to his designation as a combat scout for the 35th when it and the 29th swept over Saint-Lô; then as combat liaison officer for the Rhine and Marne crossings of the Fourth Armored; then "pioneer" for a sweeping flank of Patton's Third Army, then for the Seventh Army in the Bache Mountains, and briefly for the First Army. The repressed Burn Man was under fire for three hundred days without opportunity to burn any brush. But his long-time and intuitive skills as a woodsman made him "quite a war hero." One of his fellow officers reminisces: "Orval picked himself a very handsome chest salad, including the Bronze Star. But his greatest worth to our outfit was in keeping the Fourth Armored from running us over and Patton from taking us over . . . that Faubus is a terrific frontiersman!"

Back in Arkansas, political rumor had it that the Congressman had decided it would save work and trouble to set up the terrific frontiersman and self-envisioned Abe Lincoln as a postmaster rather than having him free to do reckless things—such as running for Congress. Major O. Faubus took separation from the Army on November 10, 1946, and five days later took over as acting postmaster of Huntsville, Arkansas. Though Orval proved to be a creditable postmaster, it was not the job but his use of his savings from it which was destined to set the fires which opened his way to fame or infamy. Orval planked down his savings from his first six months of postmastering as down payment on the weekly *Madison County Record*, the county's only newspaper.

The Burn Man had become one of the paper's local correspondents when he first took to schoolteachering at Ball Creek; allegedly one of his first reportorial nougats dealt with a local flowerbed contest . . . "The more the judges looked, the more pretty bloomers they found." But the Ball Creek correspondent's prose improved with time, and after Orval went off to war he "favored" *The Record* with an Army Letter which won him local note as the Ernie Pyle of the Ozarks. "They shouldn't have called me that," Orval confides, but adds, "Guess it didn't hurt me any." Neither, obviously, did the feat of reviving the feeble but respected little paper which, with Alta's able help and Orval's readable editorials, centered strongly on the immortal merits of Lincoln, Jefferson, St. Paul and the needs for better roads, schools and welfare services, and soon began winning friends and influencing local history.

Faubus' editorials came to the attention of Sid McMath, then Arkansas's youthful "Reform Governor." McMath astonished friends and foes by making the "Crusading Squirrel Chaser" a state highway commissioner, without pay but with a lot of power. Orval took the job and hired his most gifted country correspondent, Myrtle Clark, to ride herd on the paper. Myrtle still rides herd, though the masthead lists "Orval E. Faubus, Editor, Publisher & Owner." He left Alta as acting postmistress (though he did not actually recommend her appointment, "the Congressman just gave it") and hied forth to burn out a way for a "decent" highway system.

To the amazement of many, Faubus made an exceptionally good and impartial highway commissioner. He burned red tape, political brush piles and impeding departmental debris with effectiveness, even while avoiding bribes and bosses, including the subtle ones. After a brief salaried tenure as governor's assistant, Faubus took post as Nonpolitical Director of Highways. Commentators laughed heartily at the "nonpolitical," but not for long. When

Orval went back to Huntsville and his newspaper in 1953, the
highway department was beaver busy, roads were appearing like
veins in Maytime oakleaves, and the department kept an unprecedented cash balance of nearly fifteen million dollars—as Orval
noted, approximately a million times his personal savings from the
job.

An appointment as permanent postmaster waited his homecoming. But when another April came, Faubus resigned the post-
mastership and blandly announced for the governorship. The
moved appeared to be lunatic. The incumbent was free-loading a
second term in keeping with Arkansas tradition. Faubus had
never run successfully for state office, and as highway director
he had alienated plum pickers and "influential citizens" throughout the state. His weekly newspaper was barely breaking even.
Astutely, Alta had deposited their scant savings in an escrow
account to make sure Orval didn't squander them on something
silly—such as running for governor.

But Orval, "feeling the air for himself," had composed what
is still his basic campaign speech and felt obliged to use it "before it sp'iled." The key chat is a rather schoolteacherish exhorta-
tion for government of, by and for the people with some recognizable sprinklings from the civic philosophy of Thomas Jefferson.
Such as, "I am for preserving for the states the powers not specifically yielded by them to the Union." Or, "the wit of man
cannot devise a more solid base for a free, durable, and well-
administered republic than the self-governing township, county
and state . . ." The perennial Faubus "chat" also pleads for state
facilitation of better roads, schools, and welfare agencies to serve
all citizens in line with local needs and in answer to specific local
legislation.

Otherwise the perennial document is surprisingly lacking in
spellbinding qualities or devices, so much so that it causes many

216

A BALLET SINGER BEARS A SON

listeners to marvel that the slow-moving monologue can win votes, even to wonder how it keeps audiences awake. Yet somehow in Arkansas it does both. This became undeniable during the discouraging summer of 1954 when Faubus plodded forth for what appeared to be one of the worst-organized campaigns in Arkansas history. Yet when the run-off primary vote was counted, Orval was governor. As he had softly predicted, he had put his "aigs" under the hens and watched them hatch.

Even more astonishingly, he next set out to raise figurative chickens by changing the tenets of his basic speech to workable legislation. As a first step, Faubus set about changing the normally pompous and funereal Governor's Office Suite to an oversize version of a country court-house office. With rural disregard for union hours, the new governor instituted a personalized "tending" of his callers whereby he talks with each one "country-preacher style," usually closing with, "Glad we could have this nice visit."

As governor, Faubus directed one of his first burning jobs at Arkansas's century-old tradition of the unofficial, non-elected but long-dictatorial Big Bosses. In earlier times news seekers were accustomed to bypassing the governor and going directly to the reigning Boss who usually knew the answers because he made them. The traditional strategy of the Big Boss was to raise up the governor and take key appointments to boards and commissions. Faubus reiterates that he is "beholden only to the voters." With no political machine to feed or grease and with a primitive's distrust of self-projected Mister Bigs, the hillbilly deftly fired around the previous Big Boss and burned the successor's ladder. That much was almost childishly easy, but the job of changing specific recommendations of his basic speech to accomplished deeds was the opposite of easy.

Following New Year's, 1955, when Faubus officially "feathered into" the governorship, Arkansas, one of the most agrarian as

217

well as the poorest of our states, was depressed and floundering from four years of pitiless drought and was, as Faubus had privately noted, "sad as a sheep tick in a barrel of creosote." Yet his preachments for better schools, roads and welfare required drastic tax increases, invariably bitter medicine for the nation's second-poorest state (in average per capita income). The only way he could accomplish the "strong financing program" was by raising taxes and this he could do only by gaining and holding the support of the legislature. To attain this, as he did immediately, Faubus set out to "sell" the philosophy of local sovereignty with state aid accurately gauged to local services, including, of course, deft ego massage for the local representatives.

Orval plunged into the complex task with a canny merging of rustic skills and intuitive expediencies. He got close to his legislature; persuadings became intimate as a country washday. The new governor began "materializing" new tax monies, first to public-school teachers, who drew an inadequate but unprecedented uppance averaging $800 per year—twice as much as Faubus ever earned in any year as a teacher. He maneuvered desperately needed raises for highways, asylums, health services and welfare funds, the University and state colleges. He diligently encouraged a referendum move which presently placed all Arkansas legislators on annual salaries of $3600 per year, more than many of the peripatetic horde had ever earned, seen, or concretely imagined.

Most appraisers were chary of labeling Faubus a great governor. But more and more legislators began idolizing him and relishing his sometimes acrid jibes at himself. A favorite: "Don't confuse me with the facts. My mind is made up!"

Faubus grinned at this writer while directing at him the partly rhetorical question, "How's the old Burn Man doing?"

In view of the integration holocaust which has raged in Little

Rock, threatening and smudging half the earth, the question still holds an ironic pertinence. The most direct and revealing answer this reporter has dug out comes from one of Orval's long-time and sincerely admiring country neighbors:

"Orval really is a crackerjack burn man. He's smart as a wild-cat oiling a clock and he's got guts enough to wear for suspenders and water his garden with the leftovers. It's a double pity he let that Little Rock blaze get out of hand. Orval's got no personal feelin's of race. He truly likes Negroes; he's worked alongside them as a day laborer. When we were young'uns there was only one colored family in the county. Orval liked 'em fine, treated 'em real nice. That family didn't seem to want any school integration. They chose to move off to Nigger Town in Fayetteville, next county. It looks like most Arkansas colored folks still don't choose school integration, but it shore is pitiful to close up *all* public schools to them, like in Little Rock."

Faubus continues to side-step this basic issue, fibs easily and impishly, intermixes rather childish untruths with items of fact —including the reality that one of his first moves as governor was to gain authorization for six additional members for the State Democratic Central Committee and to appoint Negroes to all the new posts as a move "to take the Party fairly to the people." He made Dr. Lawrence Davis, Negro president of Arkansas A.M.N., the state's Negro college, his representative to the Southern Regional Education Board. He encouraged Arkansas's Department of Education to appoint qualified Negro supervisors of Negro schools. During his second term, Faubus sponsored and obtained for the state's Negro college more money than that institution asked for and the largest increase granted any college or university in Arkansas.

There is no real doubt that Faubus has picked up (sometimes he still says "pecked up") most of his firsthand and reasonably current observations on Negroes and Negro opinion in the Arkansas capital. Of Little Rock's 118,000 people, about 23,000 or twenty percent are Negroes. Back in Reconstruction times, Little Rock was one Confederate capital which never had a Ku Klux Klan, and it presently became a stronghold of the Society of Southern Women Opposed to Lynching. Rearing of Negro children as equals in white homes is an old Little Rock custom. For one instance, Delia Davis, the revered American Negro missionary to Liberia, was brought up in and sent away to college from the family home of the late John Gould Fletcher, Arkansas's Pulitzer Prize poet.

By 1957 experts tended to agree that Little Rock's best public school, in terms of physical plant and faculty qualifications, was the Horace Mann High School for Negroes. Its principal, Dr. L. M. Christophe, was one of the two high-school principals in Arkansas with a Ph.D. Fifteen of its regular faculty of twenty-eight have master's degrees or better. The plant, completed in 1956 to accommodate 1,000 students, has been cited for excellence by the American Institute of Architects and, according to respected accrediting groups, Mann may well be the highest ranking high school in Arkansas.

But why did the Big Trouble, the earth-smudging wildfire break in Little Rock, the "good town for Negroes?" Faubus reveals no integrated answer. As a devotee of what he terms "local-option government of, by and for the people," he reminds one that Little Rock citizens originally expressed their views by ballot at the ratio of nineteen against public-school integration to seven in favor. Yet the Burn Man from Greazy Creek grants that the sordid, selfish, badly reported, fact-twisting Little Rock story is certainly not of the "spirit fire" of Lincoln or the "mind fire" of Jefferson; also that "it has set back integration a mighty far ways." Faubus is not happy about the situation as a whole, nor is he repentant.

In the manner of most primitives, and true to the environmental traits of which he is currently a most noticed prototype, Faubus is a complex and subtle man. Like the mind he wishes to exemplify, the Burn Man is devout, stubborn and self-reliant to the fringe of mania. As a public official he functions without machine, brain trust or inner sanctum. His country-housewifish devotion to conventional honesty in the handling of money, particularly other people's, is typical backhills ethics. So is his dogged disregard of wealth as a mark of eminence. He not only lacks but he willfully defies the popular reverence for personal fortune which has made the American plutocrat, however lacking in integrity or intelligence, the most secure royalty now remaining on earth.

Like his backhill neighbors, Faubus' belief in the implicit merits of local government and the "feelin's" of the individual local community is deep and sincere. He speaks honestly, I believe, when echoing his backhill kind in declaring his homeland is a last stand in the ancient struggle of the democracy of the community versus the autocracy of the central government.

The hillbilly governor believes with apparent sincerity in Jefferson's devotion to basic democracy by way of the local community, the township, the town, and the county. Yet, arbitrarily, he violates this belief when he fabricates and forces legislative enactment which would or could, Faubus decreeing, obliterate the integrity of local viewpoint and the democratic effectiveness of local election. Similarly and knowingly, he defies the firmly stated directives of his idolized Abraham Lincoln, who repeatedly disagreed with and opposed the decisions and opinions of the United States Supreme Court, insisted that the will of the people in democracy must and will transcend that of courts or of Congress, yet exhorted, even commanded that no patriot openly defy either the courts or the Congress.

The Ozarks yeoman's private view of courts, judges, Congress and enforcement officers remains an almost habitually disapproving view. But the backhill commoner rarely practices open defiance of direct orders of a court. Faubus does. Again and again he has defied Federal authority without political motivation; he does not need the resulting or probable harvests of votes. With the world looking on, Orval has continued to exhibit the more lamentable paradoxes of traditional Ozarks behavior. He dreams nobly, fights dirty. Like a mauling participant in a woodcutter's brawl, the Burn Man finds himself fighting dirty for the brutish lust of it, not for rational cause or principle.

Faubus has never denied, in this writer's presence he has repeatedly confirmed, his acceptance of the fact that in the Ozarks, in Arkansas, or anywhere else in this nation the Negro is a citizen with all the obligations and rights thereof. And he points out that the Ozarks as a whole have "done better" by Negroes than most like-size regions of the United States.

This statement is somewhat on the smug side. The fortunes and status of Ozarks Negroes are generally up-bound. But school integration is still incomplete. Church integration is only now in the borning. In the writer's boyhood at least a dozen Ozarks towns (Rogers and Springdale, Arkansas, were ready examples) boasted that no Negro ever spent the night within their corporate limits. This is no longer literally true, but the division of Ozarks towns where Negroes are not welcome and where Negroes are merely tolerated remains far too conspicuous. By welcome contrast, most Ozarks villages and country communities are far more just toward Negroes than are most of the towns.

Faubus agrees with this observation and adds that Christianity has no place for the segregation of races. In calm moments the primitive from Madison County enjoys discussing religion and demonstrating his competence as a Bible scholar. And, perhaps, his competence as a pantheist who sees God in all living things. This is a typifying viewpoint of the backhill Ozarks at large.

One of the Arkansas governor's former neighbors remembers him as a very young pantheist. "One day when he was about six, little Orval came over to bring us some spareribs; his folks were butchering hawgs that day. I was out on the hillside choppin' an old apple tree. Little Orval said, 'Mister Evans, you hadn't ought to be choppin' that apple tree.' I asked why not. He said, 'That apple tree is part of God, Mister Evans. Every time you whack it with that ax you're hurtin' God!'"

More and more people, with more and better reasons, state or at least feel that Faubus hurts God when he moves to keep God's children, of whatever skin color, from attending public schools, whether in Little Rock or elsewhere. Reminded of this, Orval reiterates his belief that his people, "in God's time" will accept integration as a Christian as well as a civic principle—"on a basis of Lincolnlike enlightenment and Jeffersonian democracy," but not on a basis of "political autocracy of the U.S. Supreme Court."

The latter phrase has an Ozarkian ring. It also typifies the Burn Man's stubbornness which is almost mysteriously deep and distinctly melancholy. As a governor, Orval Faubus is an unhappy man. He confides that he "can't truly feel for any public office outside Arkansas"; he adds wistfully and convincingly that if he had his "rathers," he would very much prefer just to "keep" his county newspaper and get in some wood chopping, brush burning, hunting and trapping on the side.

The rational question, at this point, would seem to be, So why not take your rathers and get out of public office?

Faubus does not take this as a rational question. But he plainly

223

indicates that the mere fact of being asked it adds to his ever growing load of unhappiness. In his darker moods, Orval reminds fellow Ozarkers of olden backhill legends about good men mysteriously changed to werewolves, or willipus-wallipuses, or other fancifully destructive monsters.

The primitive, recurring warmth of the man presently melts away these or any other marrow-chilling fantasias. Even so, images linger. I, for one, see Faubus as an inherently adroit trapper who nevertheless finds himself securely and, in fact, painfully caught in his own trap. Faubus ridicules the image, vows that as a Burn Man he can fire, or "far," his way out of any number of predicaments.

The pooh-poohing is not entirely convincing, for one quickly gathers that O. Faubus is a primitive with ample perceptive intelligence to see himself as such and plenty of experience to confirm that a trapped creature almost never leaves a trap without injury to itself. The Burn Man points out with some degree of objectivity that if he is, as some insist, a prisoner of the mob, "I'm shore not beholden to no prisoner."

Orval is completely silent regarding the fact that his most vociferous support has never yet been from home countrysides. Rather it is from what Faubus admits are fanatic or lunatic fringes, both far and near. This adds to the Faubus burden of unhappiness. So does the realization that, as years follow, he is being accepted or rejected as a symbol of hates which Orval professes not to possess or accredit. Though a contentious fighting man, he is not a hating man.

But he is an own primitive son of the primitive Ozarks. As such he is a typically baffling paradox. He is too old to regret the past; yet too young to refrain from eye gouging or from gut-dripping personalized frays. He is broadly of the Lincoln prototype; yet, as an Ozarkian Lincoln, he is no more than a warped caricature of the Man of the Ages. Perhaps, had Orval Faubus clung with home country as devotedly as his father has, he could have been a rather interesting miniature of the one and only Abraham Lincoln.

In part deliberately, in part by unholy contrivances of others, Orval Faubus has taken the wrong road for himself and for his beloved backhill Ozarks.

CHAPTER XIX

Everlasting Ozarks

THERE ARE GOOD REASONS for living in the Ozarks or, at very least, knowing the Ozarks. One is that they are somehow the most definitive frontier now remaining within the first forty-eight states of this Union. Another is that the Ozarks continue to link past, present and future with a strange and rare continuity. Still another reason for knowing the Ozarks, or joining them, deals with the timeless appeal of the humble and amiable merged as a pre-eminent way of life.

One of the better rewards of being a reporter is the capacity of that querulous trade to draw on the talents and labors of others for translating fuzzy thoughts into comparatively rational opinions. Or, put another way, to turn the grindstone on which others may sharpen their wits, if any.

A good many years ago, in the reporter's purgatory which is Washington, D.C., I was interviewing a then eminent U.S. Senator. He was Joseph Taylor Robinson of Arkansas, Senate Majority

Leader under both Woodrow Wilson and Franklin D. Roosevelt. Mr. Joe was very sick at the time. He bellowed the declaration that he felt just fine and added with a flurry of forthright Arkansas profanity that the damn fool doctor who kept nagging him about his heart condition was plain off his four-dollar rocker. The Senator added that as a matter of conceivable possibility he could drop dead in his bathtub that very night. As a matter of record, the Senator did exactly that two nights later. Meanwhile Mr. Joe told me that the possibly less than completely steadfast behavior of his pumping system was pathological only to the extent of the pathology of Washington, D.C., and of his personal failure to keep with a life he could honestly love.

"I come of a one-love clan," the Senator rumbled. "My father was a country doctor down on the south shank of the Arkansas Ozarks. He used his profession as a living expression of his real love, which was farming and village living. I was never that lucky. Politics simply won't be sublimated to any other love, and politics ain't a love."

The Senator sighed loudly. "I never could understand human motivation, particularly my own. I can't explain my own course, even to myself. I only know for sure that I've always wanted to be a country man and to keep some kind of a farm—on account I see farming as the only truly creative work there is, and therefore the only truly rewarding work. Likewise the only remaining expression of opportunism which can be both honest and reasonably kind to all parties concerned. That, of course, is just another way of admitting that I'm a rustic, and never could be otherwise."

The Senator paused to drop a selzer tablet into a glass of water which waited ominously on his desk. He scowled deeply and began sipping the bubbly mess. "Never could understand why I ever let myself be hogtied into politics . . . much less in this moldy mausoleum of a Senate Building. Always wanted to be a man with a hoe, with a sunset behind me and a south wind to my right side."

When I inquired of his retirement plans, the Senator belched disgustedly. "I already retired once—into the Ozarks. I was nineteen then and it was the happiest year I ever knew. Pappy let me go up to Fayetteville—Arkansas, that is—for a year in the college. I didn't think too damn much of the so-called college. But I fell head over heels in love with the Ozarks and the Ozarks people." He glared at me and belched again. "Not excepting your Aunt Nellie. She was my age. She was the square-dance queen, back in those times. One frosty night she agreed to let me take her out in the hills to a square dance at some back-creek schoolhouse. I rented a team and buggy from Vaughan's Livery Stable, and I never got over it."

The Senator's scowl abated. He emptied the remaining contents of his medicine glass into his brass spittoon. "I never got over that square dance. It was partly your Aunt Nellie. She was quite a package back in those days; for all I know she still is. She was the best dancer on the floor, and naturally I was the worst. In some little part it may have been the music, though remembering back I expect the music was nothing to brag about too much. As I recall, the fiddle player was drunker'n a hoot owl and probably couldn't have scraped a tune any other way. The banjo player was a pale little boy with the slobbers who kept breaking strings."

The Senator smiled for the first time. "It was the country people that really won me over. They were country folks, mostly in blue overalls and calico dresses and plow shoes. But they were happy inside, and they warmed like a fireplace burning locust logs. They made me feel as one of them, and like I'd never by any stretch of the imagination be anything else. . . . But being a yes boy, as I was back in those days, I said yes to driving my lady home, yes to going back to my father's drug store, which he kept on the side, yes to cuddling law books in Little Rock, and yes to running for the bloody legislature, yes for tackling the governorship, yes to running for Congress, and so on."

The Senator pushed back his chair unsteadily and hobbled across the room to turn off an angrily banging radiator. On returning he sank to a straight chair beside my own.

"Look, boy, let's me and you remember something else together. It was the last free day I spent in the Ozarks. You were there, too, at that crazy mountain town called Eureky Springs. They were having a homecoming party for one of the Congressmen; you were reporting for some damn newspaper and you came barging in my hotel room after I'd laid down on the bed. Just as you left the damn bed fell all to pieces. Well, next day, as you should remember, they had a real old country-style reunion shindig.

"I got blasted awake when the school band started a concert in the little chicken house of a bandstand just across from my hotel window. I jumped out of my collapsed bed like a shot cat and raised the window. I swear to God that sounded to be the prettiest music this side of heaven. It wasn't of course, but it began sounding like Gabriel and his complete line of trumpeters the minute I saw who was playing. Those country school kids were themselves a wonderful concert, even without one horn or drum. One could say, and truthfully should, that all young'uns are interesting and mostly likable, because they are.

"But these young'uns were at least a little different. Along with being appealing young human animals, they were the living Ozarks, same as those country dancers were—fifty years earlier. The whole day through those sleepy old hills just came alive in the likable shapes of a kindly people . . . carefree, trustful, happy inside. When night came we had a spread supper out in the open on a chiggery hillside. Beforehand, we'd done a bit of sipping of waterlike mountain-dew whisky straight out of glass fruit jars.

229

The supper was mostly split cornpone with fried catfish . . . on good days, I can still taste it . . ."

The Senator answered the telephone and yawned. "So here goes the rat race again! Willie will tell you the rest of what you came to ask about. Meanwhile I got work to do."

The Senator yawned again and tapped my shoulder. "You know, I sometimes wonder if the deep-down appeal of people and places . . . if finally analyzed, isn't in the food they eat . . . the catfish and cornpone or whatever. Not entirely the food maybe. But also the way they cook it and the way they get it, whether by earning, rustling, or just grabbling . . ."

Maybe the Senator had something. To speak quite tritely, food is the staff of life and life must lean on staffs. This goes for Senators, for higher forms of life and for lower forms, including reporters. While taking handouts of routine buncombe from the Senator's man, Willie, I continued to reflect that like the Senator I had never really parted with my intentions to become an Ozarks country man.

Now that my real or imagined causes for straying were no longer wholly compelling, I began feeling the ageless urge to return to home pastures. The urge is timeless, as primitive as springtime mating, frequently as obvious as a country washday, and sometimes as mystical as the urge to find one's soul. I reflected, as millions of others have, that country living is infinitely wasteful of work and convenience and that, measured financially, farming anywhere in the United States is in what appears to be a state of permanent depression. As an agricultural region the Ozarks are considerably poorer than average. Their principal economic virtue is the opportunity to make oneself modestly self-sufficient. The particular charm and distinctions of Ozarks foods are born of the opportunities not of abundance as such, but rather of raising, foraging or stalking down what one eats. The same holds for the less tangible resources of living speech, humor and wit, tempos of speech and movement, and the quasi-dream world of backhill viewpoint.

I am again homeward bound to learn again of my native land. This page is being written on a gold-dusty October day on an Ozark hilltop. As an old man driving an old auto along paved roads which I first traveled afoot when they were mere forest trails or bouncy wagon lanes, I reflect that the Ozarks remain a land of yesterdays and tomorrows in unbreakable wedlock. They are still a frontier, of tangible land and intangible spirit; of people who come in and people who go out. I note again that the coming of the through road has been a recognizable—by all logic a completely overwhelming—force of change. Yet in what, offhand, seem miraculous ways, great areas of the Ozarks have withstood the domination by roads. Great areas of backhills have somehow remained backhills. In this instance "great areas" means at least 12,000 square miles, almost a fourth part of the total area of the basic Ozark plateau.

From the highway the perpetuation of the backhills is difficult to see and even more difficult to explain. Granted, the Ozarks backhills are not nearly so far back as they used to be, and their total areas are barely half of what they were during the 1920's. But even that half is as big as, say, the state of Vermont.

The central Ozarks plateau or "uplift" currently covers approximately 50,000 square miles; an area almost the size of the big and sprawling state of Arkansas. When the hilly fringes of the plateau, including such lands as the Ouachita Hills of western Arkansas, the Osage Hills of Missouri and the Blackoak Ridges of western Oklahoma are included (as geologists vow they should be), the Ozarks plateau covers almost 75,000 square miles—considerably more than the entire state of Missouri. That, obviously, is a sizable block of land and, as noted, it is striated with through roads which lead to other long-settled regions on every side. Even so, and in all principal sectors of the Ozarks, literal remoteness endures. There are still isolated countrysides in the Ozarks.

I have been revisiting one of these embryo lost worlds. The place is called Hemmed-in-Holler. It is in the lower Arkansas Ozarks, specifically in Newton, the sparsest-settled county in all the Ozarks. When one checks with a contour map, one notes a deep oval chasm in a rather wildly tumbled range of hills. The length of the deep dip is about fourteen miles, and its total area is somewhere near that of Manhattan Island.

Nowaday one can drive an auto to within about three miles of the Holler; at least as far as the weather-grayed crossroad called Compton. From there on one does best to walk. The Holler is walled by rims of limestone bluffs which are separated by a swift, deep-channeled river, Little Buffalo. The latter's course is one of pell-mell rapids; its gradients are so very steep that in winter or spring or after heavy rains in any season one fords the main channel at considerable peril. As a completely rational and year-around alternatives, settlers continue to enter and leave the Holler along roof-steep foot trails which avoid crossing the river and follow wavery diagonals up the steep hillsides.

First land takers went into the holler during 1833. For the first half a century or so the human population grew slowly. For the past three-quarters of a century the Holler's census has been declining to a current level of nine families and two, or perhaps three, unattached individuals.

Subsistence remains the living way. Gardens, melon patches and scattered fruit trees help yield the necessary provender. These supplement the garden-size field crops—corn, wheat and oats, and the open-range livestock, principally swine and beef cattle. "Milk ain't healthy," an old settler recently assured me. "It never was meant to be drunk by growed-up peoples."

Yet the health and mortality rates of Hemmed-in-Holler appear to be fairly close to national averages. (Apparently childhood mortality is slightly above current averages; the adult death rate is slightly below.) Ironically, appendicitis remains the foremost menace to adults; there is no local surgery and no assured or punctual means for removing the sufferers to outside hospitals. The other day a settler got to the hospital at Harrison while the getting was still good and had a belligerent appendix removed. "They shore 'nough was a sarpent inside me, a sort of grayish viper. When they tooken it out it looked about as mean as it had been a-feelin'."

The mental health appears to be better than national averages. There is only one contemporary instance of insanity. That was Chaddy Kent, flower of the Holler's youth and a particularly likeable rural Adonis. Riding home one day, Chaddy was overtaken by a springtime thunderstorm. He ducked for shelter at the cabin of the Widder Williams. The Widder had lately acquired a young ram. Terror-stricken at the oncoming storm, the young wool-bearer lunged down a steep ravine. Chaddy ran after him. Just as the youth pinned down the ram, a great blast of lightning splintered a pine tree not five yards away. Man and ram sprawled to earth. Presently the ram got to its feet and limped away. Chaddy rose too, and weeping, pointed to the ram and vowed it was a brazen image.

To the Widder Williams, a storm-frightened ram was only that and nothing more. But Chaddy insisted that he had beheld a Divine Parable, his particular "call" to go forth to all the world and preach. He went forth to preach and turned violently insane. The sheriff took Chaddy in tow and dutifully delivered him to the state hospital where the beholder of the parable prayed and died.

Earlier generations of Hemmed-in-Holler settlers never bothered about keeping a school. At present, though by gradual stages,

233

literacy is increasing as more and more of the children are put to school, at least briefly, at Jasper, the county-seat town some eighteen miles away. But the scholastic impediments stay strong.

A Holler father tells me why he felt it unwise to "put" his eleven-year-old daughter, Rosy Faye, to schooling: "She'd shore love to go schoolin', and I'd cherish to leave her go weren't it fer jest one thing. That chile ain't nowhere near so spry and nimble as she looks; she ain't yet well-growed enough to make a fast getaway. And them Hembrees is still got a mean, free-roamin' bull on the loose. The rest of my young'uns, everwhen that bull takes after 'em, can easy outrun hit. But little Rosy ain't yet capable to do so. That's why I'm keepin' her close about the homestead."

Back in 1912, the Holler people got together and built a one-room schoolhouse which they still use as a community church. But there never was enough tax money to keep school longer than two months a year. There were other impediments. One summer (1923), a strolling evangelist came into the Holler and "lead" a series of perspiring and spirited revival meetin's in the schoolhouse. During his prolonged course of exhortations, the son of Higher Truth announced his appalling discovery that there didn't appear to be any more than three or four lawful marriages in the entire Holler. Accordingly, most of the parents were living in sin and most of their offspring were you know what.

Resentful at being cited as bastards, even by a preacher man, several young blades of the immediate countryside planted several sticks of dynamite in front of the schoolhouse, and directly following the services, set it off. The blast shattered the windows and sent the man of Higher Truth high-tailing up the mountain rim. The parson never came back. But the religious life of the Holler goes on, an engaging pantheism sincerely colored by a highly personalized Christianity.

234

Hemmed-in-Holler remains a haven of prevailing honesty and order. During the past quarter-century there is no record of a murder, burglary, rape, or other felony. The homes continue to stand open, latchstrings hanging free. The agrarian sequence remains admirably effective. The farms are small, averaging no no more than twelve acres in cultivation, with several times as much space in pasture and woodland. The tillage season usually begins in April and ends in July. During this exceptionally busy period, working days for family heads last as long as nine hours, chores included. By year-round averages, the women work considerably longer hours than the men.

In the main the males are the gayer and the better dressed— including high-brimmed, cowboy-style hats banded with colorful ribbons or processions of gold-painted stars. For dress-up days and dancing nights boots come into the picture, slim-toed boots, handsomely stitched and polished. In general, the young men are more conspicuous than the girls, granting the latter have their charms and purposes, including an impressive prowess for getting married between their thirteenth and eighteenth birthdays; thereafter the matrimonial chances range from slight to virtually nonexistent.

Hemmed-in-Holler is also a musical countryside. Of the nine resident families, all but one own and use one or more musical instruments. Pianos, foot-pump organs, guitars, fiddles and banjos are the most favored; guitars are the most used. Local musicians, preponderantly innocent of "musical literacy" play mostly for the fun of it and revel in old-fashioned waltzes and plantation songs, also hoe-downs and jig songs, ballads of maidens wronged, wandering boys, and mothers who pray for sons dying on far-off battlefields. Also, overhauled ballads of long ago, song hits of the 1920's and before, and comic ditties improvised for the occasion and the amusement or embarrassment of the immediate listeners.

THE BODACIOUS OZARKS

The Holler people are also a dancing folk, light of foot and heart, and short on rules. But their premier asset is the superlative luxury of free time; time to putter, eat, sleep, or rest, to talk and be friendly; time to inquire how you are feelin', and even more important, to listen while you tell them.

Hemmed-in-Holler has lived on without benefit or disadvantage of through roads. Such a feat was fairly typical of hundreds of backhill communities a century ago. Today the Holler is a truly exceptional phenomenon even in the farthest-back of the enduring Ozarks backhills. Even so, and speaking and pondering as one long-time viewer and cherisher of remote backhills, Hemmed-in-Holler stays a living symbol of the amazing and all but timeless Ozarkian talent for sustaining remoteness.

CHAPTER XX

You Take That There Road

OZARKS ROADS GIVE and take away. For better or worse they change, restore, erase, and build. They also define and reveal. As I ramble through my home country once more, I note that the revelations of the roads are more numerous and emphatic than before. Nowadays it is not only possible to learn about the Ozarks by following the roads; it is virtually compulsory.

We are no longer a pedestrian people. In the Ozarks as elsewhere, the auto replaces feet; the plane is our stride for distance. At present, according to the pamplet-exuding Ozarks Playground Association, the majority of Ozarks tourists, perhaps twelve million per year, enters from the north and east. Missouri U.S. Highway 66, which tends to parallel the way of the Indians' Southwest Trail (eventually renamed the Old Spanish Trail), is the most used entry route. Between St. Louis and Springfield, Missouri, the self-admitted Metropolis of the Ozarks, U.S. 66 is also one of the most interesting and efficient of toll-free roads. Its dual ribbons of pavements, separated by intervening acres of grasslands and woods, swerve and bypass through the far-spread fringelands of the plateau. One is thereby encouraged to ask or at least to ponder where the Ozarks begin and for good measure where the West begins. There is no absolute answer to either query. But anybody is entitled to his own surmise. Mine is that one enters the real Ozarks when he crosses the Osage River. Further, that the West begins directly to the sunset side of the Missouri town called Carthage. This, as you may recall, was the home town of Belle Starr, the female bandit, and the "Saturday Swappin' Town" of the magnificent George Washington Carver.

My father always contended that the Ozarks begin precisely when and where one meets the first roadside sign proclaiming FRIED CATFISH AND 'COON HUNTIN' COFFEE—and end where and when one shuffles into some roadside eating place and finds himself staring at or sniffing boiled collards and grease-fried hushpuppies. This is shortly north of the Chitlin's-Bayous or the Grits-for-Breakfast Lands. When one encounters the Great Barbecued Plains, he is too far west. But when fried catfish and black coffee come fortified with slabs of white cornpone and a platter of wile greens, then a person is just bound and beholden to be in the True and Everlastin' Ozarks.

Highway 66 provides some revealing confirmation. It permits the follower to note that as the terrain grows more markedly uphill and downhill, so do the speech and postures of the people. The fringeland language becomes an intriguing mingling of the Ozarker's verbal inventiveness and the Westerner's drawl. One begins to notice, too, that the inhabitants tend to walk and gesture in the tempo of their speech; they sit and lean with great thoroughness, and show a visible disposition to yawn and stretch in the shapes of capital X's and Y's. One also observes a persistent increase in tight-fitting blue jeans which would offhand indicate

238

either the return of the cattle era or an irrespressible tendency not to take shrinkage into account when buying blue breeches.

Next one begins to notice big and garish road signs which tell of caves. When it comes to telling of caves in the Ozarks, this writer is a sort of broken-down authority. Again and again I have been lost and waterlogged in Ozarks caves; still more frequently I have been bored to the very bloomers in and by Ozarks caves. My Uncle George Ezekiel Wilson, who sometimes overreached the family talent for making stupid generalities, used to vow that every farm should have its own cave for constructive uses such as storing butter, cooling summer-slain game and hell-raising women. My uncle George had at least five caves on his farm; perhaps coincidentally, he had a wife and four daughters, all strong of will and voice.

During the middle 1920's, while stringing along as Ozarks reporter for the St. Louis *Post-Dispatch,* I covered the ballyhooed openings—to the tourist trade, that is—of several dozen Ozarks caves. In line of occupational hazards I sloshed, goosepimpled and skidded through more dank caves than better-gifted citizens ever dreamed of. I listened to more cribbed recitations about outlaws, bandits, train robbers, bank robbers, spies, feudists, night riders and treasure hiders in caves than the generality of writers could dream up collectively, even if employed by Hearst.

At best, which is less than excellent, Ozarks caves are not particularly Ozarkian. Neither is the stall-run of roadside catering goods, which along with factory-made quilts and rugs and corncob pipes made in Japan, include Chinese temple bells and Alaskan totem poles. I could never understand the reason for the foregoing. But I do understand a bit or two about picture postcards. I can and do understand why one finds in the Ozarks a special and continuing preference for satirical cards. For one long-time example, more than a quarter-century after the heyday of the New Deal,

239

one of the better-patronized Ozarkian postcards remains the Political Definitions number:

Socialism: You have two cows. You give one to your neighbor.

Communism: You have two cows. The Government takes both and gives you the milk.

Fascism: You have two cows. The Government takes both and sells you the milk.

Nazism: You have two cows. The Government takes both and shoots you.

New Dealism: You have two cows. The Government takes both, shoots one, milks the other, and throws the milk away.

Capitalism: You have two cows. You sell one and buy a bull.

The adventure of getting into the Ozarks proves interesting primarily because the people are interesting. Even on the fringes one can make the acquaintance of a cautiously friendly people with a unique and engaging candor. Should your auto develop the flutters or splutters, the garage man is likely to tell you quite frankly what ails the contraption, or what he believes ails it. Chances are he will not tear asunder the carburetor or replace the sparkplugs unless he truly, even if mistakenly, thinks they are causing the trouble. He will very probably conclude by inviting you to "come back and see us." When and if you do come back and see them, you are likely to be surprised by the warmth of your reception, quite regardless of your buying or not buying what the inviter may have to sell.

Other memorable revelations are provided by the placards exhibited in shop windows. The "winder cards" reveal beyond reasonable doubt that the traditional Ozarkian social events, including square dances, old settlers' picnics, old settlers' and old soldiers' reunions, fish fries and "pioneer frolics" persist. But

240

they are being interspersed more than occasionally by such new-fangled innovations as dam dedications, speed-boat races, water-ski shows, summer theatres, Boy- or Girl-Scout encampments, and fireworks displays.

And even more impressively by rodeos (pronounced *road-ee-oh*). Many of these are sponsored officially by towns and cities. The contemporary list leaders include such headliners as the three-day Indian Capital Rodeo held annually in Muskogee, Oklahoma; the four-day Western Festivities and Annual Rodeo at Joplin, Missouri; the four-day Rodeo of the Ozarks in Springfield, Missouri; Oklahoma's Sequoyah State Park Rodeo; the three-day Annual Rodeo of Sallisaw, Oklahoma; the three-dayer at Cassville, Missouri; the four-day Finlay River Rodeo of Ozark, Missouri; the three-day annual Roundup Club Rodeo of Tallequah, Oklahoma, and many others.

The rodeo's triumphant entry into the Ozarks is a particularly noteworthy revival. The marathons of roping calves, riding wildly bucking horses, bulldogging rebellious steers, manipulating "cutting" horses (trained deftly to separate individual cattle from the herd), bareback and acrobatic horsemanship, athletic clowning, and so on by the hour and evening, are frequently as exciting as they are demanding of gumption and skill. They are being adopted or reinstated by Ozark people as enthusiastically as the play parties, community picnics, "weddin' chiverees," fox hunts, fish-gig drives and brush-arbor meetin's of a century ago. The rocketing rodeo returns to visible life the gifts of a persistently range-riding West which spilled over into the Ozarks in bygone generations and once more is finding a brawny but generally graceful resurrection.

The highway traveler also notices that Ozarks housing is undergoing historic changes. The era of the log cabin has vanished like last April's snow. The slab-board shack persists, but it is

THE BODACIOUS OZARKS

waning. The rock house is in renaissance, though it tends to use rock veneer instead of bona fide stone. Praise goodness, the flat, squat-roofed, Iowa-styled bungalow is no longer rampant (granting that the low-sprawling, Western-style ranch house is mushrooming).

Entering or re-entering the Ozarks by auto reminds one of recessive as well as allegedly progressive developments. There are far fewer roadside farms than there were a half-century ago. An actual majority of the villages and smaller towns and many county seats continue to lose people or at best to "stay put" in census. Many of the old-time crossroads stores wait in abandonment.

Yet there are also evidences of agrarian re-awakenings. In numerous valleys and on some of the prairies one sees abandoned farms which are once more tenanted and tilled. More and more frequently one notes rocky hillsides or scenic hilltops newly adorned with modest-sized cottages or ranch houses. For the most part these "view homes" are being built and occupied by retired people or those anticipating retirement.

The newcomer or the returner notes, too, the peculiar coherence of the Ozarks, the exceptional talents for merging contrasting terrains into a distinctive environment. You keep encountering "typical" Ozarks towns and farm communities which are not in hill country, not otherwise typical. A conspicuous example is Springfield, Missouri, the largest town in all the Ozarks. Back in 1812 Springfield materialized as a hillbilly town without hills. Through succeeding generations it has remained a self-modeled Ozarks capital, with colleges, museums (one of which houses the only eminent collection of early Ozarkiana), an art gallery, and various other facilities which enhance the cultural resources of the Ozarks. Otherwise the Metropolis of the Ozarks is remarkably non-Ozarkian. Even so the old town provides a flourishing example of the talent of the Ozarks to integrate and keep living union

242

with communities which for one cause or another decline to merge with the more extensive countrysides about them.

The Ozarks road-follower keeps meeting such former colonies as Tontitown, the original Italian settlement in northwest Arkansas, and Friestadt, a noble old-line German community in southwest Missouri. Both are convincingly of the Ozarks now; yet both perpetuate and honor their respective countries of origin.

The Ozarks traveler also notes the recent emergence of highway outposts. For example, directly below the Missouri-Arkansas boundary one may follow U.S. 62 along the topmost rim of the central Ozarks plateau. This skyline drive, one of the most beautiful routes in all the nation, presently eases into the sprawling old county seat, Harrison, Arkansas. During my boyhood this town was listed as the end of the through road. Beyond Harrison one traveled by horseback or preferably a-foot; or else he settled in Harrison.

At present the erstwhile end-of-the-road town assumes the rather surprising function of highway hub for what, until the past decade, was the most extensive roadless stretch in all the Ozarks. From Harrison one may now travel a generous variety of auto roads which lead into successive and heretofore lost countrysides, some of almost unbelievable beauty and charm.

The new roads head for a still greater variety of water sites. They touch into magnificent and heretofore little-heeded river valleys, such as those of the Big Buffalo and Little Buffalo rivers. They open travel routes to a far-flung succession of magnificent surface springs, including several of the biggest in North America. They also lead to a series of federally built river impoundments which are changing great intervals of river channels to inland lakes that are acquiring dozens of resorts, hunting and fishing camps, and various other recreational facilities.

Today, even as in very early pioneering times, new roads and

243

trails keep heading for water, thereby evidencing the persistent awareness that surface water remains a prime decider of Ozarks destinies. The foregoing is more than an abstract deduction. The new river lakes are already adding impressively to the competence of Ozarks tourist catering, easily the biggest as well as the fastest-growing industry of the area.

The expanding water impoundments are providing other benefits of importance. They are contributing splendidly to fish and game resources which are fast improving throughout the region. The federally financed dam building is strengthening regional potentials for manufactures, which can put to industrial uses the hydroelectric power of the impressively huge water impoundments.

The new era of river damming bears still more directly on agricultural futures. It already provides water for some interesting ventures in crop irrigation which, thus far, feature the use of supplementary watering by means of light pumps and portable pipe lines as attainable insurance against ruinous drought. There is no present likelihood that the Ozarks will ever develop irrigation practices comparable to those of the intermountain West or the Rio Grande Valley. But there is good reason to believe that, at least in the more fertile valleys, supplementary irrigation will help in producing more foodstuffs on fewer acres better tilled, and will safeguard farmers against complete ruin by cyclic drought.

But one who would discover or rediscover the Ozarks is almost certain to deduce that country living, "foundationed" by subsistence farming is bound to be the preponderant destiny of the Ozarks of tomorrow, even as it was yesterday and is today. From the highways, as well as from the back roads and foot trails, the onlooker notes that the earth writing continues to stress the role of the small farm, or the even smaller plot of land, for use as home and refuge rather than as a typically commercial farm plant. The road-follower with an eye for productive lands will note, too, that the over-all reach of Ozarks farming is tending to improve. Though only about one-fourth of the "family farms" which were being tilled as of 1900 are still so tilled today, by averages the contemporary farms are more productive than those of a generation ago.

Though population losses in most rural areas were severe during the 1940's because of wartime demands for industrial and military workers, and even more severe during the early 1950's because of the virulent drought cycle, the Ozarks census is once more beginning to rise—slowly but surely. The inflow of retired people and returning natives or former residents is increasing, though not competitively with such retirement Meccas, as, say, Florida, New Mexico and Arizona. Because young people continue going out as middle-aged and elderly people continue coming in, the Ozarks continue as a land of the elderly more than of the young.

Also by majority but with exceptions, the Ozarks remain a poor man's country; less drastically poor than a generation ago, but at least comparatively poor. If the Ozarks were a single state, it would almost certainly rank among the lower half-dozen in per capita income. Even so, the perceptive viewer of the region will doubt that any great part of it is doomed to be a regional slum. Like the Ozarks census, the total economy is stubbornly and slowly upward bound. The same holds for average lifespans and the general health of Ozarkers.

The old uplift smiles more and laughs less as it grows older. But the spirit of the frontier stays planted in the land, in the people and in their vital partnership with earth, rain and sun.

Road-following reiterates that Ozarks remoteness will continue to dwindle; in major areas it may fade entirely. But the pondering

245

onlooker will almost certainly find himself or herself reflecting that the Ozarks language, and wit, and inventive noncomformity of viewpoint will endure for many years to come.

Discovery or rediscovery of the Ozarks continues to tell that the Ozarks will keep on providing refuge for those who seek refuge, revival of spirit for those who require it. The Ozarks are old and in great part slow and silent. But they are also a land of singing winds, racing shadows and brave young leaves. And of yesterday wedded with tomorrow.